J.K. LASSER'S™

REAL ESTATE
INVESTING

Look for these and other titles from J.K. Lasser™—Practical Guides for All Your Financial Needs.

J.K. Lasser's Pick Winning Stocks by Edward F. Mrkvika Jr.

J.K. Lasser's Invest Online by LauraMaery Gold and Dan Post

J.K. Lasser's Year-Round Tax Strategies by David S. De Jong and Ann Gray Jakabin

J.K. Lasser's Taxes Made Easy for Your Home-Based Business by Gary W. Carter

J.K. Lasser's Finance and Tax for Your Family Business by Barbara Weltman

J.K. Lasser's Pick Winning Mutual Funds by Jerry Tweddell with Jack Pierce

J.K. Lasser's Your Winning Retirement Plan by Henry K. Hebeler

J.K. Lasser's Winning With Your 401(K) by Grace Weinstein

J.K. Lasser's Winning With Your 403(b) by Pam Horowitz

J.K. Lasser's Strategic Investing After 50 by Julie Jason

J.K. Lasser's Winning Financial Strategies for Women by Rhonda Ecker and Denise Gustin-Piazza

J.K. Lasser's Online Taxes by Barbara Weltman

J.K. Lasser's Pick Stocks Like Warren Buffett by Warren Boroson

J.K. Lasser's The New Tax Law Simplified

J.K. Lasser's New Rules for Retirement and Tax by Paul Westbrook

J.K. Lasser's New Rules for Small Business Taxes by Barbara Weltman

J.K. Lasser's Investor's Tax Guide by Elaine Floyd

J.K. LASSER'S™

REAL ESTATE INVESTING

Michael C. Thomsett

John Wiley & Sons, Inc.

This publication is designed to provide accurate and authoritative information in regard to the subject matter covered. It is sold with the understanding that the publisher is not engaged in rendering professional services. If professional advice or other expert assistance is required, the
services of a competent professional person should be sought.

Library of Congress Cataloging-in-Publication Data:
Thomsett, Michael C.
   J.K. lasser's real estate investing / by Michael C. Thomsett.
     p. cm.— (J.K. Lasser—practical guides for all your financial needs)
   Includes index.
   ISBN 0-471-39776-8 (pbk. : alk. paper)
    1. Real estate investment. I. Title: Real estate investing. II. J.K. Lasser
Institute. III. Title. IV. Series.

HD1382.5 .T5643 2001
332.63'24—dc21   2001046887

Printed in the United States of America.

10 9 8 7 6 5 4 3 2 1

Contents

Introduction

Land is a limited commodity. There is only so much land to go around, which is what gives it value. In other words, we cannot increase the land supply; we can only develop what's already there. This is the appeal of real estate investing.

Other investments—stocks, bonds, and mutual funds, for example—have unlimited supplies. Companies can issue additional shares of stock to raise more capital, bonds can be issued as long as investors are there to buy them, and mutual fund companies will take any and all investors willing to buy up shares. Land, though, is in limited supply no matter what. In cities, the problem is solved by building up; in rural areas, undeveloped land can be developed, but only to a limited extent.

Land development is limited by several factors. Topography prevents the development of some land, and practical considerations limit the rate of growth. Essential services, such as water and sewer, electricity, gas, streets, and police and fire protection, cost money. Antigrowth forces can prevent development through the political process. Thus, development into *new* areas is a balancing act between demand and cost. There is a tendency to develop in existing built-up areas and to leave the open countryside alone. Even where little growth has occurred, the supply of land remains limited in a practical sense.

What does this mean for would-be investors? Whether you want to speculate in raw land, hoping for future development interest; to build homes and resell them; or to invest in rental properties; you will be dealing with a commodity of limited supply. This is the real appeal to real estate investing. Part of the long-term growth potential comes from the limited supply of the commodity itself. As populations increase over time, two things happen in response. To some degree, more construction meets part of the demand. Beyond that, greater demand for more residential space forces prices upward. As more people move into an area, demand also grows for commercial and industrial land uses.

Some features of real estate make it an investment unlike any other. For example, when you own rental property, you can keep an eye on your investment from day to day, making sure that tenants are treating your property well and maintaining the home and yard; you can insure your investment against loss; and you can actually hold the property with little or no cost, because you pay the mortgage and other expenses with rental income.

All of that assumes that you select tenants carefully, that they pay the rent on time, and that they care for your property. Thus, as long as demand for rentals is strong in your town, you will be able to choose from among a pool of tenants. These are broad assumptions, however; there can also be a downside to real estate investments. For example, if laws in your state protect tenants to a greater degree than landlords, you are placed at a disadvantage. This becomes a problem if you need to evict a tenant who is not paying rent or taking proper care of your property. As an investment in a more general sense, real estate is *illiquid,* meaning your capital is tied up in the property and cannot be removed easily for emergencies. Real estate cannot be sold easily, either; it takes time, and, if the market is not strong, selling might not even be profitable.

Thus, there is good news and bad news about real estate. All investments have characteristics of opportunity and risk, and you need to weigh each in deciding whether any investment is appropriate for you, given your financial situation and risk tolerance—your ability and willingness to live with particular risks.

You may take a speculative approach to real estate investing. This means buying up land or developed property with the idea of reselling at a profit in the shortest possible time. For example, some houses need only cosmetic improvements, which cost little but vastly improve the appearance, so investing some time and money makes it possible to earn a profit quickly. Or you can assume a long-term approach to real estate. This usually means buying rental property and keeping tenants in it over many years. If you select properties carefully and at the right price level, it is possible to have your mortgage, insurance, and taxes paid from rents.

This book explores the various ways you can buy real estate, either as a primary investment for profit and tax benefits or as a method for diversifying your investments for the long term. The book is divided into two parts: how real estate investing works and managing your property. The purpose of this book is to provide you with the basic requirements for real estate investing, the major benefits to look for, and the drawbacks you should be aware of before going forward.

Real estate—like all investments—has specific characteristics that, when considered as a package, determine whether or not real estate is right for you. Like all investments, these characteristics should be mastered before you proceed. One of the common pitfalls for all investors is being aware only of opportunity, but not of the associated risks of a particular investment strategy. These risks extend far beyond the easily understood financial and market risks. They include the less tangible but equally important personal risks related to dealing with tenants. This book deals with both types of risk and is designed to present you with the full spectrum of questions you should ask before you proceed.

Real estate certainly can be used to develop and maintain a long-term base for your investing future. By its nature, real estate value tends to rise over time as long as it is well selected, maintained, and improved. The demand for real estate is not likely to go away, since shelter is one of the basic necessities. As long as people need a place to live, real estate investors will have a market for their product.

This book is based on the assumption that most first-time real estate investors will begin by buying a single-family house. This is the most common way that people start out, mainly because houses are more affordable than duplexes, triplexes, and apartment complexes. While you might want to trade up into multiple-family dwellings later on, single-family housing is a sensible and logical place to start.

In addition to becoming a landlord with single-family rental houses, there are numerous other ways to become a real estate investor. These include speculating in raw land, buying fixer-upper properties and turning them around quickly, buying commercial or industrial properties, and buying "distressed" properties, meaning investing in property in foreclosure. In all of these highly specialized areas are distinct problems and opportunities. However, considering that most first-time investors are more likely to opt for the relatively tame single-family housing market, this book emphasizes that area only. Other markets are beyond the scope of this book.

Many web sites are provided throughout this book for your convenience. A referral to a web site is not an endorsement or a recommendation for any advertisements or products being sold by the sponsors. Web sites also change or become inoperative over time. You may want to perform your own search by entering key words on a search engine. One site that allows efficient searching with second-level search capabilities is *http://www.searchalot.com/*—many other sites offer search capabilities as well.

How Real Estate Investing Works

CHAPTER 1

The Real Estate Market

I s real estate a practical investment for you? How does it compare with stocks and mutual funds, for example? What are the relative risk and safety features to be aware of, and how does risk affect the decision?

One of the biggest problems in comparing two investments is that the risks often are vastly different. As a result, the comparison is not valid. You need to make a qualified comparison, weighing opportunities and risks in relative terms. The study of risk is always a good starting point whenever deciding whether to place money into an investment.

The most obvious difference between real estate and other investments is the amount of capital required to get started. You can buy shares of stock for a small amount per share, often only a few dollars. Real estate requires significantly more money. Even if you finance most of your purchase, you are still required to make a down payment, in most situations. To invest in a single-family residence, you probably will be required to put 30 percent down, in many cases.*

The fact that real estate requires more capital just to get started makes any comparison difficult. The question "Should I invest in the stock market or real estate?" does not have a simple answer. First you need to determine the purpose in investing, how much money is available, and whether you are suited to real estate management. This brings up the second area of risk.

Stocks require no direct maintenance at all. You buy shares and wait. "Maintenance" for stocks means keeping an eye on the market price as well

---

*While owner-occupied housing often can be purchased with as little as 10 percent down, investment property usually requires a larger commitment. Typically, this is 30 percent. More liberal terms can be found but often involve more cost, such as a higher interest rate and up-front fees.

as any developing news about the company and its sales and profits. You can buy stock and literally forget about it, hoping for long-term appreciation. However, if you buy a rental property, you need to screen tenants, ensure that rent is paid on time, keep an eye on the property to make sure it's being cared for properly, pay periodic property taxes and insurance premiums, and more. In other words, the level of commitment is far different for real estate than for the purchase of a few shares of stock.

The commitment is a form of risk. These two areas—capital investment and commitment—are only the obvious areas where comparison is dissimilar for real estate and other investments. Virtually all aspects of real estate present different levels of risk and opportunity. One important advantage to rental real estate is that it produces a stream of income, which covers all or part of your mortgage payment. Stocks may provide a quarterly dividend payment. This, too, is an area of dissimilar risk and opportunity. As a landlord, you risk being unable to find a suitable tenant, meaning no cash is coming in. At the same time, your mortgage payments continue from one month to another. However, stocks provide very little income stream. Again, the comparison between stocks and real estate cannot be made easily. The two investments are different in many other ways as well.

Because most of the aspects are different between these two major areas, it is impossible to say that one or the other is better as a choice. Some people are willing and able to assume greater risks, so they can select stocks that are more volatile than average, for example. Others might be unwilling or financially unable to expose themselves to the long-term commitment of real estate or to the higher cash flow risks. In a balanced portfolio, real estate often is an appropriate alternative to keeping a larger portion of investment capital in one market, such as stocks, so, as a means of diversifying a capital base, you might want to have some money invested in stocks (directly owned or through mutual funds, for example) and some in investment real estate.

How Real Estate Is Different from Stocks

Consider the differences between stocks and real estate in five primary ways:

1. *Changes in value.* Stocks change in value from day to day, often dramatically. This is both an opportunity and a risk. For the short-term trader, a big change means big profits or losses in a short time, often a matter of minutes or hours. Real estate investors, in comparison, do not think about value from day to day. They tend to be long-term investors, out of necessity. While real estate prices often are compared to long-term trends in stocks, they are less volatile.

2. *Buying and selling.* Shares of stock are traded in big volume from day to day. You can buy shares of stock in the morning and sell at a profit later the same day. The process is streamlined; buy and sell orders can be executed with a telephone call or online with little effort. Real estate transactions are far more complex. The buyer needs to obtain financing or come to the table with a large amount of cash. Inspections and approvals take time, and the typical period from acceptance of an offer to closing will run from six to eight weeks, sometimes more.

3. *Cost.* Stock trades are fairly low-cost. Brokerage firms compete with one another to get investors' business, especially for Internet trades. You can buy or sell 100 shares of stock for under $20. Real estate, in comparison, involves much more cost. Sellers using real estate agents pay a fee for finding a buyer. On top of that, closing costs include filing fees, excise taxes, and loan origination fees and charges. The cost is vastly different because shares represent very small portions of a company, whereas real estate normally involves trading the entire property in a single transaction.

4. *Insurance.* The market value of stocks is not insured or protected in any way. You can lose a lot of money buying stocks, whether directly or through mutual funds. In comparison, real estate can be completely protected through the purchase of homeowners' insurance. In the event of a loss from fire, for example, the value of improvements is reimbursed by the insurance company. This protection extends to sudden and unexpected losses from fires, theft, and other events; however, no investment can be insured against market price reductions, and real estate, like most investments, is cyclical, so values are going to change, sometimes rapidly and at other times very slowly and over a longer period of time.

5. *Pricing.* The stock market is described as an auction marketplace because the current prices of stocks are set by buyers and sellers from moment to moment. This varies as the number of buyers and sellers changes, and as news (or rumors) about a company float around. In addition, specialists in the major exchanges ensure a market by buying stock for sale when no other buyers are available or by selling stock to buyers virtually on demand. Of course, scarcity affects price, but given that, every buyer and seller in the market can make a transaction at will. Real estate prices, while also subject to the desires of buyers and sellers, do not see the volume of trading activity due to the larger size of a transaction. Real estate does not operate by auction, but through contract. A buyer makes an offer, and the seller accepts, rejects, or counteroffers. The fact that stocks are available in fairly small dollar-value shares makes auction marketplace activity practical. Real estate is not traded in shares in the same manner. In some markets, a seller may have several buyers bidding on a property. In others, a seller might not receive any offers whatsoever. (See Table 1.1.)

STOCKS	REAL ESTATE
Values change daily—both up and down.	Values change over time, rather than daily.
Shares can be bought or sold immediately.	Buying and selling take time.
Transactions are fairly low-cost.	Trading is expensive and more complex.
Shares are not insured or protected.	Property values are insured.
Prices are set by an auction marketplace.	Prices are set by supply and demand.

TABLE 1.1 Differences between Stocks and Real Estate

Landlords and Tenants

Some of the obvious differences between stocks and real estate are easily evaluated in terms of risk. Given the capital requirements to buy real estate, property values, and other attributes of the market, a comparison of risk features is executed without trouble. However, one of the features about rental real estate that distinguishes it from stocks in a very big way is that the real estate owner deals with tenants.

This fact has both positive and negative features. As landlord, you have the right to select the tenants for your property. Your selection has to be made on a nondiscriminatory basis, meaning you cannot exclude a tenant because of race or nationality, for example.[*]

The selection of tenants has to be made within the law; however, you are allowed to discriminate in certain ways. For example, you can check a tenant's background and determine whether he or she has ever been evicted, has been convicted of a felony, or has had credit problems. And if you discover

---

[*]Discrimination renting property is illegal under federal law and state laws. The Federal Fair Housing Act states that it is illegal to refuse to rent to a person because of "race, color, religion, sex, familial status, or national origin" (Sec. 3604).

anything negative in a person's background, you can refuse to rent on that basis. If a person's income clearly is not high enough to afford the rent you are asking, you can exclude him or her for that reason. If you have a number of applicants for a single rental, you can select from among qualified people. Landlords enjoy the right to make the final decision about whether a particular tenant will be allowed to reside in their property.

Once a tenant moves into your property, both you and that tenant have a series of obligations and rights, and these are spelled out in your rental agreement. This agreement will be explored in considerable detail in Chapter 7. The major obligations of the tenant are to pay rent each month and to maintain the property. The landlord has to keep the property safe and secure and agrees to provide notice before entering the property occupied by the tenant.

The relationship between landlord and tenant can be peaceful and satisfying for both sides. This assumes that everyone keeps his or her contractual promises and respects the rights of the other. This is not always the way things work out. While the majority of renters are responsible people who want to live in peace and not have problems with their landlords, some people either do not understand the landlord's point of view or simply don't care. If you end up with a tenant who is chronically late paying the rent, who does not take good care of your property, or who violates other terms of the rental agreement, you will need to deal with the problems of being a landlord. That often means giving notice to someone that you want him or her to move; if the person does not move, it could mean having to evict the person. These are extreme measures, however. If you check on a tenant's background and screen potential tenants before renting to them, you have a good chance of experiencing a positive relationship in most instances.

For most people who would not want to become a landlord, the tenant issues are the major sticking points. The potential problems of dealing with unhappy tenants does cause many people to avoid directly owned rental property. However, there are a number of solutions. You can invest in rental property and protect yourself from direct contact with tenants. Among these solutions is hiring a resident manager (in the case of apartment units) or placing a rental under professional management. Companies specializing in rental management charge a fee, often based on rents. The fee averages 10 percent of all rents due each month.

Tenants look at the rental agreement from a completely different perspective than landlords. They do not realize that most landlords depend on rental income to pay their monthly mortgage on the property, for example. They also are unlikely to realize that rental increases occur because the landlord's expenses have risen. For example, if your local county raises your property taxes on the rental, you probably will pass on that increase to your tenant in the form of higher monthly rent. You will probably not be able to explain your position to a tenant who is unhappy about higher rent; even when you present the facts, the tenant knows only that *you* are raising the rent.

Responsible landlords have positive experiences with most tenants, most of the time. Even with the need to raise rents and deal with occasional problem tenants, the relationship is going to be positive when you select tenants carefully, when you respect their tenancy rights, and when your policies are fair and reasonable. When you own stocks, you do not have to deal with the corporate managers and employees, customers, and vendors; you are far removed from the daily operations and corporate problems. When you own real estate, you are on the front lines. This can be enjoyable and satisfying, or troubling, depending on the people on either side, the way that each addresses problems, and the goodwill of both landlord and tenant. While many people stay away from real estate due to the direct contact attribute, this is not the sole consideration. You need to consider the tenant risk in context with the other benefits and opportunities associated with real estate investing.

Special Tax Benefits and Limitations

As a real estate investor, you enjoy special federal tax benefits (as well as state benefits, in most cases). In the 1970s, it was possible to use the tax laws to avoid taxes altogether, by buying units in tax shelter programs. Today, virtually all tax shelters have been eliminated, with one exception: real estate investing, the only remaining legitimate tax shelter available to virtually everyone.

The days of abusive tax shelters are over. There were many schemes. For example, an investor could buy a piece of art for $1,000, along with an appraisal of $5,000; then the artwork was donated to create a tax write-off of $5,000. That produced a tax benefit as high as $2,500 (if the person paid taxes in the 50 percent tax bracket). Thus, for an investment of $1,000, taxes were reduced by $2,500.

The artwork scheme was one of many ingenious ways that existing tax laws were misused. Of course, the consequence of such schemes was that many Americans avoided taxes, while others paid more than their fair share. The laws were changed during the 1980s to eliminate such schemes. Among the more significant changes was one new requirement: that a tax deduction cannot exceed the amount of money actually invested.[*] Losses in in-

---

[*]The rule is referred to as at-risk limitation. The maximum deduction is the amount of money invested plus any obligation the investor is required to pay, such as a promissory note. The combination of cash and debt is the total amount at risk.

vestments can no longer be deducted unless they are offset by gains in other investments. This rule is called the passive loss limitation.

One important exception to the limitation of loss deductions was introduced in the new series of tax reform laws. Real estate investors can deduct up to $25,000 in annual losses from real estate investments; this is the key benefit that distinguishes real estate from most other investments. It is possible to have a positive cash flow (meaning cash income is higher than cash expenses) and still report a legal loss for tax purposes. That happens when you deduct depreciation on real estate investments.

The exact workings of the tax rules are explained in more detail in later chapters. The purpose for introducing this information now is to make the point that tax rules for real estate are unique and far different from similar rules for stocks, mutual funds, and other investments. In analyzing risks of various investments, one of the most important points to keep in mind is the difference in tax rules.

Stock market investors can control when they sell their stock, so that they can time their profits and losses from investment with their tax situation in mind. They also are provided tax benefits in the form of capital gains rates, which are lower than the usual tax rates paid on income in general. Real estate investors also benefit from the same rules: They can time the sale of real estate, and profits are taxed at capital gains rates. However, real estate investors can deduct losses up to $25,000 per year. All other capital losses are limited to $3,000 maximum, and any excess has to be carried over to future years.[*]

SIDEBAR

For more information about passive loss rules, check the information at the IRS web site *http://www.irs.gov/prod/tax_edu/teletax/tc425.html*

Real estate investors can deduct all of the normal business expenses they experience: interest on mortgage loans, insurance, property taxes, transportation, utilities, advertising, and tax consultation fees, for example. In addition, they are allowed to claim depreciation for the value of real estate (on buildings and improvements, but not land). This noncash expense creates a legal write-off; this is how tax-based losses can occur even when you bring in more cash than you spend.

---

[*]This limitation applies in full if your adjusted gross income is lower than $100,000. Above that level, the allowance is phased out.

The tax benefits of owning investment real estate have to be considered as part of any valid comparison between investments. Because these benefits are significant, the after-tax income are different as well; this affects your expectations of return from an investment. For example, if you expect to earn a net profit of 7 percent per year from either stocks or real estate, the comparison cannot stop there. You also need to analyze how stocks or real estate would affect your federal (and state) taxes. Only then would the comparison be realistic. The tax rules and limitations that apply to real estate investing are explained in more depth in Chapter 4.

Direct Control of Market Value

Tax benefits are a significant consideration when comparing real estate with other investments; another is your ability to control market value directly. No other investment provides this capability to the same degree.

When you buy shares of stock, you have no participation benefits. The corporation that issued the stock is operated by its management under the supervision of the board of directors. Your only rights involve voting for major decisions once or twice per year. Thus, if the corporation fares poorly in the market, you do not have the ability to add your voice to management's in determining whether decisions are wise. In other words, stockholders in publicly listed companies are not able to directly control the value of their investment; they depend on the company's management for that.

When you own real estate, the story is different. As landlord, you pick your tenants, and, if you do so wisely, you will probably have overall satisfying experiences. By checking the references and financial resources of tenants, you are likely to find people who pay rent on time, care for your property, and honor their contract. If you do not select carefully, you are likely to have problems.

Even beyond the selection of tenants, you have a high degree of control. By caring for your property, you maintain and even improve its market value. If a house is in need of painting, and has not been landscaped for many years, with garbage in the front yard, a falling-down fence, and other visible problems, its market value will be relatively low. However, by fixing up the same house—painting, landscaping, hauling away junk, fixing the fence—market value is maintained and improved. Real estate investors have direct control over the value of their property and can do a lot to increase market value.

You also protect your investment by purchasing homeowners' insurance. In the event of a fire or another loss, the insurance company will reimburse you. As long as you finance your purchase through a conventional lender, you will be required to carry homeowners' insurance. After your loan has been paid in full, you are no longer *required* to pay insurance premiums, but it is unwise to let insurance drop. Considering the value of improvements, it just makes sense to protect yourself against catastrophic losses.

Direct control means even more than these points. The steps you take to put responsible tenants in your house, maintain its value, and protect yourself against loss are all basic requirements for smart investing. However, control goes beyond this. When you invest in the stock market, you are supposed to pick stocks of companies whose fundamentals are strong. This means that sales and profits are supposed to be healthy over a number of years, and all signs point to a company that is well managed and competitive in its sector. The same rules apply to picking real estate investments, even though some people buy property without looking at the real estate fundamentals. That is a mistake.

Even seasoned stock market investors, who know what stock fundamentals mean, may be puzzled at the idea that the same rules apply to the real estate market. What are real estate fundamentals? They are the basic features of real estate that determine whether a specific property has the potential for long-term appreciation. These fundamentals include the following:

1. *Location.* The location of property is the most important of the fundamentals. Two identical properties will have vastly different values when they are located in different areas. For example, a house on a very busy street will be limited in potential growth values, whereas the same house one block behind that busy street will see much more appreciation in value. Location also refers to zoning and neighborhood condition. Mixed zoning is less desirable, because it means that owners have little or no control over the land uses nearby. A nice house sitting next to a construction company or trailer court loses much of its value because of mixed use. And when a neighborhood is in decline, that affects all property values. Decline is seen in terms of how other owners care for their homes (or let them go into disrepair) and in rising rates of crime in the area.

2. *Condition and age.* You would expect to pay more for a well-maintained, newer property and less for a poorly maintained, older property. As a general rule, older houses require more maintenance. Electrical and plumbing systems might be outdated, and many older houses are poorly insulated by modern standards, meaning that heating and cooling bills will be higher than those in newly constructed houses. It may be a mistake to invest in older properties just because the price is lower, if, in fact, you need to spend a lot to bring that property up to minimum standards. Some houses in

disrepair can be improved cosmetically with minimal work, but when a house is profoundly out of shape, you need to compare the savings in initial purchase price with the cost and time that will be involved in repairing it. Inexperienced real estate investors often overlook this all-important fact.

3. *Conformity.* The concept of conformity is important to you as a real estate investor, because it will affect the long-term value of your investment. Generally speaking, property is expected to be similar within an area or a neighborhood. Thus, if you own a three-bedroom, two-bath house, it conforms to the neighborhood standard if most other houses have the same number of bedrooms and baths, lot size, overall square feet in the house, and outer appearance. A nonconforming house in such a neighborhood tends to be overimproved, so a six-bedroom house twice the size of the standard house, located on a double lot, and of unusual architectural style would definitely be a nonconforming property. A nonconforming property is not going to realize its full market value over time. The average sales price and market value of conforming properties will hold down the value of the nonconforming property, so that the investor will be unlikely to realize the kind of returns on investment that he or she would have earned buying a conforming property.

4. *Price.* Finally, the best-known of the fundamentals is price. The amount a seller asks for a property and the amount a buyer pays often are the features that receive the most attention about property. It is the most popular feature for comparisons between similar properties and for analyzing statistical information about the health of the real estate market in your area. As revealing as price information is about the condition of your local real estate market, it can also be misleading. It is not necessarily the price of property that determines the value of rental investments but some other features. For example, what is the *spread* of the property? What is the difference between the seller's asked price and the price actually paid by the buyer? The wider the spread, the more weakness there is in the market. Another point worth observing is the time properties are on the market. In very hot markets, properties sell on average in three months or less. In conditions where properties take six months or more to sell—or when properties are pulled off of the market without selling at all—the market is very poor for real estate investing.

Another point to remember about price is that the real price you pay for property is not related at all to the stated selling/buying price of the property. The real price is the total you pay over many years, including interest. In the typical 30-year loan, you pay two to three times more than the stated selling price, with the difference representing interest. Thus, rather than argue over a few thousand dollars' difference between what the seller wants and what you want to pay, you are wiser to look for a better financing deal. Even a small reduction in the interest rate translates to a significant reduction in overall price over the long term. A more comprehensive study of interest rates and their effect on pricing is found in Chapter 3.

Historical Prices and Values

Any analysis of real estate investing should take place on a *regional* basis. It's a mistake to review national figures, except for a broad view of the market as a whole and over many years. The status of the market in your city or town is going to be entirely different from the market even a few miles away.

Real estate values and the prices of property are cyclical and local. This means that the relative degree of supply and demand is constantly shifting over time, and that supply and demand where you live are not going to be the same elsewhere. One of the most common mistakes new investors make is to review national statistics only, forgetting to look down the street to see what is going on in their neighborhood.

The real estate cycle reflects the supply and demand. Remember, these two forces are changing constantly, and it might take many months or years to recognize a significant shift in one side or the other. Real estate, like all cycles, contains the two components. *Supply* is the inventory of property available and for sale, whether existing housing or new construction. The more units available and for sale, the greater the supply. *Demand* is the buyer market. The more buyers, the higher the demand. There is rarely a perfect match between supply and demand, because so many factors affect both sides, such as the following:

- The level of construction activity in your area
- The number of jobs available versus the number of qualified workers (translating to the number of people moving into the area or leaving it)
- New employment opportunities coming up in the near future
- Prices of property in your area, compared with those in other areas

These are but a few of the economic factors that make the real estate cycle change over time. Because real estate operates on a market economy—meaning that prices change as supply and demand change—prices of all property reflect the condition of the market. As the supply of properties for sale increases, that change tends to cause prices to level out, or even fall. For example, if too many houses are built in one year,

there will not be enough buyers, so the demand will absorb only a portion of the supply. Buyers can afford to offer less for houses, and builders
or current owners will not be able to sell for their full asking price. If the
opposite happens—not enough houses are being built to meet the
demand—then sellers have the advantage, and prices rise.

Supply and demand levels tend to change in unpredictable ways, rising and falling in reaction to one another and, often, in overreaction.
The classic example is that an area experiences many new jobs and people begin moving in as the economy picks up. In response, builders start
more new home building activity than in previous years. However, the
demand is not indefinite, and too many housing units are built. The consequence is that, following a run-up in prices, the demand levels out and
prices stabilize or fall. In the process of this classic sequence, many
short-term changes take place. In hindsight, a real estate cycle is fairly
easy to identify, because all of the sales information is in hand. However,
when you are in the middle of a real estate cycle, it is difficult to forecast
which direction will come next.

The supply and demand cycle can be reviewed on a chart like the one
in Figure 1.1. The line represents the changing level of demand in the
housing market. Remember, though, that in practice, supply and demand does not necessarily move in such a predictable manner. This
chart is only a representation of the six stages in the cycle:

1. At the beginning of the cycle, demand begins rising. This usually occurs when the local population increases beyond the current supply
   of housing. Thus, prices edge upward as more buyers appear.

2. In response to growing demand, construction of new houses begins.
   This activity is a normal reaction to increased demand in all markets.
   The supply side responds to demand.

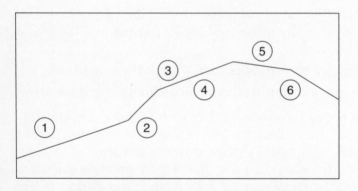

FIGURE 1.1 Supply and Demand.

3. As the supply increases, demand gradually slows down. In other words, new housing units are constructed to the point that supply and demand are well matched. Incidentally, this is a difficult effect to recognize in advance. The change in demand is difficult to see in the middle of activity. Even though demand slows down, it does not disappear, but continues to rise to a peak.

4. Supply eventually exceeds the supply, so that too many units are available. Not enough buyers are coming into the market. This point is also referred to as the peak in the cycle.

5. As demand diminishes, building of new units stops. The supply exceeds demand, so there is no incentive to continue building new housing units.

6. Demand for new houses is at a low point. No new supply is being placed on the market. Ultimately, demand will return to a level that begins the cycle anew.

This sequence applies to all markets, not just real estate. In the stock market, the fast trading activity can create a sequence like this one in a single trading day. Real estate cycles tend to be longer term. While not as orderly as this example, the general sequence is predictable; what cannot be known in advance is how long the cycle will take. Some real estate cycles go for one year or less, so that the interim building activity takes place over one season; other cycles last for several years. While a cycle is underway, it is impossible to know which direction will take place next, because the peaks and valleys of the cycle are identified only by looking back. This is comparable to the prediction of stock price movements. Studying a chart of a stock's price history, it is easy to explain how and why prices changed; predicting what will happen next is far more difficult.

The fact that real estate trends are different by region makes any broad-based prediction difficult, to say the least. Even as population trends continue to rise, a particular area might experience falling demand. Population shifts are always part of the mix of any demographic change. The U.S. Census Bureau has predicted that the population of the United States will double from 1996 levels by the year 2050—this certainly translates to higher demand for housing.[*]

Even with a doubling of the population, no investor can know with certainty where and exactly when changes will occur. You can make informed judgments based on your local economy, and that is all you can do. Base

---

[*]*Population Projections of the United States . . . 1995–2050,* U.S. Bureau of the Census, 1996 midrange prediction.

your estimates on the economy and past trends. If a particular area depends on only one or two major employers, it is vulnerable. If those companies were to relocate or close down, the job market would dry up. When that happens, housing inevitably follows. Remember, trends in real estate follow overall trends in the regional economy—notably, available jobs. A widespread demand for new homes does not occur in areas where there is no work.

In reviewing overall statistics over a 20-year period, we can see that the demand for housing has risen steadily. A review of the average sales prices of homes shows increases in 17 out of 21 years between 1980 and 2000, as summarized in Table 1.2, based on information from the U.S. Bureau of the Census.

These average sales prices are national, of course, and do not reflect the extremes—those areas suffering long-term low prices or those areas experiencing big run-ups in price, where home sales exceed $400,000 (the San Francisco Bay Area, for example). A study of specific regions is interesting in what it reveals: a wide disparity from one area to another. The averages show only that real estate prices rise over time *on average.* They do not show what is happening locally.

TABLE 1.2   Average Sales Prices of Single-Family Houses

YEAR	AVERAGE SALES PRICE	% CHANGE	YEAR	AVERAGE SALES PRICE	% CHANGE
1980	$ 76,400	6.4%	1990	$149,800	0.7%
1981	83,000	8.6	1991	147,200	-1.7
1982	83,900	1.1	1992	144,100	-2.1
1983	89,800	7.0	1993	147,700	2.5
1984	97,600	8.7	1994	154,500	4.6
1985	100,800	3.3	1995	158,700	2.7
1986	111,900	11.0	1996	166,400	4.9
1987	127,200	13.7	1997	176,200	5.9
1988	138,300	8.7	1998	181,900	3.2
1989	148,800	7.6	1999	195,800	7.6
			2000	206,400	5.4

Source: U.S. Bureau of the Census, Manufacturing & Construction Division, Residential Construction branch.

It is also interesting to compare the average real estate prices to changes in inflation, as measured by the Consumer Price Index (CPI). In the majority of years, real estate values have exceeded the CPI, so that long-term real estate investing is a good hedge against inflation—again, considering the record overall and for many years.

A summary of the Consumer Price Index is provided in Table 1.3, summarizing information from the U.S. Bureau of Labor Statistics. When you compare the rate of increase in average sales prices of houses with the rate of increase in the Consumer Price Index, it is clear that housing investments beat inflation consistently—*on average.* Because these statistics are national and not regional, they are useful only insofar as they demonstrate how real estate and inflation compare on a broad base.

TABLE 1.3   Increase in the CPI

YEAR	CPI INCREASE (%)	YEAR	CPI INCREASE (%)
1980	13.5%	1990	5.4%
1981	10.4	1991	4.2
1982	6.1	1992	3.0
1983	3.2	1993	3.0
1984	4.3	1994	2.6
1985	3.6	1995	2.8
1986	1.9	1996	3.0
1987	3.7	1997	2.3
1988	4.1	1998	1.6
1989	4.8	1999	2.2
		2000	3.4

Source: U.S. Bureau of Labor Statistics.

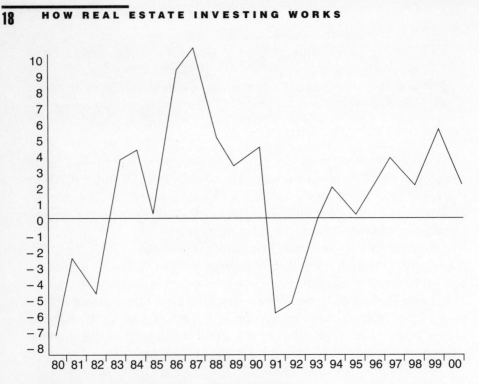

FIGURE 1.2   Housing Growth Over- or Underinflation.

SIDEBAR

The web site for the Bureau of Labor Statistics is worth visiting. It is *stats.bls.gov*

A summary of the rates of increase of housing over- (or under-) inflation is summarized in Figure 1.2. A general overview of national trends in housing (especially when compared with growth of inflation) is instructive, as it shows that real estate investing makes sense as a long-term proposition. This assumes, of course, that

- You invest in an area that is growing at or above the national average.
- The rate of growth will continue in the future.
- The investment is suitable for you in all respects.

Predictions about the future for real estate, as for any investment, are made with available information but are reliable only to a point. Historical and future growth rates can never be known, but an educated guess is possible if you review the economic status in your area. A diversified employment base, historical strength in demand for real estate, and other positive economic indicators certainly make any real estate investment viable based on what you know today. To judge whether or not real estate is a suitable risk for you requires additional study, definition, and analysis.

Real Estate and Risk Tolerance

Every investment can be defined in terms of how well it matches your risk tolerance, the kind and amount of risk you are willing and able to take with your money. Risk tolerance refers not only to how much risk you are willing to take but also what you can afford and what makes you comfortable or uncomfortable. Some people require safety and insurance in all of their investments, whereas others are willing to speculate and risk losses for the opportunity to earn bigger profits. No two people are the same in terms of risk tolerance.

The definition of your individual risk tolerance depends on several factors:

1. *Your long-term investing goals.* If you are investing to save for a child's college education or to start your own business, for example, you are likely to pick specific types of investments; however, if you have longer-term goals, such as retirement security, you need a different type of portfolio. Because real estate tends to be a long-term investment, you may need to look further into your financial future if real estate is going to play a substantial part in your overall investment portfolio.

2. *Your family and marital status and age.* A married couple with young children probably need to think about insurance, college education, and their personal housing costs. In comparison, a single person can afford to forego those specific concerns. Younger people have more time to invest before retirement, so they can take greater risks if they are so inclined. The business of owning rental properties, particularly if they need fixing up, may also require more elbow grease than other types of investments, so people in their 30s and 40s are most likely to be attracted to real estate investing. This does not exclude other age groups. However, people in their 20s might not have the financial and credit strength to qualify for financing, and older investors might not be interested in working with tenants and directly managing properties.

3. *The amount of capital available.* Every investment is going to depend on the amount of money you have available. It's not just the initial cash outlay that matters, either. You need to be able to afford to pay for property taxes, insurance, and a mortgage payment, in addition to unexpected repairs to properties; you also need to make monthly payments even when the property is vacant. These requirements can place a strain on a tight family budget.

4. *Your experience as an investor.* Everyone has to begin somewhere, and a first-time real estate investor will learn a lot of the important lessons by going through the experience. However, experienced investors in the stock market will be better equipped to analyze risk and opportunity. An investor who already owns a family residence also is familiar with mortgage rules and conditions, property taxes, homeowners' insurance, and the types of ongoing maintenance involved with owning property. All of this experience helps the first-time investor overcome the initial apprehension when trying something for the first time.

5. *Your attitude toward risk.* Are you willing to take higher than average risks, in exchange for higher than average profits? If so, you are more a speculator than an investor. However, if you are more conservative, you will be attracted to insured investments (such as real estate). It is one of the few investments that provides a cash flow, supplies insurance, and beats inflation—all while providing you with a tax-sheltered income. Thus, in defining your attitude toward risk, consider all of the attributes of real estate (and other investments) before deciding that a particular course is too risky or does not provide enough financial incentive.

Risk tolerance defines a range of important questions that every investor needs to address. It often is boiled down to the point of view that divides all investments into yes or no columns. In practice, though, your risk tolerance might be far more complex and finely defined. For example, a real estate investor may further define risk tolerance by type of property, location, price, condition, and other features.

If you intend to buy rental properties for the combined benefits they offer—positive cash flow, tax shelter, long-term growth, and appreciation of your net worth—then you also need to understand the risks you face along the way. As an informed investor, you improve your chances of success in the financial sense, as well as your chances for personal satisfaction with the decision to become a landlord. As with any investment, the more you know before you put your capital at risk, the better you will fare afterwards.

CHAPTER 2

Buying Rental Property

S election of the right property is the key to success. As a real estate investor, the time you spend looking for the best possible rental is time well spent. Just as stock market investors emphasize the importance of research, analysis, and comparison, real estate investors also need to pay attention to the fundamentals.

Applying the Fundamentals

In a buyer's market—that condition where prices are low and a lot of properties are for sale—it would seem, at first glance, that you would have an array of desirable properties from which to choose. While a lot of properties are on the market, many at bargain prices, you are still in jeopardy. Another comparison to the stock market makes this point: After a large sell-off, many stocks are underpriced, and bargains can be found. However, stocks with weak fundamentals such as poor sales history and low profits, will also be low-priced relative to previous price levels. Whether stocks are high or low, it is still essential to remember the rule of selection: *Valuable investments are identified by comparison, analysis, and observation.*

The same is true in real estate. Some experienced stock market investors may observe the commonsense rule when applied to stocks yet fail to realize that the same rule applies in real estate investing. By not going through the methodical process of comparison, analysis, and observation, it is all too easy to buy a property that will not be a good rental and that will be unlikely to appreciate in value. Apply the three steps in the following manner:

1. *Comparison.* Every investor makes educated choices by comparison. In the stock market, a particular company reports many years of growing sales and consistent profits, is well managed, and leads its sector. The stock's price history has been strong and steady. Another stock reports erratic growth, low profits, and inconsistent fundamentals. Its price is volatile and prediction is difficult. These extremes make the selection easy. The same rule applies in real estate: One property is well located, well cared for, and reasonably priced. Another is run-down, in a poor location, and in questionable condition. Investing in the second property would require considerable additional work to fix the problems. Again, the choice is easy with such extremes. In practice, comparison is more subtle between similarly priced properties, but the point remains: Only through comparison between properties can a wise selection be made.

Comparisons also need to be made for the overall market. By studying the condition of your real estate local economy from one period to another, you are able to make value judgments. For example, if properties are selling more quickly today than they were six months ago, that is a sign that demand is on the rise. If listed properties are taking longer to sell, it means that demand is soft. This information, usually available through Multiple Listing Service (MLS) or local brokerage firms, provides you with a wealth of information about the overall local market. Remember, too, that it is the local and regional market that counts, not the national averages. Your regional economy is likely to be completely different from the economy of other areas of the country.

2. *Analysis.* Successful investors are invariably oriented toward analysis. This does not mean you need an accounting degree to study markets, but it does mean that it pays to respect the fundamentals and to watch them carefully. Analysis usually means interpreting comparative information. For example, you compare price, location, condition, and other features of two or more properties; you calculate your monthly mortgage payment and other costs; you estimate the rent you are likely to receive; and you determine whether the investment is feasible.

Beyond the analysis of a specific property, the entire market should be studied as well. Using areawide information about recent sales, you can discover a lot of information about past trends and current ones. Look for length of time properties are on the market to decide whether today's conditions are improving or declining. Also observe the spread between asked and selling prices of residential properties, information usually available on MLS records. Finally, compare prices for similar properties. Are they rising or falling in your area? Also observe vacancy rates in your area for rentals. A very low vacancy rate—under 3 percent, for example—indicates a very strong market and the likelihood that current rental rates are well supported by rental demand. However, if vacancy rates are climbing, it can indicate an excess of rental units above current demand levels, which can also mean that current rental rates are likely to fall in the future.

3. *Observation.* To succeed as an investor, become a keen observer. Recognize the importance of learning from what you see. Are a lot of new homes being built in your community? What does that mean in terms of the real estate cycle and timing of your plans to purchase rental property? Should you buy older houses or new ones for rentals? Compare the prices for the same-size houses in different areas of your town or city. Also watch other factors that affect real estate values: crime statistics, traffic, the job market, and the local political climate. Do your local and county governments discourage growth or invite industry to your area? Are the number of jobs rising or falling? All of these economic factors are going to affect future real estate values.

Overall, what is the likely demand for rentals in your area? Is there a large university in your city, and what percentage of total population is represented by students? Is there a large number of apartment units in the area? If so, how will rental houses be able to compete with those units? (The market for houses and apartments often is quite different, so a comparison is not necessarily for the same tenant base.) It often is not difficult to find information, but it might be harder to interpret it. You should check with a local banker to get help in better understanding real estate trends. Bankers—who lend money to people to buy property—are in a good position to understand the local market economy. You can also consult with real estate agents and brokers. However, remember that agents tend to be less objective, since they usually are compensated via commissions; thus, they are likely to advise you to invest in real estate, regardless of whether the timing is appropriate.

Price Calculations

In selecting a property, the most obvious criterion is price. A preliminary analysis reveals quickly whether a particular price range will work for you, based on monthly payments versus likely rental income. Thus, a property on which the mortgage payment will be far above rental income should be eliminated easily. The first method for selection of property is price range.

To determine the monthly payment level, consult a book of mortgage amortization tables. These books list monthly payments for specific loan amounts, given interest rates and the number of years to repay. Typically, a table shows the monthly payment amount in a series of columns. For example, Table 2.1 shows a section of a repayment table. The table shows a section of the page for the monthly schedule of 7.00 percent loans. By

TABLE 2.1 Mortgage Amortization Table

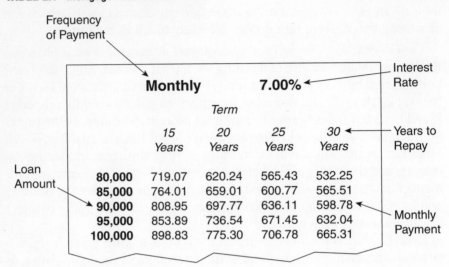

Frequency of Payment

Interest Rate

	Monthly		7.00%	
	Term			
	15 Years	20 Years	25 Years	30 Years
Loan Amount				
80,000	719.07	620.24	565.43	532.25
85,000	764.01	659.01	600.77	565.51
90,000	808.95	697.77	636.11	598.78
95,000	853.89	736.54	671.45	632.04
100,000	898.83	775.30	706.78	665.31

Years to Repay

Monthly Payment

locating the loan amount in the first column and the number of years for repayment across the top, you will find the required monthly payment. For example, a $90,000 loan to be repaid over 30 years requires a monthly payment of $598.78.

You might be looking at a property selling for $125,000 and requiring a $35,000 down payment, which would leave a mortgage of $90,000. However, if the level of monthly rental income can be reasonably expected to come in at only $400, it makes no sense to purchase this property. The mortgage amount is nearly $200 per month above rental income; in addition, you need to be able to pay property taxes and insurance, not to mention repairs and maintenance for the property. In order for such a purchase to make sense, the amount of monthly rent should be at least as much as the mortgage payment.[*]

The monthly payment is a determining factor in identifying the price range of rentals. In some areas, real estate prices are too high to make rental income investment practical, unless you can put a lot of down payment money into a property. In other areas, rents are so low that it

---

[*]When rental income covers the mortgage payment, it is a good starting point. However, any periods of vacancy mean lost cash flow, because the mortgage payment continues whether or not you have a tenant.

SIDEBAR

You can find numerous mortgage calculators on the Internet. Search on "mortgage amortization tables." Three typical sites are
http://www.anchormortgage.com/mortgage_calculator.html
http://ray.met.fsu.edu/~bret/amortize.html
http://nt.mortgage101.com/partner-scripts/1007.asp?p=youronlyn

is difficult to find acceptable properties that are supported by likely rental income.

A number of calculations can be made concerning rental value. Among these are the so-called cap rate and the gross rent multiplier. In practical terms, when you invest in real estate, your concern should be with the practical question of cash flow affordability. What is the monthly mortgage plus property taxes and insurance versus the rental income? And what would vacancies mean in terms of drain on your family income or reserves?

Even though your concern should be with the cash flow comparisons, it also helps to understand the more technical calculations and how they affect real estate investment values. The *cap rate*, an abbreviated term for *capitalization rate,* is a method for estimating the market value of income property. This is used by appraisers when evaluating rental properties, basing value on rental income, more often used for apartment complexes and other multi-unit complexes than for rental houses. To calculate, divide annual income by market price. For example, if the market price is $300,000 and current income is $22,800 per year, cap rate is

$$\frac{\$22,800}{\$300,000} = 7.6\%$$

Cap rate would be used to compare several different properties. Obviously, the higher the cap rate, the better the cash flow and, from an investor's point of view, the more desirable the property.

The gross rent multiplier (GRM) is similar and is used for the same purpose: to evaluate and compare income-producing property values in terms of income generation. An appraiser may set the estimated value based on comparisons between similar properties' sales prices and rents. For example, the appraiser might look at three comparable properties with the following sales prices and rents:

Property	Sales Prices	Monthly Rent
1	$211,500	$1,250
2	$225,000	$1,500
3	$207,950	$1,175

Gross rent multiplier is calculated by dividing the sales price by monthly rent. For example, GRMs for the three properties are

$$\frac{211,500}{1,250} = 169.2$$

$$\frac{225,000}{1,500} = 150.0$$

$$\frac{207,950}{1,175} = 177.0$$

The appraiser next finds the average of the three comparable properties:

$$\frac{169.2 + 150.0 + 177.0}{3} = 165.4$$

Finally, value of the property being appraised on this basis is estimated by multiplying the average GRM of three comparable properties by the monthly rent. For example, if you are selling a rental property generating $1,400 in monthly rent, value would be set using the GRM calculation:

$$\$1,400 \times 165.4 = \$231,560$$

Knowing the various methods used to set value in investment real estate is useful, if only because appraisal of property often is complex and confusing to the novice. An appraiser makes a best estimate based on several factors and may choose the income method, replacement cost, or market comparison to make a final value judgment. Some appraisals use more than one method, giving more weight to one over the other.

Income property calculations might be insignificant in terms of setting value for rental houses because an appraiser will know that a new owner might not necessarily use the property as an investment. Thus, using the income method could distort value, and it would make more sense to base value on market comparisons, in which sales of comparable properties in the past few months are used as the basis for setting current value of your property.

Establishing value comes down to an agreement between buyer and seller. How much is the buyer willing to pay, and how much is the seller willing to accept? When the two sides can agree on the right number, then the transaction is made possible. However, valuation is made more complex when the property is in run-down condition because some money will have to be spent to make repairs. This is important when looking for so-called bargains, because some repairs can be too expensive to make the investment practical. If you will need to invest thousands of dollars just to bring a property up to minimum condition, then a low price is not a bargain at all. The balance between price and value can be a delicate one. The ideal rental property is one in fair to excellent condition (needing little work) for which rental income will exceed the monthly mortgage payment.

Cash flow from single-family housing might be too tight to meet this requirement. In such cases, you might consider duplex investment, or even triplex and fourplex housing, as an alternative. Apartment units may be too expensive for first-time investment, but smaller, multi-unit housing could work out. These units tend to be closer to single-family housing in cost, but cash flow often is far better. It depends, again, on rental demand levels and vacancy rates, housing prices in your area, and the mortgage cost. The amount you are able to invest in the form of down payment is also a factor. The higher your down payment, the lower your mortgage payment. Thus, when you invest more cash up-front, you reduce the need for ongoing cash flow and broaden your likely market.

Many first-time investors do not have the luxury of a large pot of cash to invest in property, so more creative approaches need to be taken. However, you need to be aware that lower-priced housing often will require more maintenance and repair; such housing also tends to demand less in rental income. A careful analysis of likely rents versus mortgage payments is an important first step, even when you are thinking about buying a fairly inexpensive first property.

Characteristics of Property

While price and mortgage payments are crucial first considerations, you also need to think about the specific characteristics of a potential investment property. What features will help the property grow in market value, and what features will inhibit value?

We have already mentioned property as a top determining factor. An old real estate adage states that the three most important considerations for real estate value are location, location, and location. This emphasizes the fact that some properties will increase in value along with overall market changes in the future, whereas other properties will not grow in value.

Situations such as an overly busy street, high crime, and poorly maintained properties in the area contribute to a negative location problem. When houses are located too close to airport flight paths or train tracks, the noise factors hurt property value. In fact, buying residential properties in close proximity to noise and other nuisances is a mistake.

Properties located near schools might seem to be worthwhile investment properties at first glance. Certainly, if you attract tenants with children of the right age, the convenience of the school's location serves as a short-term advantage. However, some other problems are also associated with properties close to schools. These include the noise factor, as well as possible vandalism, littering, traffic volume, and loitering.

A similar argument can be made for proximity of properties to churches, shopping areas, and other facilities. What at first appears to be a convenience can be offset with high traffic volume and noise factors, which in the long run detract from property value and may prevent a property from growing at rates of similar houses in quieter areas, perhaps only a block or two farther removed.

The modern trend in the location of dissimilar land uses affects the way that you will locate and buy property. The United States was largely a rural country until the invention of the automobile, with few people ever traveling more than 20 miles from their homes. Industrialization resulted in the migration of people into big cities, followed by the post–World War II development of suburbia. Today, the country is going through another revolution, described as the development of edge city patterns.

The edge city is one designed and planned carefully, with residential neighborhoods free of any nonresidential use. Shopping centers have replaced downtown centers, and many people work closer to home, rather than commuting into inner cities. As this trend continues, land use becomes sharply defined and distinguished, while mixed land use downtown areas of the past are disappearing. The charm of town life is a casualty of the edge city movement. It ensures that land uses are not mixed, meaning that edge city life tends to be sterile and consistent. The pattern also requires that you drive a car to go anywhere, even if only for a quart of milk or to see a movie. While the edge city social trend does away with the problems and dangers of mixed land use, it also gives over the charm and quality of small-town life to the less creative, colder, planned community designed and engineered by bureaucrats. The new edge city is described in a book on the topic:

> Their characteristic monument is not a horse-mounted hero, but the atria reaching for the sun and shielding trees perpetually in leaf at the cores of corporate headquarters, fitness centers, and shopping plazas . . . Their land-

mark structure is the celebrated single-family detached dwelling, the sub-urban home with grass all around . . .[*]

Older neighborhoods still tend to be characterized by mixed land use. For example, you will find older stores with street-level entry and the owner's residence above; a gas station next to a general store; and other mixed uses that would be strictly prohibited under the modern guidelines. If you decide to invest in neighborhoods or towns with more traditional land use features, you should be keenly aware of how location will affect the current and future value of your property.

Some characteristics relate to the property itself, rather than to its location. A house that is small in comparison to other houses in the area will naturally tend to attract less rent, even though the price might not be much less than larger, roomier houses. A house with poor insulation will be priced lower than others, but tenants will suffer with higher utility bills and will tend to look for other dwellings more frequently. Such features might save money in the initial purchase, but will cause higher tenant turnover. That is a recurring expense for you as landlord, because in between tenants you will have vacancy costs. If you rent a property for $600 per month, your loss of rent is $20 per day, which can add up quickly. A half-month vacancy costs you $300. If that occurs two or three times per year, then the money you saved by not insulating an older house will be absorbed quickly in lost rents.

Properties that have been poorly cared for in the past will also cost more in the future. As problems arise due to what is called deferred maintenance, you will have to spend money to keep your end of the landlord-tenant agreement. The cost of repaired furnaces and water heaters, a new roof, and failing plumbing systems adds up to a substantial drain on your resources, so you often are better off spending more for an updated and renovated house than for a run-down older one—unless you are handy and enjoy working on those problems.

Property Types and Tenants

The location, age, and condition of a property define its potential as a rental. Beyond that, the property and its characteristics also define the kinds of tenants you will be able to find. The conventional belief is that landlords pick their tenants; in practice, though, tenants tend to pick the kinds of houses that are suitable for them. This is an important distinction.

For example, if your property is located in a run-down neighborhood, the house is old and poorly cared for, and the yard is overgrown with weeds, chances are that the tenants will be the type of people who will not take care

---

[*]Joel Garreau, *Edge City: Life on the New Frontier* (Anchor Books, New York, NY 1992, 4.)

of your property. If your house is in a neighborhood of well-manicured lawns, it has been painted recently, and all systems are in excellent shape, you are more likely to attract tenants with an attitude that a home should be cared for and who are more likely to keep your property in its good condition.

These are generalizations, of course. It is also possible to find excellent tenants even for the run-down property or to end up with poor tenants in the nicest of houses. As a rule, however, your property is an advertisement for the type of tenant you seek (and for the type that is a likely fit for the house itself).

Going along with the observation about tenants and properties, first-time investors might not be able to afford a nicely appointed house. It might be a financial necessity to start with a small house in a poorly maintained neighborhood, fix it up, rent it out, and hope that property values improve over time.

Buying a house in such a neighborhood can be a problem, however, because property values are less likely to rise than in a better kept neighborhood. Areas are characterized by the way that houses are maintained. Even in the well-kept neighborhood of today, a transition can occur, and the character of the area can change. An area tends to go through a transition when properties turn over. For example, a neighborhood is developed and people of a similar age buy houses, most of whom remain in those houses while they raise their children. Many years later, the same original owners begin to move to other areas or pass away, and a new generation of buyers takes over. When that happens, an outdated neighborhood may go through modernization and updating and gain a new, vibrant character, or it may fall into disrepair and decline.

In identifying property for investment, it helps if you can identify the overall character of an area and assess the potential for transition in the near future. Are most of the people on the block elderly, or are they primarily young families? Are most properties owner-occupied, or are there many rentals? Are there any empty lots that appear to have been that way for a long time? All of this information helps you determine what kinds of tenants are likely to be attracted to a property in the area.

Rather than buying a house in a run-down neighborhood, another approach is to buy a house needing only cosmetic repair, located in an otherwise well-maintained area. In other words, look for properties needing only cosmetic repair. This is likely to represent the best value. The old adage advises: Buy the worst house on a good street. That means you will do best by looking for a property that can be brought up to neighborhood standard with little effort. Some painting and landscaping often is all that is required to transform a run-down shack into a charming cottage or starter home.

The condition of a property reflects the level of care exercised by a previous owner, so when you look at properties on the market, you can identify a bargain in terms of price by recognizing the difference between major problems and cosmetic neglect. Looking in low-priced areas is a mistake if *all* of the properties are run-down and poorly maintained, because there is no obvious reason for property values to go up in the future. Few people want to move into poorly cared for neighborhoods. The poor investment value, coupled with the potential for higher crime and other problems, makes such a decision ill-advised.

Thus, two distinctions need to be made. First is the distinction between characteristics of the neighborhood itself in comparison with other neighborhoods. Second is the distinction between the condition of a specific property in relation to other houses in the same area—notably, on the same block. Seek properties needing only cosmetic repair but located in an otherwise nicely cared for area. That is the most likely scenario to make your investment a profitable one.

As a general rule, cosmetic repairs add value instantly. When a property is on the market and those relatively easy improvements have not been made, you should wonder as a potential buyer why the current owner has not bothered. When people list properties, a competent real estate agent will advise them to clean up the yard and apply a coat of paint, if needed. At the very least, they will tell people to pick up any debris lying around in the yard, so when you view a property for sale in poor condition, what does it mean? It is most likely that the current owner does not care about appearance and does not realize that a few simple repairs would improve the property's marketability *and* market value.

Knowing what to look for, and being patient until the right property comes along, increases your chances to profit as a real estate investor. Stay away from run-down neighborhoods characterized by empty properties, an excessive number of empty lots, poorly maintained houses, and high-crime statistics. Look for run-down houses in nicer neighborhoods. The cosmetic repairs you perform will bring that house up in value as soon as they are completed, and you will be likely to attract tenants that are a good match for the area.

SIDEBAR

Check your local police or sheriff's department to find current crime statistics for a neighborhood. Compare low-crime areas to find modest neighborhoods with well-priced properties for sale. Remember that there are likely to be *more* properties for sale at lower prices in run-down and high-crime districts.

Finding the Best Deal

Most good deals are defined in terms of price. In other words, negotiating a few thousand dollars off the asked price means the buyer gains a small profit at the point of purchase. However, a good deal often is not connected to price at all. At times, what seems to be an attractive price is not a good deal at all.

Consider the case of a property so in need of repair that it has no equity or even potential for equity in the future. In other words, the property is totaled, in the sense that its current equity cannot possibly match the repairs needed to bring it up to par with other properties of similar size and location. These properties should be avoided altogether. You often will find that sellers are the most willing to negotiate on their price when the property has such severe problems that they cannot be corrected economically.

One way to identify problem properties is when a seller is willing to finance the sale. In other words, you won't need to go to the bank because the seller will act as lender to you. For a specified down payment, you will make payments to the seller instead of to an outside lender. When this occurs, the seller is said to "carry" or to "take back paper" on the property. This jargon is real estate terminology for seller financing. Why, though, would a seller take such a step if he or she could cash out instead? Some sellers see an opportunity to earn interest over several years and are willing to assume the small risk of a secured loan to earn that money.[*] However, the reasons could also be due to problems with the property itself.

Most lenders will not be willing to approve loans for properties that do not meet minimum standards. If a lender requires that a house have a permanent foundation, for example, a house with post and beam supports will not qualify for a mortgage loan. A bank would require that outdated foundation work be replaced. That's an expensive capital improvement, which the current owner may be unwilling to undertake just to be able to qualify for financing, so one solution for the owner in such a situation is to offer to carry a loan for a new buyer.

An inexperienced real estate investor, especially one whose own credit would not qualify for outside financing, is likely to be attracted to seller financing. It could be viewed as the only practical way to begin investing in real estate for someone whose income and cash resources are too low to invest in more traditional ways.

---

[*]A secured loan is a reference to the underlying value of the property. If the buyer were to default, the seller could foreclose and recover the property in satisfaction of the secured loan.

Thus, a likely match can be made between a seller and buyer without the involvement of a conventional lender. However, as a first-time investor, you are more likely in this situation to acquire properties with intrinsic problems—perhaps expensive ones as well. When you buy property in this manner, you also buy the seller's problems with the property. At one point in the future when you want to sell that property, you will have to face the same decision: Fix the problem preventing outside lenders from approving loans or carry the financing yourself for another buyer.

What might look like a deal and an opportunity could end up being an expensive mistake. A truly good deal is locating property that meets current standards in the lender's eye. That is always a smart starting point, because lenders do not want to acquire someone else's problems any more than investors do. You will probably need to invest some amount of cash, usually 30 percent of the sales price for investment property, and then be able to make mortgage payments, even if you have a period of vacancy in the property.

The conventional requirement of 30 percent down is not a hard and fast rule, just a common requirement. By shopping around, you could discover that more favorable terms are available, but often in exchange for a higher interest rate or more up-front origination fees or loan points. Some people, recognizing the restrictions on low down payment for rental property, have decided that a more practical route involves buying a new primary residence and renting out a previous one. In that way, the newly acquired home—as a second primary residence—can be financed with 10 or 20 percent down, and the original home can be converted to a rental property.

Conversion of property from one use to another makes sense if you are seeking income, for a number of reasons. Because you have been living in your residence, you already know its condition, so no surprises are going to come up after you place a tenant in the home. This step also enables you to upgrade to a larger home, one with a more desirable location, or one with more market value. This idea is the most practical way for many first-time investors to get into the market. If you cannot come up with the down payment required to buy a rental property, you simply buy yourself a new primary residence and convert your current home to a rental property.

If you have been living in your home for several years, you might also find that current rental income is comfortably higher than your mortgage payment. That means you will have positive cash flow, always a desirable trait for an investment. You also create tax benefits by converting your present house to a rental. All of your insurance and other investment expenses become deductible, in addition to depreciation. As a homeowner, you are allowed to deduct interest on your mortgage loan and property taxes as itemized deductions; however, as a real estate investor, your tax benefits are more expanded.

Good Rentals versus Poor Ones

Whether you buy a rental property or convert your present home to an investment, you will need to manage your rental to maximize returns, protect your equity, and ensure that tenants are caring for the house and grounds. Some properties lend themselves to rentals by their very features, but other properties are not ideally suited for rental uses.

A large, expensive house might not generate rental income adequate to cover your mortgage payments. That is always a problem for real estate investors, because a primary limitation to expanding your real estate portfolio will invariably be cash flow. Thus, any negative cash flow impedes your investment's profitability. Each month that you pay out more than you bring in you erode your capital base. If this problem goes on for several years, you end up losing money even when market values rise.

A house with three bedrooms and two baths is considered traditional by modern standards, so any house with fewer bedrooms (or with only one bath) will be more difficult to rent out and to keep rented. The market for rental houses usually involves people who want to live in a house instead of an apartment. Many renters are new to the area and will be looking for a house to buy and, in the meantime, want to live in a rental house. This type of tenant will expect three bedrooms and two baths, essential for a family with children.

Houses without a garage are similarly difficult to rent. The lack of such a feature limits your market, because people want the garage, either to park their cars or to store their belongings. Many renters looking for houses will not even consider properties that do not have a garage.

A large yard might attract some people and discourage others. If the yard requires a big investment in time to maintain, a tenant might be unwilling to rent such a house. There seem to be two reactions to a large yard. One group wants the land and has big plans to put in a vegetable or flower garden; such plans often do not work out. The second group wants a house but prefers a no-maintenance situation. For the second group, the big yard is a problem. In rural areas, land presents an even greater difficulty. For example, many rural areas have houses on five-acre plots. That area is said to be too large to mow and too small to hay. The result, of course, is that the land is difficult to maintain and often is ignored. The result is that it does not show well, presents a potential fire hazard, and leads to disagreements between landlord and tenant.

A final determining factor in distinguishing between good and bad rentals is the noise factor. First-time real estate investors are looking for bargain properties, so they often find themselves buying houses near schools, highways, railroad tracks, or airports. Bargain prices often translate to poor investments, unfortunately, because such properties do not gain value, as do similar properties in quieter neighborhoods.

The noise factor also affects the rental prospects for a property. Tenants, like real estate investors, seek bargains, so they might apply for houses with lower rents, even when in a noisy area; however, the nuisance of the noise itself leads to more turnover in the rental, presenting the landlord with a triple problem: having a property in a poor location, which doesn't command top rents, and characterized by high turnover. Thus, a real bargain requires a careful study of the house and its features, *as well as* of the neighborhood and its features.

You need to assess properties critically, with several levels of concern in mind. Not only should the house be built properly and according to building codes. It also should be located in a nicely maintained neighborhood free of noise and other nuisances. The house should conform to the traditional features of a house. This usually means three bedrooms, two baths, and a garage. Having more bedrooms is just as much of a problem as having fewer, because most families simply don't need the extra room.

The ideal property also should be well priced relative to the other houses in the area. As long as any repair needs are merely cosmetic, they will have an easy fix. As a buyer, you have an advantage in looking for the worst house on a good block, because the problems can be fixed with little investment of time or money, requiring no special skills. Compared with having to fix the plumbing, electrical, or heating systems; the roof; or the foundation problems; the cosmetic repair is far easier. If you invest in a lawn mower, weed eater, and some painting supplies, most cosmetic problems can be resolved without having to pay anyone else to help.

Checklist of Features

What features are worth seeking to find a bargain property? The following are the important features for properties and one for neighborhoods.

Property Checklist

SUITABLE FOR RENTAL USE

Not every house works well as a rental. Does the house in question have the typical number of bedrooms, baths, and other features? Is there a garage? Is there a yard? Most tenants looking for houses expect features that are typical for people living in houses, either as tenants or as owners.

HOUSE LAYOUT

Most houses have been planned well, so that inside traffic makes sense. However, other houses are poorly planned. Do you need to walk through bedrooms to access a bath? Are rooms located oddly? Seek houses with sensible layouts. They are more likely to resell and to hold value over time.

LIKELY TYPE OF TENANT

Remember, tenants are attracted to houses that suit them, so a house sometimes described as an "executive" house (modern, well-landscaped, relatively large) is probably going to attract tenants with higher than average income, who are new to the area, and who will be buying or building their own homes within a year or two. A run-down house with outdated features, deferred maintenance, and a poor paint job is going to attract a far different type of tenant. While these are generalizations, they are important ones for real estate investors; the rental income you are likely to earn and the relationship you will have with your tenants depend to a degree on the appearance and quality of your rental property.

POTENTIAL CASH FLOW

What is the relationship between rental income and cash outlay? It is not a question of how much rent you will bring in but one of how well the rent covers expenses and other payments. If your payments are going to exceed rental income, then the investment makes no sense. If you cannot afford to continue making your mortgage payments if your property is vacant for a few months, then you cannot afford the investment. You need to compare the potential income versus cash outlay to decide if the investment works for you.

RENTAL INCOME LEVEL

How much rental income will you receive for each month that the property is rented? This question relates not only to the immediate level of income but also to longer-term investment feasibility. For example, if you expect the property to grow in value only modestly, and for very little income each month, is it worth the risk? If you believe that your income from owning rental property will not be substantial, there might be other alternatives for investing your capital—and these might involve less hands-on maintenance and perhaps lower risk. It does no harm to consider placing your cash in a mutual fund and letting someone else manage it, as one possible alternative.

The level of rental income you will receive is a good indicator of whether or not the property is a valuable investment. In some areas with high demand for rentals, monthly income can be significant, perhaps exceeding mortgage payments and other outlays by a nice margin. In other areas, where the market is relatively soft, the viability of real estate investing makes the idea less attractive.

CONDITION VERSUS PRICE

The real test of investment value is condition in comparison with price. This is the same rule for all types of investments. For stocks, for example, *condition* refers to financial health of the company, and you would not want to pay top dollar for the stock of a company with weak sales and profits. For real estate, *condition* refers to the appearance of the house and yard, the systems (heating and cooling, electrical, and plumbing), the roof, need for paint inside and out, and other situations requiring attention. The price of the house should reflect the condition, and vice versa.

COMPARISON TO OTHER HOUSES

How does the property compare with other properties nearby? Remember the advice to buy the worst house on a good block. That means that the potential for increasing value quickly is greatest when cosmetics are the main problems. If *all* of the houses in the area are run-down, that is not a promising sign for you. It means that the neighborhood is in decline, and the properties are not likely to grow in market value until that trend is reversed.

Think of the neighborhood as a sector, as described in the stock market. Cyclical stocks tend to go out of favor as a group, so most investors stay away from sectors that are in decline. By the same argument, real estate investors should not be interested in properties in neighborhoods in decline. Look for cosmetically run-down properties in otherwise upscale neighborhoods; that is where real values can be found.

CONFORMITY

Is the property similar to other properties in the area? This applies in terms of lot size, the design and appearance of the house, the number and size of rooms, and the treatment of the yard. As a general rule, conforming properties tend to grow in market value at the same rate as other houses in the same area and in similar areas. Nonconforming houses, especially those overbuilt for an area, tend to not gain the market value that they would elsewhere. In other words, a six-bedroom house in a four-bedroom neighborhood is not going to grow in relative market value at the same rate as other properties. This is due to its nonconformity with the neighborhood or street. Avoid nonconforming properties to maximize the return on your investment.

LEVEL OF NEEDED REPAIRS

A bargain property might not be a bargain at all. If you would need to spend so much money fixing its problems, then you would end up overspending for the property. Remember, the relationship between property value and rental investment value cannot be overlooked. If you put too much money in a house to fix it up and bring it up to minimum standards, it will be difficult, if not impossible, to recover your investment.

Repairs should be cosmetic or a match for your skills. As soon as you need to bring in professional help, the costs will begin to rise. For example, if you purchase a house for $85,000 in a neighborhood where the average property sells for $95,000, the difference should be thought of as the maximum budget for fix-up costs. You should not spend more than the $10,000 in this example. If you do, then you are paying more for the house than it is worth, and that means you will have problems recovering your investment. As other properties increase in value, the overspent condition of your house will remain ahead of the average until other properties catch up. That is not a wise investment scenario.

LOCATION AND FUTURE MARKET VALUE

The all-important location of the house dictates its future market value to a large degree. The only advantage of owning property on a busy street is that it's easy to find. First-time investors often buy such houses without realizing the problems, because they see the "for sale" sign as they drive by. They also see that the property is lower in price when compared with similar houses nearby. Remember however, that, over the long term, poorly located houses will *not* grow in value at the same rate as well-located houses.

Location problems include not only traffic but also levels of crime; mixed zoning; noise due to train tracks, airports, and other public facilities; and any other features of land use that detract from the value of the house.

Neighborhood Checklist

OVERALL CONDITION

Neighborhoods, like individual properties, can be defined in terms of their condition. For example, an area containing several vacant lots, many houses for sale, and a run-down appearance is obviously not a desirable one for investment. In comparison, in an area whose properties are obviously well cared for, with no vacant lots, and with other signs of "health," property values are being maintained and probably are on the rise.

AREA LAYOUT

How is the neighborhood arranged? Some areas are planned for practical use, and are easy to move around in; others can be described as poorly planned, and the signs show. An area that used to have through streets, but that now is interrupted with a freeway, is laid out poorly. Inevitably, when a neighborhood is cut in half in that manner, one aspect of the area dies: its identity as a desirable place to live. Not only does the freeway represent a noise intrusion; it also ruins the character of the original neighborhood.

The same argument is applied in areas that have grown haphazardly rather than in a well-planned manner. When one series of streets is added onto, the signs are apparent. One set of houses belongs to a new generation, whereas others are older and out of style. Streets that once were used for quiet residential access now have heavy traffic patterns. The character of an area affects its investment value directly; changes over time often are called improvements, but from the investment point of view, they might have the opposite effect.

ZONING

Today's standard calls for isolation of land use by type. Typically, in newly developed areas, residential neighborhoods are set up as satellites around shopping malls, and freeway access is removed from both residential and commercial use. Light industrial, heavy industrial, rural, and agricultural zoning are strictly isolated to specific areas deemed appropriate for such uses. Under modern zoning methods, mixed use is discouraged and, quite often, forbidden as a matter of local ordinance.

In some, older and well-established communities, mixed zoning is allowed because it has been there longer than the planning department. To some, mixed use is charming and appealing and is a desirable attribute, especially for historical areas. To others, it presents a problem for investment purposes; mixed zoning could be a problem when investors want to sell their land. For example, a house located behind a service station could be difficult to place on the market, considering the levels of traffic, noise, and environmental hazard.

CRIME LEVELS AND TRENDS

The study of an area's crime statistics is always revealing about the recent direction of the real estate cycle. When neighborhoods begin to decline, that decline often is characterized by a rise in crime, if not actually caused by such crime. Pay special attention to crimes of violence and property crimes; these usually indicate the overall direction of an area. If crime has been on the rise in the past year or two, chances are it will get worse in the future as well.

In areas where citizens are determined to not let crime take hold, the crime statistics usually reflect the facts. Crime begins falling as people become concerned about the safety of their families. The origins of gang activity, such as tagging graffiti, are quickly removed as people work to prevent the development of other gang activities. To a large extent, the amount of crime in an area is a direct reaction to the level of citizen concern. A falling crime rate indicates that investment in the area is a smart idea.

CONVENIENCES

How close is the property to conveniences, such as houses of worship, libraries, schools, shopping areas, and transportation? If the property is in an isolated rural area, its likely market value will be limited (unless growth overtakes the area in the future), and you will limit your potential tenant market as well. Many would-be tenants will decide against a remote location for a variety of reasons. While many people would like to live in a rural setting, they also want to be close to schools, shopping, and other outlets.

Conveniences can work against your property as well, especially if they are accompanied by nuisance factors. For example, it might be convenient to live near an airport, but the noise and traffic factors hold down property values. And living near a high school is a great convenience for high school–age children, but noise levels, traffic, and potential vandalism have to be considered as offsetting factors.

PRICE TRENDS

A basic requirement for all investors is to study recent trends in prices. Just as a stock market investor should review market share price along with sales and profit history, a real estate investor should consider potential rental income in light of current market value and recent price changes. If property is increasing in value, and you believe the trend is going to continue in response to demand, then investing in real estate makes sense. However, if the area is overbuilt and houses move slowly, that is a sign of a soft market.

Ask questions and get the facts. How long has the average property in your price range been on the market? What is the spread between asked price and sales price? How much has the typical price range increased (or decreased) in the past year or two? In other words, get your facts and compare different neighborhoods. Don't take the word of a real estate agent, who is likely to tell you that the best time to buy is right now. Go to the Multiple Listing Service, which may be online in your area; check with local lenders; and consult with the local Association of Realtors, which often collects local sales and market statistics.

RENTAL DEMAND TRENDS

A lot of emphasis is placed on studying the current market for property in terms of market price, which is appropriate. But it is only part of the analysis. You also need to determine how much demand exists for rentals. Check with the local landlord's association, if your community has one, or with lenders specializing in investment properties. Real estate agents who specialize in investment properties may also be able to provide you with selective information from their firm or the MLS records about rental trends.

Remember that apartment and house markets often are different, at least demographically. Renters seeking houses tend to have larger families, have high income, and are somewhat older. Apartment tenants tend to be limited to one or two people or to be young couples with one child, and they tend to be younger. These are important differences because they are completely different markets.

In some communities, a large number of apartment complexes address the younger market and, in fact, could even be soft. That doesn't mean the market for houses is soft as well. To a degree, the two markets cross over; however, as a general rule, the demand for apartments and the demand for houses are distinct. In a college town, for example, there might be a strong demand for smaller, cheaper apartments available for six- to nine-month leases, paralleling the school year. At the same time, families might be looking for three-bedroom houses, with longer tenancy in mind. In such a market, cross-over could consist of groups of students wanting to rent houses and share rent as an alternative to buying separate apartments.

LOCAL ECONOMY

The demand factors of real estate are related directly to economic realities in your community. When a lot of jobs are available, people move into the community; when major employers close their doors, workers sell their homes and move elsewhere. This brings up several considerations for you. If there are only one or two major employers in your area, what will happen to the real estate market if they close down or move? A diversified job market provides more economic health and safety for you as an investor.

Besides jobs, other economic facts affect the real estate market. For example, if your community has a lot of retail activity, are the shoppers coming from the same community or somewhere else? Are you located near a border with another state or with Mexico or Canada? If so, what influence does that proximity have on the real estate market? If, for example, there is no sales tax in your state, are neighboring state citizens coming across the border to shop in your city?[*] If that is the case, how will the real estate market change if the shopping situation changes? In other words, the demand for real estate may be affected by the demand for jobs, which could change if the local economy were to change.

---

[*]An example of such an economic condition is seen in Oregon, which has no sales tax. People from neighboring states have an incentive to visit Oregon for their taxable purchases.

POLITICAL CLIMATE

One factor often overlooked in assessing real estate investing is that of the political climate. Certainly, the climate will change from time to time as people are voted out of office and replaced by others. However, the *current* political climate will have much to do with real estate values. For example, if your local lawmakers determine to raise property taxes and increase government spending, that will make real estate investments less practical. Higher property taxes mean you have to pass on rent increases to tenants; higher rents drive people out of the market.

Some generalizations can be made about the political climate; these rarely apply in the strictest sense because there often is a balance between political forces with opposite points of view. However, it is accurate to say that, when politicians in power are against growth, that also means they will not encourage new businesses to relocate in the community. Such leaders also will be opposed to expansion of housing or commercial real estate inventory, on the theory that creating those jobs brings people into the area, along with more traffic and other undesirable outcomes. However, from an investor's point of view, an antigrowth government usually means that existing housing prices rise. Politicians cannot really prevent growth; it will happen on its own terms, in spite of what politicians hope to achieve. However, when the local government resists growth, the tendency is that real estate prices rise, because increasing demand for housing will not be met with new construction. When a local government is progrowth, it will tend to encourage new employment creation. Companies will be invited to relocate in the area, and politicians will liberalize zoning requirements to speed up development. From the real estate investor's point of view, the first impression in this situation is that everyone will benefit from a more robust economy; job creation will create new demand for housing, and investment makes sense. This is true to a degree; however, there also is a tendency at such times to overbuild real estate. The consequence is that supply exceeds demand, causing a softening of prices.

A study of neighborhood and community conditions makes it clear that drawing conclusions about investing in real estate is no easy task. So many variables are at play that it is difficult to say unequivocally that now is or is not a good time to buy real estate. You need to look over the whole situation and make an informed judgment about the market.

Calculating Cash Flow

Among the more important tests of feasibility is cash flow. As a real estate investor, you commit yourself to the long term, and, in most instances, you will need to finance your investment. The typical 30-year mortgage requires monthly payments, whether or not you are able to offset those payments with rental income.

In addition to making payments on your mortgage, you also are required to pay for insurance, property taxes, utilities, and other operating expenses associated with owning rental property—not to mention the unexpected roof repair, burst water heater replacement, or broken-down furnace. The essential requirement for real estate investing is that you be able to afford to carry the financial burden of the property, even when your rental income is inconsistent, and even when you go through a two- or three-month period with no rental income.

Begin with the presumption that you will have rental income each month. On calculating the *known* costs of owning the property, will rental income be adequate to cover the cash outlay from one month to another? If so, then you will be covered as long as the property is rented out, not allowing for unexpected expenses or periods of vacancy. However, if, under your best case scenario, you cannot cover expenses, then you need to reconsider the investment itself. Your best case involves rents coming in every month without fail and no unexpected expenses. The solution when your calculations don't work out involve several possibilities:

- Put more down payment into the property to reduce mortgage payments.
- Look for lower-priced homes to reduce payments without a corresponding reduction in rents.
- Rethink investing in real estate until your financial situation improves.

It normally is not going to make sense to accept negative cash flow, the situation where more money is going out than coming in. You need to offset the net outlay with increased market value in the property, and there is no guarantee that you will be able to achieve that goal. You have no control over the market and no way to know whether property value will even keep pace with your negative cash outlay. Because real estate should be approached as a long-term investment, it does not make sense to go in knowing that your cash flow is not going to work.

The calculation of cash flow is complex because it should include a calculation of your tax benefits. Because these benefits are significant, they have to be included to make your analysis accurate. By way of example, let's assume the following facts. You purchase a property for $100,000 with a 30 percent down payment. You have a mortgage with a beginning balance of $70,000, payable over 30 years at 7.25 percent. Your monthly payment is $477.53. We will also assume that annual property tax payments are $416 and homeowners' insurance is $224. Rental income on

TABLE 2.2 Calculation of Annual After-Tax Cash Flow

DESCRIPTION	CASH FLOW	INCOME TAXES
Rental income	$6,000	$6,000
Expenses and payments:		
Mortgage interest	5,053	5,053
Mortgage principle	677	
Property taxes	416	416
Insurance	224	224
Depreciation		2,727
Total expenses and payments	$6,370	$8,420
Net tax loss		$2,420
Net cash flow	-370	
Tax benefits (26% of net loss)	629	
After-tax positive cash flow	$ 259	

this property is $500 per month. Finally, you pay federal and state income taxes at a combined rate of 26 percent.

Given these facts, what is the cash flow per year, net of taxes? To determine this, we need to break out the cash payments from the deductible expenses. Because the payment includes both principal and interest, it is necessary to review cash flow *and* tax deductions separately. In Table 2.2, the calculation is broken out for the example. The deduction for depreciation is based on the requirement under the current tax code, providing that real estate is to be depreciated over 27.5 years using the straight-line basis.[*]

Table 2.2 shows a full year's tax calculation and cash flow, based on the first full year the property will be owned. Rental income is estimated at $500 per month ($6,000 per year), assuming it will be rental for the entire year. This is the starting point. Two calculations follow: First is cash flow, where the after-tax outcome is determined, and second is the actual

---

[*]*Straight-line* simply means that the same amount is deducted each year. In the example, we are assuming that, for the $100,000 purchase, one-fourth, or $25,000, represents land value, and the remaining $75,000 represents the value of the buildings. Only buildings and other improvements can be depreciated; land cannot.

tax calculation, including income and deductions. Remember, in the example, your average federal and state combined rate is 26 percent.

Mortgage interest and principal is calculated for each month by multiplying the ending balance due on the mortgage, by the interest rate; dividing that by 12 (months) to arrive at interest; and deducting interest from the total payment to arrive at principal. As a final step, principal for the month is deducted from the balance due to end up with the balance due at the end of the month.

In the example given, the beginning balance of the mortgage was $70,000.00. To calculate interest for the first month,

$$\frac{\$70,000,00 \times .0725}{12} = \$422.92$$

The second step is to deduct the month's interest from the total payment:

Total payment	$477.53
Less: interest	−422.92
Principal	$ 54.61

The third step is to deduct principal from the balance forward to determine the new mortgage balance:

Mortgage balance, beginning of the month	$70,000.00
Less: principal paid	− 54.61
Mortgage balance, end of the month	$69,945.39

The same series of steps is carried through for the whole year and summarized in Table 2.3. This table shows the source for the annual dollar amounts for interest and principal payments. These values will change each year. During the course of the mortgage term, interest declines gradually, and principal increases from one year to the next.[*]

Having calculated the first year's principal and interest, you are ready to enter the largest cash outlay on the form. Returning to Table 2.2, note that interest is deducted from both columns, but principal is deducted only from the cash flow column. This is accurate. Principal payment represents a cash outlay, but it is not a deductible expense; thus, it has to be treated in a different manner than interest, which is both an outlay and a deductible expense.

---

[*]To double-check the accuracy of calculations for a one-year breakdown of mortgage payments, add principal and interest together; the sum should equal total payments. A second calculation also checks mathematical accuracy: Subtract the mortgage balance at the end of the year from the balance at the beginning; the difference should be equal to the total in the principal column.

TABLE 2.3 Mortgage Amortization

MONTH	TOTAL PAYMENT	INTEREST	PRINCIPAL	BALANCE FORWARD
				$70,000.00
1	$ 477.53	$ 422.92	$ 54.61	69,945.39
2	477.53	422.59	54.94	69,890.45
3	477.53	422.25	55.28	69,835.17
4	477.53	421.92	55.61	69,779.56
5	477.53	421.58	55.95	69,723.61
6	477.53	421.25	56.28	69,667.33
7	477.53	420.91	56.62	69,610.71
8	477.53	420.56	56.97	69,553.74
9	477.53	420.22	57.31	69,496.43
10	477.53	419.87	57.66	69,438.77
11	477.53	419.53	58.00	69,380.77
12	477.53	419.18	58.35	69,322.42
Totals	$5,730.36	$5,052.78	$ 677.58	

Property taxes and insurance are both cash outlays and deductible expenses for the year. Both are shown at estimated annual levels in Table 2.2. Depreciation is shown only in the tax column, since it is a calculated expense; however, no cash is paid for depreciation. This is calculated on the basis of the $75,000 value of improvements (excluding the $25,000 land value, which cannot be depreciated). The annual allowed depreciation is $2,727 (straight-line depreciation over 27.5 years).

The total comes to $6,370 (payments) and $8,420 (deductible expenses). This creates a net loss for tax purposes of $2,420 during the first year. Since the example uses 26 percent as the average tax bracket, that means that all net losses provide a tax benefit at the same percentage. Thus, 26 percent of the $2,420 tax loss equals $629. When this benefit is used to adjust the negative cash flow, the after-tax cash flow result is $259 for the full year.

While the best case outcome is on the positive side, remember that this also leaves no margin for unexpected circumstances. A single month of lost income consumes the year's meager positive cash flow and more. An unexpected expense will do the same. This calculation allows nothing for other expenses; in practice, landlords normally pay some of the utilities, such as water and sewer. Thus, for the average of $22 per month positive cash flow, the feasibility of investing in real estate in the example is slim at best.

This is an example only, of course. While it allows no provision for the unexpected expense or for any period of vacancy, it also excludes the potential growth in real estate property value during the year. This cannot be known, of course. Unlike the stock market, the growth in property values over a single year can only be estimated. Latest figures from the Census Bureau show that the *average* value of single-family houses has exceeded $5,000 per year for the past decade (see Table 1.2 in Chapter 1.) Average sales price in the year 2000 was $200,400 and $149,800 in 1990. The difference of $56,660 averages out to $5,660 per year. This does not mean the trend will continue, nor does it mean that the average applies to the house in which you invest.

In addition, increases in market value from one year to the next are of no immediate value to you if you are suffering from negative cash flow. In the example given, your house might grow in value by $5,000 per year, but if in the meantime you are paying out more than you are bringing in, that creates a hardship from month to month. When you multiply that situation by three or four houses—or more—it soon becomes apparent that cash flow is a limiting factor in how far you can go on buying and renting out property. The venture has to be affordable, not only in terms of qualifying for loans but also in managing cash within your family budget each month.

CHAPTER 3

Financing Your Purchase

More important than the stated price of real estate, more critical to the very success of your investment and your ability to be a player in real estate, is the question of financing. The vast majority of real estate owners, both investors and homeowners, have to borrow the larger portion of the purchase price. Few people have a large enough reserve of cash to simply buy property outright.

Most people are familiar with conventional financing, loans provided by banks, savings and loans, and other traditional lenders. Alternatives include seller financing, in which the seller of the property agrees to lend money to the new buyer, and various creative methods of financing real estate investments. You are likely to find a variety of methods for financing investment property. The ultimate question becomes one of affordability.

Affordability doesn't mean the purchase price of the property itself. That is a rather limited point of view concerning the larger picture for real estate investors. The question of affordability relates, instead, to three more important concerns:

- What terms are available and what monthly payments are involved?
- How much actual equity is grown through a particular financing plan?
- How long does the arrangement last?

These three concerns are, of course, the crux of the affordability question. Terms and payments, equity, and timing define whether you will be able to afford to invest in real estate.

Terms include interest-only payments, graduated payment plans, variable rate interest contracts with periodic and lifetime caps on the rate, and other similar ways to reduce the initial payment if only for the purpose of qualifying for the loan. Because lenders operate on a strict analysis of qualifying conditions, this criterion is central to just getting the loan, regardless of whether the arrangement makes fiscal sense. In other words, lenders analyze the monthly payment in relation to your income; if you meet the ratio requirements, you qualify for the loan, and, if you do not, you will be rejected. The amount of the monthly payment, of course, is the determining factor. Thus, even if your payment represents interest only, you might qualify, even though you will not be paying down the loan amount itself. This is ludicrous, since the purpose of investing in property is to grow equity over time. Thus, when you finance the purchase with an interest-only loan, you are depending on the property's market value to increase, since no equity will accumulate over the term of your interest-only loan. Such loans also have a deadline, at which point you will need to refinance the loan, negotiate a continuation of the interest-only deal, or sell the property.

Equity is the second of the three concerns. How much equity are you accumulating in the property over the term of financing? Because longer-term loans accumulate equity more slowly than shorter ones, very little equity is accumulated during the first few years of a loan term. For example, with a 30-year loan paid at 7 percent, you pay about 6 percent of the loan during the first five years, and the loan is still only half paid off in the twenty-second year. A $100,000 mortgage actually costs more than $239,000 to repay over 30 years. Of course, if the property only doubles in value during that period, then you will not have accumulated any equity whatsoever; the bank, rather than the investor, makes money on the property through its collection of interest. This is one of the troubling aspects of financing property. As an investor, you need to ensure that mortgage payments are essentially covered by rental income. The combined coverage of payment and tax benefits will make the real estate investment worthwhile, but only if you are able to achieve the positive cash flow required to make the numbers work out.

Timing is the third leg of the real estate tripod. No matter how attractive the financing is today, if the loan becomes due within a few years, you need to plan ahead to refinance or sell. For example, an interest-only loan often is due in three or five years. The lender is not willing to commit to longer terms, because the market interest rate levels are likely to change after many years. The lender would rather be able to get out of a deal if it wants, or at least to raise its rates for a refinanced loan. Of course, on refinancing, you would have to pay loan origination fees and other costs, so the lender would make yet more money in addition to interest on the loan.

From the lender's point of view, real estate loans are a winner. They are secured by property, so that, in the event of default, the lender can simply take over ownership and recapture its investment. The interest the lender earns ensures that the investor's equity is converted to interest, all or in part, so the lender makes a significant profit without having to manage property, deal with tenants, or make repairs.

Financing and Your Credit

The lender in a rental property situation is not going to approach the review of a loan application in the same way as when you buy a house for your family. Owner-occupied housing is the most desirable type of real estate loan from the lender's perspective. These are the least likely types of loans to default. The vast majority of owner-occupied homes are paid for faithfully and regularly, so the bank's risks are minimal.

For this reason, qualifying for a loan for your primary residence is a relatively simple matter. As long as your income is sufficient to meet the lender's ratio, and as long as you have the down payment, you qualify. The only remaining question is that of your credit.

In order to operate as a real estate investor, you will need an excellent credit rating. Credit is going to serve as an essential element in operating your real estate investments, because you are going to need to work with lenders over and over again, unless you have a large supply of available cash and plan to buy properties outright. If you have any problem areas in your credit report, including late payments or debts in collection, you need to get these cleaned up before embarking on your real estate investment venture. Many people have undeserved negative entries on their credit reports, and cleaning them up is a matter of writing to the credit agency, explaining the circumstances, and asking to have the problem entries removed from your file. As long as you are correct and the problem was the result of error, it will be removed.

SIDEBAR

To check on your credit status, order copies of your credit report periodically from *all three* national credit unions. The cost is $8.50 or less in most cases. If you have been denied credit in the past 30 days, a credit report is free from the agency whose report was used for the decision. The web sites of the three national credit agencies are

Equifax—*https://www.econsumer.equifax.com/*
Experian—*http://www.experian.com/*
Trans Union—*http://www.tuc.com/*

Typically, errors occur on credit reports when creditors provide inaccurate information. For example, you might pay off a balance due but it is reported as being outstanding. Or an account that was paid on time could be mistakenly classified as paid but delinquent. It is also possible that someone else's debt is assigned to your file in error. Even when a debt is yours and it was paid late, there often are reasonable explanations. A payment could have been lost in the mail, bills were sent to an old address, or you disputed items on a credit card and it took several months to resolve the problem. All of these situations can lead to negative or erroneous information on your report; by writing a letter to the credit bureau, you have a good chance of getting the report cleaned up.

It also helps to know your rights under the Fair Credit Reporting Act, the federal law that covers all matters concerning how credit bureaus handle your file and disputes that you bring to their attention. As a real estate investor, your good credit is one of your most important assets; it should be protected with great care.

SIDEBAR

The Fair Credit Reporting Act (FCRA) spells out your rights under federal law in dealing with credit agencies and in having inaccurate information removed from your file. To review the full text of the FCRA, check the Federal Trade Commission web site, at *http://www.ftc.gov/os/statutes/fcra.htm*

It will be difficult to accomplish the financing goals you need to pursue without excellent credit or the ability to borrow money through affordable channels. Real estate investors whose credit is less than perfect may be forced to seek out alternatives; these may not only prove to be expensive but also may limit the scope of real estate investing possibilities.

When you cannot qualify for traditional financing through conventional lenders, you will find it difficult to purchase properties that might be described as mainstream—well-built, conforming properties in desirable neighborhoods. Such houses usually are financed through conventional lenders, and, as long as such financing is available, investors trying to break into that market through unconventional means will find it difficult, if not impossible. Such investors often end up using seller financing as their only alternative.

Seller Financing

The inexperienced real estate investor is likely to view seller financing as a great opportunity. At first glance, it seems so. When a seller agrees to carry a loan for you, especially if the deal includes a low down payment, you avoid the usual expenses of going through a traditional lender—the need for an appraisal, inspections, loan review and approval, filing of applications, credit reports, tax returns, and other paperwork. In other words, the seller could make the deal very fast and easy.

However, there usually is more to the story. Why would a seller be willing to carry financing if it were possible to find a buyer who qualifies for conventional financing? In other words, if the seller has the chance to get all of the money out of the property at the time of sale, why agree to remain at risk by becoming a lender? Most sellers want to cash out, so you need to take a careful second look when sellers are willing to carry a loan for you.

Some properties do not qualify for conventional financing because their construction is below minimal standards. For example, a lender might not be willing to finance a property that does not have a complete foundation. A post-and-beam–constructed house, under those rules, would not be qualified for financing, so a seller with minimal equity could be in a difficult position: knowing about the problems of the property but unable to afford to repair those problems without spending all or most of the equity. In such a case, the seller has the choice of looking for someone to take on his or her problems; that means carrying a note.

The seller who takes a note and accomplishes a sale can also discount and resell that note to someone else. This means that, as a real estate investor, it would be difficult or impossible to require the seller to pay for repairs on discovery. If you buy property without getting an inspection, you take a big chance. Even though the law might support the idea that you can sue the seller to get needed repairs paid for, it is most difficult if that seller has since resold the note and, perhaps, left the area altogether.

Private financing could present a problem, but there is another side to it. Some people recognize the advantage of lending money and come to realize that they can profit from real estate by being a lender rather than owning the property. As an owner, you need to find tenants; manage the property; juggle cash flow; and pay property taxes, interest, upkeep, and unexpected repairs. As a lender, you only need to collect your payment; if that doesn't happen, you can foreclose and take back the property. Thus, some people will be willing to convert their position from owner to lender to maximize their income without having to deal with tenants.

If you do come upon an opportunity to buy real estate with seller financing, follow these guidelines:

1. *Get all needed inspections, without fail.* When you go through a conventional lender, inspections are part of the normal routine. You

cannot get a loan until the property has passed inspections. These should include a pest control inspection and a building inspection. Even if you live in a northern area where termites are not common, pest control inspections are important and necessary; beetles can damage property as much as termites, and a range of possible pest-related problems can be revealed with an inspection. A building inspection should be conducted by a qualified and independent home inspector. Don't use anyone who would also perform needed repairs, since that presents a conflict of interest. Get inspection reports in writing.

SIDEBAR

Seek a licensed inspector who is a member of the American Society of Home Inspectors (ASHI). This national organization tests and licenses individuals, and members cannot also perform repair services. To find a member of ASHI in your area, check the ASHI web site, at *http://www.ashi.com/* or call toll-free 1-800-743-ASHI (1-800-743-2744).

2. *Negotiate a low down payment and favorable interest rate.* Approach a seller financing situation like any other negotiation. Negotiate terms that are going to be favorable to you, so that the deal is a good one in comparison with other financing avenues. Try to get as low a down payment as possible. Also try to bring down the interest rate to a level that makes it worthwhile for you to keep the loan in effect, as opposed to refinancing it later. In addition, a lower rate makes it less likely that the seller will discount and sell the note to a third party; it does not ensure that this will not happen, but it makes it less practical.

3. *Make sure the contract is in writing and all terms included.* A contract for a real estate transaction has to be in writing, without exception. You need to write out all of the conditions in the promissory note, including amount due, interest rate, monthly payments, due date, late charges if applicable, and all other terms and conditions.

4. *Have your attorney or an escrow company review the note and other conditions before you sign it.* When you take out a loan with a bank, the loan is a formal document, and the lender's escrow department or an outside escrow company takes care of all the details. The practice varies by state. You want to ensure that all of the conditions in the note are legal and that all required stipulations are included. In addition, the note and a deed have to be recorded with your county. You also should make sure that a title search is performed and that you get a title insurance policy. This protects you against any undisclosed liens against the property. To guar-

antee that the whole transaction is done properly, go through a real estate attorney or an escrow company.

5. *Include a clause making the note assumable.* Make sure that the contract specifies that someone else can take over the note in the event that you sell your property. This gives you as much flexibility as possible. When you advertise a property for sale, one attractive selling point is that the property comes with assumable financing. That means a new owner can simply be named to take over payments on the note. An experienced seller might require you to include a clause providing approval before allowing someone else to assume the note; in a sense, this gives your seller the right to deny someone the assumable provision. However, if the person trying to buy your property has a poor credit history, it is not unreasonable to allow for credit review.

6. *Perform your own financial preview.* In all of the hurry to get a transaction completed, don't overlook the all-important financial preview. Will rental income be high enough to cover your monthly payment? How do property taxes and utilities fit into the picture? How much work needs to be done on the property, and how will you perform it? In short, before closing the deal, make sure you have reviewed the whole thing realistically and that it is affordable. Watch out for the trap of wanting to get a rental property at any cost, even if that means that the numbers don't work. The numbers *have to work*, or the transaction will be a mistake.

The Cost of Borrowing

Anyone who has bought a home knows that closing and financing costs can add up to a large number, often running as much as 5 percent of the financing cost. This is especially true when the cost of obtaining financing includes loan points. Each point is equal to 1 percent of the amount borrowed, and points can add up quickly.

Besides loan points and other charges, buyers have to pay transfer and recording fees, taxes, title inspection and insurance, and property inspection costs. You might be able to negotiate a deal with a seller to pay some (or all) of your closing costs, depending on how anxious the seller is to close a deal. If the market is very slow and buyers are able to call the shots, then sellers will be more likely to give up some profit to make the deal work. However, when the reverse is true, sellers have no incentive to give you a better deal.

The costs of borrowing money should be included in your financial equation, because your monthly payment will be determined by the level of closing costs. Typically, you will be required to make a down payment equal to a percentage of the financed portion. For rental property, this may be

30 percent, even though you might be able to locate a lender whose terms will be more liberal. You need to determine whether you will also be required to pay for closing costs in addition to the down payment amount. If so, you need to get an estimate of what your closing costs will be. If those costs will be financed, you need to calculate your likely monthly payment based on the financed amount plus costs. For example, if your loan will start out at $100,000, financing $5,000 in closing costs means your initial loan balance will be $105,000. At 7 percent interest to be paid over 30 years, that makes a difference of about $33 per month.[*] That might not seem like a very large number; however, if your cash flow calculations reveal that you'll be close each month, $33 each month can make a difference. If your monthly rent is $800, the $33 per month represents a half month of rent each year. Over 30 years, this adds up to $11,880 in additional payments.

The level of closing costs makes it difficult and impractical to buy and sell properties on a high-volume level. When you sell, your closing costs are likely to run 8 to 10 percent of your sales price. This assumes that you will be paying a real estate commission to list your property, and that commission will run 6 to 7 percent of the sales price. On top of that, a number of other sellers' closing costs apply, including recording fees, inspections, escrow and title fees, excise taxes if applicable, and any costs to prepare the house for sale or fix defects discovered during inspections. This means that, even when your property appreciates in value 20 percent or so, it still makes little sense to turn it around and sell it. For example, assume you purchase a rental property for $100,000 and later sell it for $120,000. To illustrate the outcome net of closing costs, also assume that rent income paid all mortgage payments and other expenses, so your cash flow ended up at zero. If closing costs were 5 percent when you bought and 10 percent when you sold, the outcome for a 20 percent increase in market value is:

Sales price	$120,000
Less: seller's closing costs, 10 percent	− 12,000
Net sales price	$108,000
Original purchase price	$100,000
Plus: buyer's closing costs, 5 percent	− 5,000
Total purchase price	$105,000
Net profit	$ 3,000

[*]The higher down payment for investment property leads many people to the conversion approach. Property is purchased as a primary residence, with the stated intention of moving into the house. Meanwhile, the current residence is converted to a rental property. In theory, you could continue converting current homes into rentals and applying for new primary residence financing with smaller down payments, limited only by income restrictions.

For an original investment of $100,000, a $3,000 return has to be viewed in light of all of the elements involved with being a landlord: exposure to risk, commitment of capital, and the time involved. In other words, how long did you own the property? If it was in your hands for six months, then the $3,000 represents an annualized return of 6 percent. However, if you held the property for two years, then the return on your investment was only 1.5 percent.

Calculating return on investment property is complicated by two factors: First, you finance the majority of the purchase price; second, return depends on how long you own the property. Since you finance the purchase, should the return be calculated on the purchase price, as in the example? Or should it be based on the *cash* you put into the deal?

If your down payment was 30 percent of the purchase price, that changes the calculation. In the example, the $3,000 represents 10 percent of the cash at risk, rather than 3 percent of the total purchase price. The traditional approach is to use the full purchase price, whether paid in full or financed. However, a valid argument can be made supporting the approach of calculating returns on cash outlay instead. The important thing is to make your financial calculations accurate and consistent, so using one method in one case and another elsewhere makes a financial system inaccurate and flawed. To be fair to yourself, you need to determine whether to use the investment or cash basis for your calculations. Because you are at risk for the full amount borrowed, meaning you have to repay the loan, your return on investment should be defined with the financed balance included. In theory, using the alternative method of counting only cash actually put into a property, you might come to believe that your rate of return is substantially higher than it really is by using more traditional calculations.

This brings us to the second problem. A 10 percent return is not the same on every property. If you hold one property exactly one full year, then the annual return is, indeed, 10 percent. However, if you tie up your capital for two years in the property, then the annualized yield is spread over the longer holding period, meaning annualized return is only 5 percent.

These distinctions are important in calculating the cost of borrowing because, when it comes to real estate investments, it is the financing cost that actually determines your long-term yield, not the purchase and sales prices of the properties. Consider the problem of how interest is amortized: With a 30-year loan at 7 percent, you have paid off less than 6 percent of the loan during the first five years. This is not a problem as long as rental income pays the mortgage for you, in one respect. As long as tenant payments make your mortgage, your cash flow is covered. But this also is a zero sum gain in another sense. You have made little headway in accumulating equity during the holding period, whereas your lender has acquired a handsome interest income. For example, on a $100,000 loan at 7 percent, the first five years in a 30-year term yield $39,919 to the bank, of which about $34,000 is for interest. That profit for the bank is a certainty; what is not as well known is how much profit you might earn in the same period.

Using the previous example of 5 percent closing costs for the buyer and 10 percent for the seller, you would not fare as well in many markets. For example, what happens if your property grows 50 percent in value, from $100,000 to $150,000?

Sales price	$150,000
Less: seller's closing costs, 10 percent	− 15,000
Net sales price	$135,000
Original purchase price	$100,000
Plus: buyer's closing costs, 5 percent	5,000
Total purchase price	$105,000
Net profit	$ 30,000

In this example, the bank would have earned a profit of $34,000, compared with your profit of $30,000 after costs. It should be apparent that the cost of the property itself is relatively insignificant in comparison with the much more important cost of financing your purchase. Thus, you are better off paying $110,000 for a property financed over 30 years at 6 percent, than paying $100,000 for a property financed for 30 years at 7 percent. Even though the purchase price would be $10,000 more, monthly payments would be $659.52 at 6 percent, versus $665.31 at 7 percent. Thus, the house costing $10,000 more has a monthly payment of $5.79 less per month. This is not much on a monthly basis, but it makes the point that looking for a better interest rate has more effect on your true cost of investing in real estate than does the stated purchase price of the property.

As a real estate investor, your real investment cost is *not* what you pay for property; it is what it costs to finance that purchase over many years. It's easy to deceive yourself that you are profiting because you sell an investment property at a higher price than you pay. Even if you come out ahead in the analysis of sales and purchase prices, would it be worthwhile to tie up capital for real estate investments?

The answer, of course, depends on how the numbers really work. If you hold property for several years and break even on cash flow, then you have neither gained nor lost money from month to month. Tenants pay rent, which in turn covers your mortgage payment, property taxes, insurance, and other expenses on an after-tax basis. If, after several years, you sell, how can you determine whether the net outcome made sense?

This is where an analysis involving actual cash outlay is helpful. It's true that, for calculation of net return on investment, it makes sense to use the full value of the property. In the previous illustration, this comparison was illustrated to show how rate of return is vastly different using the cash invested method, versus the price of the full investment, including the financed portion. However, to compare the validity of a real estate investment in terms of cost versus benefit, the cash method does show what you get (or lose) for having your money tied up over several years.

You have seen that even a 50 percent increase in market value can translate to very little actual profit, when you adjust for closing costs, so the question comes down to whether a minimal profit is worthwhile, considering the capital you tie up and the time you have to spend maintaining the property. In the example of a $100,000 property sold a few years later for $150,000, we assume that a $30,000 down payment was involved. If that money had been invested, instead, in a typical stock mutual fund yielding an after-tax rate of 5 percent per year, and the money was left on deposit for five years, how does that compare with buying real estate? Assuming that all earnings are reinvested, the mutual fund yields about $8,288.*

With this in mind, how can you make a valid comparison between real estate and other alternatives? This comparison is meant only to show what *could* happen in another investment. However, the mutual fund might not yield a 5 percent return per year; it could yield more, or it could lose value. There are no guarantees. The real estate investment could double or even triple in value, a phenomenon that has occurred in many parts of the country in five years or less. In other words, you cannot know in advance how one investment will perform compared with another; real estate investors need to be aware that financing is a major factor to be remembered in the financial equation.

As long as you finance real estate through traditional methods, you will accumulate little or no equity during the first few years that you own the property. Most of the mortgage payment consists of interest, and very little goes toward principal, so real estate has to be treated as a long-term investment, or you need a dramatic run-up in market value to justify the investment in the short term.

By definition, depending on a short-term run-up in market value makes you a real estate speculator, rather than a long-term investor. That is not

---

*This calculation was done on a straight annual return basis of 5 percent per year. The formula for this is $30,000 (1.05^5)$.

a negative aspect, only a different approach to real estate. However, as an investor, you should be in control of the decision to work as a speculator or an investor. If you simply buy real estate and wait to see what happens, then you relinquish that control. The plan to sell if and when the property doubles in value could take 2 years or 20, or it might not happen at all. A more analytical approach, including setting specific goals, makes more sense, so that your long-term plan is satisfied by real estate investing—rather than hoping for the best and making random decisions.

The financing problem is a serious one. Every real estate investor needs to determine how to deal with the problem, because, with the exception of the few who can afford to pay cash, the ultimate determining factor defining profit levels is interest expense. Of course, growth in market value is also a big part of the picture, but you cannot control market value to the degree that you can control your interest expense.

The following are some interesting facts to keep in mind about the cost of financing:

1. *Paying off the loan in a shorter period of time saves a lot in interest.* By paying your mortgage over 15 years rather than 30, you save a substantial sum in interest, perhaps as much as $100,000. The dollar value expressed in the differences between total payments makes the point. The following is a comparison of the differences at 7, 8, and 9 percent:

Total of Payments

Rate	30 Years	15 Years	Difference
7	$239,512	$161,789	$ 77,723
8	260,557	172,019	88,538
9	289,667	182,569	107,098

The savings you achieve by paying off a mortgage over 15 years adds up, because the accelerated schedule translates to much less in interest payments.[*]

2. *A 30-year loan is only one-half paid off by the twenty-fourth year.* You pay off one-half of a 30-year loan over 24 years, and the other half in the last 6 years, so every dollar of accelerated payments made early on in

---

[*]The 30-year repayment term is most often chosen because a borrower may not qualify for the higher payment levels required for a 15-year repayment term. However, you can repay at a higher rate even if you are not required to do so. At 7 percent, a 30-year loan would be paid off in 15 years by increasing the monthly payment by $2.33 for every $1,000 borrowed.

the loan term creates a compounded effect throughout the balance of the loan period. If your mortgage interest rate is 7 percent, for example, every dollar prepaid creates a compound return equal to 7 percent. You earn this compounded rate of return in reduced overall interest costs.

3. *Acceleration builds equity in the property.* When you accelerate mortgage payments, you are not only reducing interest expenses over 30 years; you also are building up your equity more rapidly. Every prepayment goes directly into principal, so that is money you will get back later when you sell the property. The profit is derived from the reduction in interest. Each payment you make toward the principal reduces the remaining balance against which interest will be calculated. Thus, a prepayment made today reduces interest for every remaining payment still due on the loan.

4. *Making one extra payment per year takes more than five years off your repayment term.* In other words, you can cut a 30-year mortgage down to less than 25 years by adding one extra payment per year. The biweekly mortgage achieves the same effect. By paying one-half of a mortgage every 2 weeks instead of each month, you end up with 26 annual payments (or the equivalent of 13 monthly payments). However, many biweekly plans are made overly complex. It is just as easy to add one-twelfth to each payment. The monthly payment for a 7 percent loan over 30 years, with a beginning balance of $100,000 is $665.31. If you increase that payment to $720.75 per month, you essentially add a thirteenth annual payment.

These four ideas demonstrate how a change in your mortgage payment dramatically affects overall cost. You could literally save up to $100,000 over 30 years by paying your mortgage in one-half the time. The savings is derived exclusively from reduced interest payments. On top of that, any increased value due to growth in market value is additional.

The critical question is cash flow, of course. You need to be able to afford to make accelerated payments, or the entire discussion is nice in theory alone. Extra principal payments are a profitable form of savings account; however, unlike an actual account, you cannot withdraw accelerated principal payments. Once you pay the money into accelerating your mortgage, you can only get it back in one of three ways: (1) sell the property, (2) refinance the existing mortgage, (3) create an equity-based line of credit.

When you refinance or sign up for an equity line of credit, you can get back the accelerated payment; however, you are also required to then pay interest on that money. By borrowing your own equity, you again convert your net worth into debt and further add to the real cost of borrowing. It's that cost that defines the ultimate profitability of investing in real estate.

Interest and Amortization Solutions

How can you solve the problem of real estate financing cost? Were it not for that high cost, the study of real estate investing would be quite simple. It is the variable that defines not only whether you make or lose money but also whether you have positive or negative cash flow. For most people, the level of interest expense defines whether they can afford to even invest in real estate as a first question.

It is important to recognize that the lender has at least an equal chance of making a profit as the investor does. The interest income earned by the lender may equal or exceed the after-tax profit for the investor, who also needs to deal with tenants, maintenance, vacancies, and unexpected capital improvements to the property. However, as a real estate investor, you have a distinct advantage over the lender. That advantage is found in the potential of real estate. The possibility that real estate market values will grow is significant enough to justify the investment—assuming, of course, that you can afford to hold property for a long enough period to realize the long-term profits. This means that you need to meet your obligations each month, even if your property is vacant and you are receiving no rental income; it also means that you are able to afford negative cash flow on a pre-tax basis and, in some cases, on an after-tax basis as well; finally, it requires that the market does, in fact, reward your well-thought-out investment decisions.

Every investor faces the same dilemma where financing is concerned. The balance between rental income and payments, between investment value and expense, is a matter of timing. How long will it take for properties to season? The answer depends on the location and the local economy, and all real estate is cyclical. Cycles vary not only in timing but also in length, so the question of how long it takes is, perhaps, the most interesting and perplexing aspect of investing in real estate. In some cases, you will get into the market at the right time, and property values will rise every month; in other cases, your timing will not be as good, and you will have to wait out the market.

The point is, with the uncertainty of the real estate cycle in mind, you will need to be willing and able to adopt a long-term point of view about real estate. Although the investment produces cash flow as long as property is rented, you probably cannot depend on real estate to the extent that you can't afford a vacancy. You need a cushion, and you need to plan for the worst case. If demand for rentals is strong in your city today, that is a good sign; however, it does not mean that the demand will remain as strong in the future. The specific risks associated with real estate investing are varied, but they invariably come back to the cost of financing. If you did not have a mortgage payment to make, an unexpected vacancy would not present a problem for you; however, your mortgage payment has to be made in a timely manner every month, with or without tenants.

The solution for most real estate investors is to find the best possible financing rate as a starting point. Then, whenever possible and practical, that mortgage can be accelerated by adding additional payments to principal each month. Finally, market value growth adds to investment value, so that, on sale of the property, you should be able to produce profits in excess of closing costs, at an annualized rate that justifies the investment.

This combination of requirements also has to be achieved while managing monthly cash flow effectively. Having more than one real estate investment will probably be desirable, but that also adds to the potential problems of cash flow. You will need to ensure that overall rental receipts are adequate to support overall rental expenses and cash outlays. You need to be able to afford any periods of negative cash flow to justify real estate as a long-term venture. If a property seasons unexpectedly before you thought it would, that is a nice surprise. You then have the choice of continuing to hold the property or selling it and using your profits to invest elsewhere, in more properties or in alternatives other than real estate.

Approaching a Lender

While most borrowers approach a lender from a passive point of view, you may consider taking a more active stance. In other words, typical first-time homeowners do not think about whether or not a lender *should* approve a loan application; they know only that they want to buy the house, and they hope the lender will give them the go-ahead.

Real estate investors need to delve deeper than the typical homeowner. Once you understand the point of view the lender holds, you will be better able to time your application, shop for the best loan, and make the kind of impression you need to make on the bank's loan officer.

As a first step, you need to determine the current status of the money supply. This can also be called the supply and demand for money. Are lenders making loans today? Are they looking for borrowers? Are rates higher or lower than they were six months ago? The money supply goes through cycles, just as real estate does. All potential lenders experience periods when they have easy access to money, which they can lend out to real estate buyers, and periods when the money supply is tight, interest rates are on the rise, and lending is not as easy for the bank. This is the flip side of the borrower's point of view—that borrowing is not as easy today as it was a few months ago.

As the money supply changes, so do interest rates. The Federal Reserve system determines how much currency to place into circulation, based on supply and demand. Banks routinely borrow money from the Federal Reserve; when they turn around and lend it out, they are required to set up a reserve. They have to keep a required amount of cash on hand to protect against bad debts; the more money a bank lends out, the higher its reserve requirements.

SIDEBAR

For information on the workings of the Federal Reserve and its role in the economy, check its general information web site at
http://www.federalreserve.gov/general.htm

A conventional lender—usually, a bank or a savings and loan institution—has to set up reserves for its loans. However, under today's lending structure, conventional lenders rarely keep a loan on their books for very long. When they do, it is called a portfolio loan. The vast majority of conventional loans are resold on the secondary market. A loan, approved under specific guidelines, is later moved from the conventional lender to another agency. Among the largest of the secondary market agencies are the Federal National Mortgage Association (FNMA), also referred to as Fannie Mae, and the Government National Mortgage Association (GNMA), also known as Ginnie Mae. These agencies form mortgage pools made up of mortgages placed by lenders and sell shares to investors. These pools work much as mutual funds do, but they deal in mortgages rather than in stocks or bonds.

This background information is crucial to you as a real estate investor for several reasons. Lenders who want to move mortgages out of their portfolios and onto the secondary market have to meet strict standards. For the most part, the secondary market accepts only first mortgages (mortgages that are paid off first in the event of a loan default). For investment property, the requirement for down payments is greater, because the risks are higher for lenders when owners do not occupy property. In other words, an owner-occupied single-family house is considered the best risk from a lender's point of view. The historically lower rate of defaults on such homes makes first mortgage loans on owner-occupied housing the most desirable of all. A real estate investor, who will not occupy the property, will therefore be required to put more money down on a property, often 30 percent, compared with the 10 or 20 percent required for many owner-occupied housing loans.

When you go to speak to a lender about financing your investment purchase, it is important for you to know all about these matters. The more knowledge you have about the current status of the market for loans, the better prepared you are going to be to apply for a loan. You need to present yourself in terms of risk profile. The bank considers every loan application on that basis, so it makes sense that you present yourself in terms of why you represent a good risk to the lender.

Being a good risk consists of many elements. The most obvious, of course, is having excellent credit. Financing is the essential element for most real estate investors, so this is a necessary starting point. In addition to credit rating, your income has to be adequate to convince the lender that you can afford to invest in real estate. The lender will look at the investment property very conservatively and will add a vacancy factor, which could be as high as three months out of the year, even if rental demand is high and overall vacancy rates are low in your community. In comparing your income to the cost of the mortgage, the lender will add together your current home mortgage payment, utilities, taxes, and insurance—plus the same items on your proposed rental. The lender then will add up your current income plus income from renting the property (minus a vacancy factor). If the numbers work according to the standards set for secondary market placement of the loan, then you have a good chance of having the loan approved. If you fall short, then the loan will be rejected. If the loan does not meet secondary market standards, the lender will not be able to move your loan out of its portfolio.

The lender has to be convinced that you qualify for a loan based on several factors. These include your credit rating, your income, the down payment you propose to offer, and likely rental income on the property. With all of this in mind, it makes sense to go through a lender's prequalification process, so that you will know how much you can afford to borrow. This involves presenting a loan application to the lender, including listing all of your assets and liabilities, and paying for a credit check. From all of this information, the lender will be able to let you know the level of loan for which you qualify. While the bank may charge a processing fee to prequalify you, it is worth the effort. By doing this before you locate a likely investment property, you save time later. A prequalified loan is likely to move through the process more quickly and easily than one that has to start from the beginning.

When you approach a lender with an awareness of the questions you will be asked, you have a better chance for approval. Be aware that bankers think about borrowers in terms of risks. Present yourself accordingly by researching ahead of time. Be aware of market interest rates, the money supply, and the bank's policies. When you visit the loan officer, make an appointment ahead of time and dress well for the occasion. It certainly improves your chances for financing on your first property and on future investments if you make a positive first impression. Develop an ongoing relationship with a banker, so that future loan applications will go smoothly. When you approach a lender for the first time, the lender has no way to know whether you are a serious investor or whether you even qualify for a loan. Once a banker knows you, however, it is far easier to return and ask for a loan on another property.

Loan Comparisons

Remember, whenever you apply for a loan, you will be borrowing in order to invest. Most types of investing should be done with available cash, and the usual advice is "Don't borrow money to invest." However, with real estate, it is different. Rental property produces an income stream, meaning that tenants repay your loan through rent, completely or in part. In addition, the direct control you exert over your rental investments makes real estate far different from most forms of investment. For example, when you buy shares of stock, you have no control over the company's market and business decisions.

Another important difference is that real estate, unlike most investments, is less likely to suddenly lose its value. Stock values can fall dramatically in a short period of time. Real estate, in comparison, tends to be stable, and market values are relatively predictable. In addition, homeowners' insurance protects you against catastrophic losses of most kinds. While real estate values can fall suddenly and unexpectedly, it is less likely than in other markets.

Finally, the unusual tax benefits available to investors make real estate a practical and advantageous move in most income brackets. As long as your gross income from other sources is between $30,000 and $100,000, real estate investments offer significant tax benefits that cannot be ignored.

All of these features unique to real estate mean that borrowing to invest is not a bad idea, as it might be to invest in other areas, so the question for first-time investors is which loan to apply for, given the market situation and lending arrangements that are available. Remember, shopping for the best financing deal means much more in terms of what you pay for property than the stated price of real estate. A $100,000 loan paid over 30 years costs $264,000 to repay at 8 percent. And a difference of 1/2 percent on your loan, while only about $35 per month, makes a difference over 30 years of more than $12,000 over the full 30 years. It is a big mistake, but a common one, to overlook the importance of loan comparisons.

To review the most popular loan arrangements, compare both rates and terms for the fixed-rate and variable-rate mortgages offered by a lender. Comparisons are difficult, given the fact that some lenders charge more points than others, so a true side-by-side comparison of loans is very difficult. Thus, the annual percentage rate (APR) is an important test, because it takes loan fees into account, making it easier for you to compare loans with dissimilar features.

SIDEBAR

For explanations of APR and related calculations, check the web site
http://www.educatedhomebuyer.com/closingcosts.htm

The comparison of loan programs between lenders is difficult, because loan fees may vary so considerably as to make a straight rate comparison misleading. This is where APR comparisons are valuable. Even though some costs might be paid up front, meaning the monthly payment is the same for two loans with the same stated rate, the real cost varies due to the up-front charges each lender assesses.

Beyond the APR analysis, you also need to consider when a fixed-rate mortgage or a variable-rate mortgage is a better arrangement. As a general rule, fixed-rate financing is viewed as advantageous because the rate is locked in for the entire term of the loan. However, this may be a deceiving feature, especially if you end up selling or refinancing the property within a few years. The typical time that homeowners keep their first home is about five years; investors tend to keep or sell property based on the demand for rents, the experience of working with tenants, and the problems associated with a particular property or neighborhood. Thus, the long-term advantages of fixed-rate financing might not be as important as they seem at first glance.

SIDEBAR

An Internet search on "fixed-rate mortgage" or "variable-rate mortgage" will lead you to links for dozens of online sources for mortgages. Shopping online for financing has become a popular way to compare rates, and you can find a good deal on mortgages through the Internet. However, the usual caution applies. When shopping online, be sure you check out the source and that you know all of the terms before you proceed.

The fixed-rate mortgage is usually offered at a higher rate than variable-rate financing, so these loans are more expensive. One reason that borrowers go with variable-rate mortgages is that they can qualify more easily at the lower interest rate. This is true even if the rate rises later due to changes in the rate itself. Ironically, the variable-rate mortgage often turns out to be more economical.

The variable-rate mortgage comes with two forms of protection. First is the annual cap, or maximum that a rate can be increased. This ensures that you will not be hit with a huge increase in the monthly mortgage payment all at once. Annual caps often are limited to 1 percent—in which case, a monthly payment would go up about $35 based on a $55,000, 30-year mortgate moving from 6 percent up to 7 percent. The second protective feature is called the lifetime cap, which is the maximum increase in interest rate that can be charged on the loan overall. For example, you might contract for a variable-rate loan starting at 7 percent with a one-year cap of 1 percent and a lifetime cap of 5 percent. This means that, in the worst case, the interest rate could rise each year by 1 percent, to a maximum of 12 percent, but never above that level.

Variable-rate mortgages are tied to interest rate indices that rise *and* fall, so when the index rate falls, so does the variable rate. The cap structure represents the maximum *increase* that could occur per year and over the life of the contract. Because owners of real estate, whether homeowners or investors, periodically refinance property, the variable-rate mortgage is not as risky today as it was in the past, when at times it was more likely that inflation could take a mortgage right up to the cap without relief.

Some investors have found that interest-only mortgages suit their needs better than either of the more traditional forms of financing. Under this arrangement, only interest is paid each month, and no reduction of the loan's principal takes place. In other words, an 8 percent loan for $100,000 would require a monthly payment of $666.67, which is interest only, according to the most popular method for computing interest. The annual rate is divided by 12 (months) under this formula:

$$\frac{8\%}{12} \times \$1,000,000 = \$666.67$$

The argument favoring interest-only arrangements is that payments are slightly lower. A monthly payment of $733.77 is required to amortize a $100,000 over 30 years at 8 percent. An investor might also argue that the property is going to be held for only a few years and then sold and that very little equity grows during the early years, anyhow, so why pay in? The argument is fine as long as market values do rise; otherwise, the interest produces only a tax write-off but no permanent savings. An interest-only loan arranged privately can be set up to go on indefinitely, but most notes also can be called after a specified date has passed; when it is done through an institutional lender, there is invariably a specific due date included. When that date arrives, the lender can insist on being paid in full, might offer to refinance with a more permanent loan including both interest and principal, or might be willing to extend the interest-only arrangement for a few more years.

A balloon mortgage is similar in the sense that a due date is involved. Some lenders set up the loan with payments that would amortize the loan over a long period, such as 30 years; however, the loan is due at the end of a specified period, commonly either three or five years. This type of contract can also be called a rollover mortgage, because the repayment term has to be rolled over at the end of the specified term. At that time, the loan has to be replaced or renegotiated. Such arrangements protect lenders writing fixed-rate mortgages in the event that interest rates rise. If those rates fall, the lender may offer to extend the period another few years rather than give up what would be viewed as a favorable interest rate at that time. For example, if such a loan is granted at 8 percent and is callable in three years, the lender will be likely to call the loan if market rates have risen, or to offer to extend the period if rates have fallen.

Yet another alternative if you want to buy property but cannot afford a down payment is to enter into a lease option. Under this arrangement, you have a lease on the property as well as an option to buy it. You make a periodic payment consisting of both rent and a form of lay-away payment toward the purchase of the property. The contract specifies that you have the option to buy the property at a specified price by a specified deadline. At that time, you can exercise the option and buy the property, which makes sense if it is worth more, or to let the option expire. A lease-option makes sense under some conditions if you are the buyer. However, as a seller of investment property, you cannot enter into a lease-option *and* defer the profit on sale.[*]

Financing is a complex matter and should be considered one of the keys to successful real estate investing. Given all of the conventional and creative ways to approach financing of investment property, it deserves considerable study and attention. You can save money by selecting the best loan deal; ignoring the potential for savings through mortgage shopping can cost a lot in the long run.

---

[*]Investors can sell property and defer the gain under federal tax rules allowing tax-free exchange of like-kind property; however, entering into a lease-option as part of a sale contract is not allowed. If you do sell property through a lease-option, you cannot take advantage of the like-kind exchange rules. (See Chapter 5 for more discussion of this provision.)

CHAPTER 4

Tax Features of Real Estate

Whenever you begin to review the tax aspects of investing, the picture becomes complex at once. Tax rules are ever changing, and the rules as well as exceptions require expertise and regular monitoring. As a real estate investor, you should rely on the advice of a qualified tax expert. The rules are difficult enough for the average taxpayer; for the real estate investor, many special rules apply. These concern passive loss limitations, depreciation, capital gains and losses, and allowable deductions.

While most real estate investors should not tackle the tax issues without professional help, it is also important to have a good overview of how the rules work and how the benefits and restrictions apply to you. Real estate could be called the last tax shelter. When massive reforms were enacted to do away with abusive tax shelters during the 1980s, Congress recognized that one tax shelter was worth leaving in place. Real estate was seen as the one form of shelter that was not abusive but an integral part of the economy; by leaving some provisions favorable to real estate investors, the tax rules help investors and support economic growth.

Limits were placed on the way that real estate investors can claim deductions, however. This ensures that real estate investments will not be made only to avoid income taxes. The benefits that are allowed include a ceiling, so that loss deductions that exceed those limits have to be carried over and claimed in later years.

Passive Loss Limitations

Tax deductions are limited when it comes to real estate. Thus, the "passive loss limitation" is at the heart of any tax discussion involving real estate. In the regulations covering real estate, there is a contradictory rule involving the concept of *passive* losses. A passive loss refers to activity in which you do not participate materially; thus, if you do not manage your investments on a day-to-day basis, they are passive investments. In general, you can deduct passive losses only by offsetting them against passive gains.

Before the passive loss rules were put into effect, investors could claim deductions without limitation, even to the point of claiming deductions far in excess of their invested basis in a program. Under those rules, real estate limited partnerships were widely popular. It was possible to invest $10,000 and claim deductible losses of $30,000 or more. Today, however, passive losses cannot be claimed without specific restrictions. The once-popular limited partnership, by definition, is a passive loss.

When you own investment property directly, you can claim a loss up to $25,000 per year, even if you do not have other passive gains offsetting those losses. While real estate is broadly defined as passive by nature, you are nonetheless required to participate materially in managing your real estate investments in order to qualify for claiming a deduction. Under the tax rules, you participate materially when you are involved in managing properties on a "regular, continuous and substantial basis."

Even though you participate materially in real estate, this continues to be defined as a passive investment. This places you under the rules governing treatment of real estate, including limitations on deductions. By imposing the requirement of material participation, real estate investors need to manage their properties to some degree; otherwise, even directly owned property would be treated much like the old-style limited partnerships. It would be difficult to establish material participation if you own property in a city far from where you live, and if you never deal with tenants directly or for any reason. For example, if you were to delegate all responsibility for managing your properties to a management company, and you did not spend any time during the year, then you would not qualify for deducting up to $25,000 per year in passive losses.[*]

Most real estate investors acting as individuals (as opposed to investing in units of limited partnerships, for example) can easily establish that they participate materially in their real estate investments. If you deal with tenants directly, you probably qualify. If you interview prospective tenants, show properties that are for rent, collect and deposit rent money, and pay your real estate expenses, these activities establish that you materially participate. If you spend 500 hours per year dealing with real estate, that meets one of the tests qualifying you under the "material participation"

---

[*]For investors whose adjusted gross income is higher than $100,000, the allowance of $25,000 is phased out.

rule. That works out to about 10 hours per week. When you consider the time you spend looking for rental property by reading ads, going to open houses, and discussing matters with real estate agents, it does not take long to accumulate the hours. Added to this is the time you spend working on investment property, meeting with tenants, and engaging in any other activity that is related to handling your investments.

If you are claiming a passive loss from real estate of $25,000 or lower (and if your adjusted gross income is below $100,000), you are allowed to deduct losses from real estate investments. If your passive losses are higher than $25,000, you can handle the excess in one of two ways. First, those losses can be deducted against passive gains from other activities. For example, if you own units in a real estate partnership and it reports a gain for the year of $10,000, you can deduct up to $35,000 in passive losses from other real estate investments in the same year. The net difference still meets the $25,000 test. The second way to handle any excess is to carry it forward to future tax years. The loss is deductible against income in the future.

One potential problem for real estate investors with many properties is that losses may exceed the $25,000 limitation every year. This means that losses in excess of $25,000 have to be taken forward indefinitely, but without any immediate prospects for taking the deduction. If your plans include investing in many properties, you can anticipate this problem by electing to depreciate the improvements to your property over a longer period than the standard time provided. You can make such an election under specific restrictions, and these are explained later in this chapter. You also can use straight-line depreciation for assets that can be depreciated using accelerated methods, meaning more depreciation is claimed in the early years and less in later years. For example, you might find it necessary to buy a truck for regular trips to dispose of trash accumulating on your property or to dispose of items left by your tenants. Or it might be necessary to buy a computer to keep records for your real estate activity. You may also need to buy lawn mowers and other yard maintenance equipment; these also qualify as capital assets. All of these types of non-real estate capital assets *can* be depreciated using accelerated methods. However, if you are concerned about the possibility of exceeding the $25,000 annual loss limitation, then you should use the straight-line method, in which the same amount is claimed each year.

Capital Asset Limitations

Capital assets are the assets used in your investment activity. They cannot usually be written off as deductions in the year they are purchased and placed into service but have to be depreciated over what is called a recovery period. This rule is applied because capital assets are not ordinary expenses, as are insurance, office supplies, and utilities. They are purchases you make for items that will be used over several years.

Some restrictions apply in the way that you depreciate real estate–related capital assets, and the way that losses can be deducted if and when you sell the asset. In most businesses, you are allowed to "expense" a capital asset in the year that it is placed into service. Under today's rules, up to $20,000 can be expensed in one year. For example, a business owner who purchases a piece of equipment can make an election to claim a deduction for up to $20,000 in the year that equipment is placed into service, rather than depreciating it over several years.

Another restriction involving depreciation has to do with the value of land. When you invest in real estate, you need to separate your investment into two segments: land and improvements. The improvements include buildings, so a house is treated as an improvement. This is necessary because land cannot be depreciated. Thus, if you invest in a house on several acres, the land portion can represent a larger share of the total than if you buy property in the city on a standard-sized building lot.

The most popular way to divide value between land and improvements is to apply the ratio used for property tax assessment purposes. You apply the same ratio to your actual purchase price. For example, you have bought a rental property for $125,000. Your property tax bill is based on an assessed value of $80,000, broken down as $20,000 for land and $60,000 for the building. Tax assessments often are lower than actual transaction cost, and, in this case, the assessment assigns one-quarter of the value to land and three-quarters to improvements. Thus, to divide your $125,000 purchase price on the same basis, multiply your purchase price by 75 percent (three-quarters of the total):

$$\$125,000 \times 75\% = \$93,750$$

The balance, $31,250, is the assigned value for land and cannot be depreciated.

It is to your advantage to have the greatest portion of your purchase price assigned to improvements, so that maximum depreciation can be claimed. However, the method you use in determining the breakdown has to be reasonable. And if you own more than one property, it also helps if your breakdown is consistent. In addition to property tax valuation, you can also use a breakdown on an appraisal or a breakdown used for the purpose of obtaining homeowners' insurance. However, it remains important to remember that you will need to support your assumptions if you are questioned about the breakdown. The property tax assessment is the most commonly used, and documentation is easy because the bill usually comes to you on a single sheet of paper.

Another tax limitation applies to the expensing of capital assets. Real estate investors do not qualify for this benefit. Because real estate is a passive activity, the expensing provision is not allowed. If you operate other businesses in addition to real estate activity, you are allowed to expense assets placed into service in those businesses, but not assets used in real estate investments.

Another restriction applies in the deduction of net losses on capital assets. When you sell a capital asset, you are required to pay taxes on any gains, and you are allowed to deduct losses. The net gain or loss is computed as the difference between the original purchase price and the sales price. However, the purchase price is reduced by the amount of depreciation that has been claimed. For example, if you buy an asset for $20,000 and depreciate $15,000, your adjusted basis is $5,000. If you later sell it for $12,000, you are taxed on the difference of $7,000.

If you report a net loss from selling a capital asset, you can deduct up to $3,000 in the applicable tax year. Losses from real estate–related capital assets can be applied against other gains; however, as long as the *net* of all capital losses exceeds $3,000 for the year, the difference has to be carried over and taken in future years.

Reporting capital gains and losses for real estate assets sold during the year is done on IRS Form 4797, which is an attachment to Form 1040. This schedule is used for the sale of assets that are subject to depreciation. See Figure 4.1 for a copy of this form. Form 4797 provides space to report real estate sales, including property and all assets used in a real estate investment (appliances, for example). In Part II of the form, seven columns are used to summarize the transaction. This part of Form 4797 is used only if you owned the property for one year or less and had a net profit. For example, one investor purchased a house at 123 Adams Street, Midvale, Ohio. The purchase date was January 6, 2001. The property was sold on December 19, 2001. It sold for $98,500. Depreciation allowed was $2,182, and the original cost was $90,500. The net gain is computed as shown in Table 4.1, which conforms to the reporting format for Form 4797, Part II. (Note that column headings have been brought down from Part I to clarify what goes in each one.) Depreciation is computed exclusive of land (remember, land cannot be depreciated). The building portion of the purchase price was valued at $60,000. The allowable depreciation for a 27.5-year period is $2,182 per year.

Form **4797**	**Sales of Business Property**	OMB No. 1545-0184
	(Also Involuntary Conversions and Recapture Amounts Under Sections 179 and 280F(b)(2))	20**01**
Department of the Treasury Internal Revenue Service (99)	**Attach to your tax return.** **See separate instructions.**	Attachment Sequence No. **27**

Name(s) shown on return	Identifying number

1 Enter the gross proceeds from sales or exchanges reported to you for 2001 on Form(s) 1099-B or 1099-S (or substitute statement) that you are including on line 2, 10, or 20 (see instructions) **1**

Part I   Sales or Exchanges of Property Used in a Trade or Business and Involuntary Conversions From Other Than Casualty or Theft—Most Property Held More Than 1 Year (See instructions.)

(a) Description of property	(b) Date acquired (mo., day, yr.)	(c) Date sold (mo., day, yr.)	(d) Gross sales price	(e) Depreciation allowed or allowable since acquisition	(f) Cost or other basis, plus improvements and expense of sale	(g) Gain or (loss) Subtract (f) from the sum of (d) and (e)
2						

3 Gain, if any, from Form 4684, line 39	**3**	
4 Section 1231 gain from installment sales from Form 6252, line 26 or 37	**4**	
5 Section 1231 gain or (loss) from like-kind exchanges from Form 8824	**5**	
6 Gain, if any, from line 32, from other than casualty or theft	**6**	
7 Combine lines 2 through 6. Enter the gain or (loss) here and on the appropriate line as follows:	**7**	

Partnerships (except electing large partnerships). Report the gain or (loss) following the instructions for Form 1065, Schedule K, line 6. Skip lines 8, 9, 11, and 12 below.

S corporations. Report the gain or (loss) following the instructions for Form 1120S, Schedule K, lines 5 and 6. Skip lines 8, 9, 11, and 12 below, unless line 7 is a gain and the S corporation is subject to the capital gains tax.

All others. If line 7 is zero or a loss, enter the amount from line 7 on line 11 below and skip lines 8 and 9. If line 7 is a gain and you did not have any prior year section 1231 losses, or they were recaptured in an earlier year, enter the gain from line 7 as a long-term capital gain on Schedule D and skip lines 8, 9, 11, and 12 below.

8 Nonrecaptured net section 1231 losses from prior years (see instructions)	**8**	
9 Subtract line 8 from line 7. If zero or less, enter -0-. Also enter on the appropriate line as follows (see instructions):	**9**	

S corporations. Enter any gain from line 9 on Schedule D (Form 1120S), line 15, and skip lines 11 and 12 below.

All others. If line 9 is zero, enter the gain from line 7 on line 12 below. If line 9 is more than zero, enter the amount from line 8 on line 12 below, and enter the gain from line 9 as a long-term capital gain on Schedule D.

Part II   Ordinary Gains and Losses

10 Ordinary gains and losses not included on lines 11 through 17 (include property held 1 year or less):

11 Loss, if any, from line 7	**11**	(	)
12 Gain, if any, from line 7 or amount from line 8, if applicable	**12**		
13 Gain, if any, from line 31	**13**		
14 Net gain or (loss) from Form 4684, lines 31 and 38a	**14**		
15 Ordinary gain from installment sales from Form 6252, line 25 or 36	**15**		
16 Ordinary gain or (loss) from like-kind exchanges from Form 8824	**16**		
17 Recapture of section 179 expense deduction for partners and S corporation shareholders from property dispositions by partnerships and S corporations (see instructions)	**17**		
18 Combine lines 10 through 17. Enter the gain or (loss) here and on the appropriate line as follows:	**18**		

a **For all except individual returns.** Enter the gain or (loss) from line 18 on the return being filed.

b **For individual returns:**

(1) If the loss on line 11 includes a loss from Form 4684, line 35, column (b)(ii), enter that part of the loss here. Enter the part of the loss from income-producing property on Schedule A (Form 1040), line 27, and the part of the loss from property used as an employee on Schedule A (Form 1040), line 22. Identify as from "Form 4797, line 18b(1)." See instructions . . . .   **18b(1)**

(2) Redetermine the gain or (loss) on line 18 excluding the loss, if any, on line 18b(1). Enter here and on Form 1040, line 14 . . . .   **18b(2)**

For Paperwork Reduction Act Notice, see page 7 of the instructions.   Cat. No. 13086I   Form **4797** (2001)

FIGURE 4.1   IRS Form 4797.

Form 4797 (2001)   Page **2**

Part III Gain From Disposition of Property Under Sections 1245, 1250, 1252, 1254, and 1255

19	(a) Description of section 1245, 1250, 1252, 1254, or 1255 property:	(b) Date acquired (mo., day, yr.)	(c) Date sold (mo., day, yr.)
A			
B			
C			
D			

These columns relate to the properties on lines 19A through 19D.		Property A	Property B	Property C	Property D
20	Gross sales price (**Note:** See line 1 before completing.)	20				
21	Cost or other basis plus expense of sale	21				
22	Depreciation (or depletion) allowed or allowable	22				
23	Adjusted basis. Subtract line 22 from line 21	23				
24	Total gain. Subtract line 23 from line 20	24				
25	**If section 1245 property:**					
a	Depreciation allowed or allowable from line 22	25a				
b	Enter the **smaller** of line 24 or 25a	25b				
26	**If section 1250 property:** If straight line depreciation was used, enter -0- on line 26g, except for a corporation subject to section 291.					
a	Additional depreciation after 1975 (see instructions)	26a				
b	Applicable percentage multiplied by the **smaller** of line 24 or line 26a (see instructions)	26b				
c	Subtract line 26a from line 24. If residential rental property **or** line 24 is not more than line 26a, skip lines 26d and 26e	26c				
d	Additional depreciation after 1969 and before 1976	26d				
e	Enter the **smaller** of line 26c or 26d	26e				
f	Section 291 amount (corporations only)	26f				
g	Add lines 26b, 26e, and 26f	26g				
27	**If section 1252 property:** Skip this section if you did not dispose of farmland or if this form is being completed for a partnership (other than an electing large partnership).					
a	Soil, water, and land clearing expenses	27a				
b	Line 27a multiplied by applicable percentage (see instructions)	27b				
c	Enter the **smaller** of line 24 or 27b	27c				
28	**If section 1254 property:**					
a	Intangible drilling and development costs, expenditures for development of mines and other natural deposits, and mining exploration costs (see instructions)	28a				
b	Enter the **smaller** of line 24 or 28a	28b				
29	**If section 1255 property:**					
a	Applicable percentage of payments excluded from income under section 126 (see instructions)	29a				
b	Enter the **smaller** of line 24 or 29a (see instructions)	29b				

Summary of Part III Gains. Complete property columns A through D through line 29b before going to line 30.

30	Total gains for all properties. Add property columns A through D, line 24	30	
31	Add property columns A through D, lines 25b, 26g, 27c, 28b, and 29b. Enter here and on line 13	31	
32	Subtract line 31 from line 30. Enter the portion from casualty or theft on Form 4684, line 33. Enter the portion from other than casualty or theft on Form 4797, line 6	32	

Part IV Recapture Amounts Under Sections 179 and 280F(b)(2) When Business Use Dops to 50% or Less (See instructions.)

			(a) Section 179	(b) Section 280F(b)(2)
33	Section 179 expense deduction or depreciation allowable in prior years	33		
34	Recomputed depreciation. See instructions	34		
35	Recapture amount. Subtract line 34 from line 33. See the instructions for where to report	35		

Form **4797** (2001)

FIGURE 4.1 IRS Form 4797.

TABLE 4.1   Reporting the Sale of Property

Part II   Ordinary Gains and Losses

10. Ordinary gains and losses are included on lines 11 through 17 (include property held 1 year or less):

(a) Descrip- tion of Property	(b) Date Acquired (mo., day, yr.)	(c) Date Sold (mo., day, yr.)	(d) Gross Sales Price	(e) Deprec- iation Allowed or Allow- able since Acquisition	(f) Cost or Other Basis, plus Improve- ments Expense of Sale	(g) Gain or (loss) Subtract (f) from and the sum of (d) and (e)
123 Adams Street Midvale OH	1-6-01	12-19-01	$98,500	$2,182	$90,500	$10,182

Note that, while the gross difference in sales prices and original purchase price is about $8,000—$98,500 versus $90,500—the capital gain is $10,182. This occurs because depreciation that was claimed from one year to the next is added back in for the purpose of reporting the gain. This is called recapture, and the higher the depreciation claimed, the higher the capital gain. The rest of Form 4797, plus its reverse side, is used to report the same information for property held more than one year and sold for a profit. If long-term property has been sold at a loss, it is reported in Part I.

These distinctions are necessary because long-term and short-term capital gains are taxed at different rates and because depreciation recapture is taxed as ordinary income. This is a complex form, and the purpose of the example in Table 4.1 is only to show how the dollars and cents are translated to the form. In practice, you should depend on a professional tax advisor to complete the reporting of capital gains from real estate.

The sum of all reported gains is carried from this form over to either Form 1040 (ordinary gains or losses) or Schedule D (capital gains or losses). Like Form 4797, Schedule D has two pages, and these are shown in Figure 4.2. Schedule D is used for reporting many different capital gains, both long-term and short-term. For example, investors report the sale of stock and mutual fund shares and capital gain distributions. Assets owned for a year or less are reported in Part I and all others in Part II. A summary of the reporting entries for these forms is shown in Figure 4.3.

SCHEDULE D (Form 1040)	Capital Gains and Losses	2001
Department of the Treasury Internal Revenue Service (99)	Attach to Form 1040. See Instructions for Schedule D (Form 1040). Use Schedule D-1 to list additional transactions for lines 1 and 8.	Attachment Sequence No. 12

Name(s) shown on Form 1040

Your social security number

Part I   Short-Term Capital Gains and Losses—Assets Held One Year or Less

(a) Description of property (Example: 100 sh. XYZ Co.)	(b) Date acquired (Mo., day, yr.)	(c) Date sold (Mo., day, yr.)	(d) Sales price (see page D-5 of the instructions)	(e) Cost or other basis (see page D-5 of the instructions)	(f) Gain or (loss) Subtract (e) from (d)	
1						

2 Enter your short-term totals, if any , from Schedule D-1, line 2 . . . . | **2** | | | |

3 **Total short-term sales price amounts.** Add lines 1 and 2 in column (d) . . . . . | **3** | | | |

4 Short-term gain from Form 6252 and short-term gain or (loss) from Forms 4684, 6781, and 8824 . . . . | **4** | |

5 Net short-term gain or (loss) from partnerships, S corporations, estates, and trusts from Schedule(s) K-1 . . . . | **5** | |

6 Short-term capital loss carryover. Enter the amount, if any , from line 8 of your 2000 Capital Loss Carryover Worksheet . . . . | **6** ( ) |

7 **Net short-term capital gain or (loss).** Combine lines 1 through 6 in column (f). | **7** | |

Part II   Long-Term Capital Gains and Losses—Assets Held More Than One Year

(a) Description of property (Example: 100 sh. XYZ Co.)	(b) Date acquired (Mo., day, yr.)	(c) Date sold (Mo., day, yr.)	(d) Sales price (see page D-5 of the instructions)	(e) Cost or other basis (see page D-5 of the instructions)	(f) Gain or (loss) Subtract (e) from (d)	(g) 28% rate gain or (loss) * (see instr. below)
8						

9 Enter your long-term totals, if any , from Schedule D-1, line 9 . . . . | **9** | | | | |

10 **Total long-term sales price amounts.** Add lines 8 and 9 in column (d) . . . . . | **10** | | | | |

11 Gain from Form 4797, Part I; long-term gain from Forms 2439 and 6252; and long-term gain or (loss) from Forms 4684, 6781, and 8824 . . . . | **11** | | |

12 Net long-term gain or (loss) from partnerships, S corporations, estates, and trusts from Schedule(s) K-1 . . . . | **12** | | |

13 Capital gain distributions. See page D-1 of the instructions . . . . | **13** | | |

14 Long-term capital loss carryover. Enter in both columns (f) and (g) the amount, if any, from line 13 of your 2000 Capital Loss Carryover Worksheet . . . . . . | **14** ( ) | ( ) |

15 Combine lines 8 through 14 in column (g) . . . . . . | **15** | |

16 **Net long-term capital gain or (loss).** Combine lines 8 through 14 in column (f) **Next:** Go to Part III on the back. | **16** | |

* **28% rate gain or loss** includes **all** "collectibles gains and losses" (as defined on page D-5 of the instructions) and up to 50% of the eligible gain on qualified small business stock (see page D-4 of the instructions).

For Paperwork Reduction Act Notice, see Form 1040 instructions.   Cat. No. 11338H   Schedule D (Form 1040) 2001

FIGURE 4.2   IRS Schedule D.

Schedule D (Form 1040) 2001   Page **2**

Part III   Taxable Gain or Deductible Loss

17 Combine lines 7 and 16 and enter the result. If a loss, go to line 18. If a gain, enter the gain on Form 1040, line 13, and complete Form 1040 through line 39 . . . . | **17** |

> **Next:** If both lines 16 and 17 are gains **and** Form 1040, line 39, is more than zero, complete Part IV below.
> Otherwise, skip the rest of Schedule D and complete Form 1040.

18 If line 17 is a loss, enter the **smaller** of that loss or ($3,000) (or, if married filing separately, ($1,500)) here and on Form 1040, line 13. Then complete Form 1040 through line 37 . . . . | **18** (   )

> **Next:** If the loss on line 17 is more than the loss on line 18 **or** if Form 1040, line 37, is less than zero, skip **Part IV** below and complete the **Capital Loss Carryover Worksheet** on page D-6 of the instructions before completing the rest of Form 1040.
> Otherwise, skip **Part IV** below and complete the rest of Form 1040.

Part IV   Tax Computation Using Maximum Capital Gains Rates

19 Enter your unrecaptured section 1250 gain, if any, from line 17 of the worksheet on page D-7 of the instructions . . . . . | **19** |

If line 15 or line 19 is more than zero, see the instructions for line 40 on page D-8 of the instructions. Otherwise, go to line 20.

20 Enter your taxable income from Form 1040, line 39 . . . . . . | **20** |

21 Enter the **smaller** of line 16 or line 17 . . | **21** |

22 If you are deducting investment interest expense on Form 4952, enter the amount from Form 4952, line 4e. Otherwise, enter -0- | **22** |

23 Subtract line 22 from line 21. If zero or less, enter -0- . . . . . . | **23** |

24 Subtract line 23 from line 20. If zero or less, enter -0- . . . . . | **24** |

25 Figure the tax on the amount on line 24. Use the Tax Table or Tax Rate Schedules, whichever applies | **25** |

26 Enter the **smaller** of:
The amount on line 20 **or**
$45,200 if married filing jointly or qualifying widow(er);
$27,050 if single; . . . | **26** |
$36,250 if head of household; or
$22,600 if married filing separately

If line 26 is greater than line 24, go to line 27. Otherwise, skip lines 27 through 33 and go to line 34.

27 Enter the amount from line 24 . . . . | **27** |

28 Subtract line 27 from line 26. If zero or less, enter -0- and go to line 34 | **28** |

29 Enter your qualified 5-year gain, if any, from line 5 of the worksheet on page D-8 . . | **29** |

30 Enter the **smaller** of line 28 or line 29 . . . . | **30** |

31 Multiply line 30 by 8% (.08) . . . . | **31** |

32 Subtract line 30 from line 28 . . . . | **32** |

33 Multiply line 32 by 10% (.10) . . . . | **33** |

If the amounts on lines 23 and 28 are the same, skip lines 34 through 37 and go to line 38.

34 Enter the **smaller** of line 20 or line 23 . . . . | **34** |

35 Enter the amount from line 28 (if line 28 is blank, enter -0-) . . . | **35** |

36 Subtract line 35 from line 34 . . . . | **36** |

37 Multiply line 36 by 20% (.20) . . . . | **37** |

38 Add lines 25, 31, 33, and 37 . . . . | **38** |

39 Figure the tax on the amount on line 20. Use the Tax Table or Tax Rate Schedules, whichever applies | **39** |

40 **Tax on all taxable income (including capital gains).** Enter the **smaller** of line 38 or line 39 here and on Form 1040, line 40 . . . . | **40** |

Schedule D (Form 1040) 2001

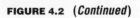

FIGURE 4.2 *(Continued)*

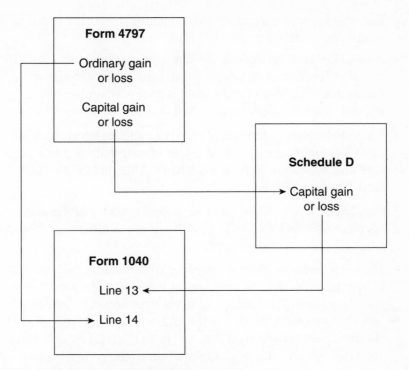

FIGURE 4.3 Tax Forms for Reporting Property Sales.

Deductions You Can Claim

You are allowed to deduct expenses from year to year that relate to your real estate investments. In general, you can deduct all ordinary and necessary expenses:

- *Advertising.* The cost to advertise property for rent or for sale is a deductible expense.
- *Auto and travel.* You can deduct these expenses, including one-half of meal expenses when away from home (for example, to tend to rental property out of town). Auto expenses can be taken under one of two methods: actual expenses or a rate per mile.
- *Cleaning and maintenance.* This is the cost of maintaining property in a condition that is suitable to rent, plus normal maintenance routines, such as winterizing or making minor repairs.
- *Commissions.* These are payments to real estate agents for listing property for sale, for example. Depending on the advice from your

tax professional, real estate commissions may be included here or as closing costs.

- *Insurance.* You can deduct the homeowners' insurance paid for on rental properties. Most people deduct the entire amount of the premium paid within each year, even if part of it applies to the following year; this is called the cash basis for reporting taxes.

- *Legal and other professional fees.* This includes tax preparation fees. Most legal fees related to real estate investment have to be capitalized and added to the property's basis. This means they have to be amortized over time.[*]

- *Management fees.* If you put your property under professional management, the fees paid to the management company are deductible as an expense against income.

- *Mortgage interest paid to banks.* This includes all interest and points (including loan origination fees) actually paid during the year. Any institution collecting more than $600 per year in interest will send you a Form 1098 at the end of the year. If the amount you claim on your tax return is different from the total reported on Form 1098, you should attach an explanation to the return.

- *Other interest.* This includes interest paid to a noninstitution. For example, if you buy property and the seller finances part of the price, you pay interest to that person each year. That interest is reported as "other" interest.[**]

- *Repairs.* You are allowed to deduct the cost of repairs to rental property. Such repairs do not add significantly to the value of property. For example, fixing a broken lock, repairing a window, or replacing a leaking pipe normally meets the definition of a repair. Major repairs that do add value, such as a new roof or furnace, have to be set up as assets and depreciated over time.

- *Supplies.* This includes items used to maintain property. For example, paint brushes, tape, rope, tarps, minor electrical parts, and small yard tools all meet the definition of supplies. Larger purchases, such as lawn mowers, are capitalized and depreciated.

---

[*]Amortization is similar to depreciation. A capitalized item, such as legal fees, is set up as an asset, and a portion is deducted each year.

[**]When you pay interest to someone else, you are required to report that interest on Form 1099-INT each year. This form summarizes interest you paid out to another individual. A copy is sent to the IRS and another copy to the recipient.

- *Taxes.* This usually means property taxes paid on rental property. If other taxes apply, they can be deducted as well. For example, if you pay excise taxes on property, that also is deductible. Excise taxes often apply as a charge when property is sold and might be included as part of closing costs; or the tax can be separated and deducted as an expense. A tax advisor should be consulted to determine the proper way to handle excise tax deductions.

- *Utilities.* You can deduct utilities that you pay for rental property. Depending on the agreement you enter with tenants, you may pay part of the utilities. Landlords often pay for water and sewer, for example, whereas tenants pay all other utility costs. You also pay for utilities while property is vacant.

- *Other expenses.* You also are allowed to deduct any other "ordinary and necessary" expenses related to your rental properties. These include office supplies, telephone, or minor landscaping expenses.[*]

If you have expenses that apply only partially to real estate investments and are partially personal, then special rules apply for deducting and documenting them. Careful recordkeeping is especially important if you rent out part of the property in which you also live, or if you use a property part of the year as a dwelling and rent it out for the remainder of the year. In some instances, investment-related expenses are not deductible if you rented out a property for 15 days or more per year.

SIDEBAR

IRS Publication 527 explains the rules for mixed use of rental property. To order this publication online, check the IRS web site at
http://www.irs.gov/prod/forms_pubs/index.html

In addition to the expenses previously discussed, you also are allowed to claim depreciation for all improvements to your property. These include a house sitting on land[**] as well as any improvements made while you own it, as well as other assets, such as appliances, landscaping equipment, or a vehicle used exclusively in your rental operations. For example, you might

---

[*]As with other expenses, landscaping expenses may be deductible as long as they are relatively minor. For example, if you buy a small tree on sale for $15, it can be deducted as a supply item. However, if you spend $2,000 to fully landscape a lot professionally, that cost has to be set up as a capitalized improvement and depreciated over time.

[**]Under tax rules, all changes to raw land are classified as improvements, including buildings.

need to buy a pickup truck to haul landscaping debris, move appliances, or dispose of items left by tenants. The amount of depreciation allowed depends on the nature of the asset.

Remember that a *loss* from real estate investment activity cannot exceed $25,000 per year. A loss above that level has to be carried over and applied against income in future years. Thus, if you buy a lot of real estate and the net loss is over $25,000 every year, your loss carry-over will grow from one year to the next.

Real estate income and expenses are reported for federal taxes on Schedule E. This is a two-sided form as shown in Figure 4.4. On the first side of Schedule E, each rental property is listed by type and location. There is room to provide details for up to three properties. If you own more than three properties during the year, supplementary exhibits should be attached, breaking down the details for each, and a summary entered on Schedule E. If a property was used during the year for personal use, special rules apply. In Part I, section 2, three questions relating to personal use have to be answered, and depending on the number of days of personal use, some deductions might not be deductible for the year.

Rents and expenses are listed on Schedule E, including depreciation deductions (line 20) for each property. The net profit or loss from real estate is shown at the bottom of the page on line 26 and is carried over to Form 1040, line 17.

The second page of Schedule E is used mostly for non-real estate activity. This includes farming or fishing, partnerships and small business corporations, estates and trusts, and real estate mortgage investment conduits. Most people investing in directly held real estate do not use the second page of Schedule E.

Depreciation of Real Estate

Depreciation is allowed for all *improvements* to land, but not to the land itself, and for capital assets used for real estate investments. Each classification of asset is depreciated differently, based on the mandated recovery period (years of depreciation allowed) and restrictions on how rapidly depreciation can be taken—some assets can be depreciated quickly through accelerated depreciation, and others have to be depreciated using the straight-line basis only.

Land cannot be depreciated at all. Thus, if your investment in rental property includes acreage, and land represents a majority of the total property value, depreciation will be less. For the typical city building lot with a house on it, land is normally a relatively small portion of total value, usually one-third or less of the overall purchase price. Such generalizations do not apply

SCHEDULE E
(Form 1040)

Department of the Treasury
Internal Revenue Service (99)

Supplemental Income and Loss

(From rental real estate, royalties, partnerships,
S corporations, estates, trusts, REMICs, etc.)

Attach to Form 1040 or Form 1041.   **See Instructions for Schedule E (Form 1040).**

OMB No. 1545-0074

2001

Attachment
Sequence No. **13**

Name(s) shown on return | Your social security number

Part I   **Income or Loss From Rental Real Estate and Royalties**   Note. If you are in the business of renting personal property, use **Schedule C** or **C-EZ** (see page E-1). Report farm rental income or loss from **Form 4835** on page 2, line 39.

1 Show the kind and location of each **rental real estate property:**

A ....

B ....

C ....

2 For each rental real estate property listed on line 1, did you or your family use it during the tax year for personal purposes for more than the greater of:

  14 days **or**

  10% of the total days rented at fair rental value?

(See page E-1.)

	Yes	No
A		
B		
C		

Income:

		Properties			Totals (Add columns A, B, and C.)
		A	**B**	**C**	
3 Rents received	3		3		
4 Royalties received	4				4

Expenses:

		A	B	C	Totals
5 Advertising	5				
6 Auto and travel (see page E-2) .	6				
7 Cleaning and maintenance . . .	7				
8 Commissions	8				
9 Insurance	9				
10 Legal and other professional fees	10				
11 Management fees	11				
12 Mortgage interest paid to banks, etc. (see page E-2)	12				12
13 Other interest	13				
14 Repairs	14				
15 Supplies	15				
16 Taxes	16				
17 Utilities	17				
18 Other (list)	18				
19 Add lines 5 through 18	19				19
20 Depreciation expense or depletion (see page E-3)	20				20
21 Total expenses. Add lines 19 and 20	21				
22 Income or (loss) from rental real estate or royalty properties. Subtract line 21 from line 3 (rents) or line 4 (royalties). If the result is a (loss), see page E-3 to find out if you must file **Form 6198** . .	22				
23 Deductible rental real estate loss. **Caution.** Your rental real estate loss on line 22 may be limited. See page E-3 to find out if you must file **Form 8582.** Real estate professionals must complete line 42 on page 2	23	(	)(	)( )	

24 **Income.** Add positive amounts shown on line 22. **Do not** include any losses . . . . | 24 | |

25 **Losses.** Add royalty losses from line 22 and rental real estate losses from line 23. Enter total losses here | 25 | ( ) |

26 **Total rental real estate and royalty income or (loss).** Combine lines 24 and 25. Enter the result here. If Parts II, III, IV, and line 39 on page 2 do not apply to you, also enter this amount on Form 1040, line 17. Otherwise, include this amount in the total on line 40 on page 2 . . . . | 26 | |

For Paperwork Reduction Act Notice, see Form 1040 instructions.   Cat. No. 11344L   Schedule E (Form 1040) 2001

FIGURE 4.4   Schedule E, Part 1 and 2.

Schedule E (Form 1040) 2001   Attachment Sequence No. **13**   Page **2**

Name(s) shown on return. Do not enter name and social security number if shown on other side. | **Your social security number**

Note. If you report amounts from farming or fishing on Schedule E, you must enter your gross income from those activities on line 41 below. Real estate professionals must complete line 42 below.

Part II   **Income or Loss From Partnerships and S Corporations**   Note. If you report a loss from an at-risk activity, you **must** check either column **(e)** or **(f)** on line 27 to describe your investment in the activity. See page E-5. If you check column **(f)**, you must attach **Form 6198.**

27	(a) Name	(b) Enter P for partnership; S for S corporation	(c) Check if foreign partnership	(d) Employer identification number	Investment At Risk?
					(e) All is at risk / (f) Some is not at risk
A					
B					
C					
D					
E					

	Passive Income and Loss		Nonpassive Income and Loss		
	(g) Passive loss allowed (attach **Form 8582** if required)	(h) Passive income from **Schedule K–1**	(i) Nonpassive loss from **Schedule K–1**	(j) Section 179 expense deduction from **Form 4562**	(k) Nonpassive income from **Schedule K–1**
A					
B					
C					
D					
E					
28a Totals					
b Totals					

29   Add columns (h) and (k) of line 28a . . . . | **29** |
30   Add columns (g), (i), and (j) of line 28b . . . . | **30** (   )
31   Total partnership and S corporation income or (loss). Combine lines 29 and 30. Enter the result here and include in the total on line 40 below . . . . | **31** |

Part III   **Income or Loss From Estates and Trusts**

32	(a) Name	(b) Employer identification number
A		
B		

	Passive Income and Loss		Nonpassive Income and Loss	
	(c) Passive deduction or loss allowed (attach **Form 8582** if required)	(d) Passive income from **Schedule K–1**	(e) Deduction or loss from **Schedule K–1**	(f) Other income from **Schedule K–1**
A				
B				
33a Totals				
b Totals				

34   Add columns (d) and (f) of line 33a . . . . | **34** |
35   Add columns (c) and (e) of line 33b . . . . | **35** (   )
36   Total estate and trust income or (loss). Combine lines 34 and 35. Enter the result here and include in the total on line 40 below . . . . | **36** |

Part IV   **Income or Loss From Real Estate Mortgage Investment Conduits (REMICs)—Residual Holder**

37	(a) Name	(b) Employer identification number	(c) Excess inclusion from **Schedules Q,** line 2c (see page E-6)	(d) Taxable income (net loss) from **Schedules Q,** line 1b	(e) Income from **Schedules Q,** line 3b

38   Combine columns (d) and (e) only. Enter the result here and include in the total on line 40 below | **38** |

Part V   **Summary**

39   Net farm rental income or (loss) from **Form 4835**. Also, complete line 41 below . . . . . | **39** |
40   **Total** income or (loss). Combine lines 26, 31, 36, 38, and 39. Enter the result here and on Form 1040, line 17 | **40** |

41   **Reconciliation of Farming and Fishing Income.** Enter your **gross** farming and fishing income reported on Form 4835, line 7; Schedule K-1 (Form 1065), line 15b; Schedule K-1 (Form 1120S), line 23; and Schedule K-1 (Form 1041), line 14 (see page E-6) . . . . | **41** |

42   **Reconciliation for Real Estate Professionals.** If you were a real estate professional (see page E-4), enter the net income or (loss) you reported anywhere on Form 1040 from all rental real estate activities in which you materially participated under the passive activity loss rules . . . | **42** |

⊕   Schedule E (Form 1040) 2001

FIGURE 4.4 *(Continued)*

everywhere, however, so in planning the cash flow and tax benefits related to real estate investing, it also makes sense to investigate the typical breakdown between land and improvements.

For purposes of depreciation, improvements include the house and all other structures on the land. Once you own the property, improvements may also consist of additional work, including replacement roofing, major repairs and cosmetic changes, landscaping, and other permanent changes. All improvements have to be depreciated under the straight-line basis, and most residential real estate is depreciated over 27.5 years.

For example, if you purchase a residential property for $100,000, and $30,000 is assigned to the value of the land, then you can depreciate $70,000 for the improvement value. If you later perform several additional improvements, those also are depreciated on the same basis. The usual method, straight-line over 27.5 years, apply to any and all improvements made subsequent to buying the property.

As a general rule, straight-line depreciation is easy to compute. You divide the depreciable value by 27.5:

$$\$70,000 \div 27.5 = \$2,545$$

Rounding to the closest dollar, annual depreciation would be $2,545 in this example.

For the *first* year that you own rental property, depreciation is calculated based on when it is bought and placed into service. Residential real estate's first-year depreciation is based on the midmonth convention. This simply means that real estate is assumed to have been bought midway through the month in which it was purchased. The applicable percentage to use under the midmonth method is summarized in Table 4.2. In this table, the applicable midmonth multiplier is shown for each month in the year. For example, in January, the midmonth convention is based on the assumption that the asset went into service midway through January, so that you are allowed 23/24 of a year's depreciation. (There are 24 half-months in the year, so in the first month, only 1/24 is excluded.) The multiplier calculates 23/24 of a year's depreciation:

$$23 \div 24 = 0.9583$$

Applying the multiplier to a full year's depreciation involves two steps. First, calculate the full year's depreciation:

$$\$70,000 \div 27.5 = \$2,545$$

Next, multiply the full year's allowance by the midmonth multiplier:

$$0.9583 \times \$2,545 = \$2,439$$

TABLE 4.2 Midmonth Convention

PLACED IN SERVICE	MULTIPLIER FOR DEPRECIATION
January	0.9583
February	0.8750
March	0.7917
April	0.7083
May	0.6250
June	0.5417
July	0.4583
August	0.3750
September	0.2917
October	0.2083
November	0.1250
December	0.0417

Again rounding to the nearest dollar, the allowable depreciation for the first year in this example would be $2,439. This applies when the property was purchased at any time during the month of January.

After the first year, the same property would be depreciated under the straight-line method at the rate of $2,545 per year. This would continue for the full 27.5 years. If the property were to be sold prior to that time, the amount of depreciation claimed over the period you owned the property would be deducted to compute the capital gain. For example, let's say you owned the property for five full years. Depreciation would total up to $12,619, using the example. If the $100,000 property were sold for $130,000 at the end of five years, the capital gain would be computed as follows (not allowing for any additional improvements or for closing costs at purchase or sale):

Sales price	$130,000
Purchase price	$100,000
Less: depreciation	− 12,619
Adjusted basis	87,381
Capital gain	$ 42,619

Although the difference between purchase and sale is only $30,000, the depreciation adjusts your basis in the property and then is taxed. The recapture portion is taxed at ordinary tax rates, rather than at the more favorable long-term capital gain rates.

Any improvements made to the property after purchase is depreciated under the same straight-line basis over 27.5 years. And their value is added to the basis of the property when sold, so that capital gains include all capital investment.

Other assets are depreciated under different methods. Any property placed into service after 1986 is depreciated under what is called the Modified Accelerated Cost Recovery System (MACRS). Under MACRS, depreciation normally is computed under what is called the General Depreciation System (GDS). GDS excludes automobiles used partially for personal and partially for investment purposes, as well as assets owned before the MACRS went into effect.[*]

SIDEBAR

Check IRS Publication 946 for further information about the MACRS. It is available on the IRS web page at
http://www.irs.gov/prod/forms_pubs/index.html

Under the GDS calculation, assets are divided into distinct property classifications. For example, automobiles or trucks, appliances, carpets, furniture used in rental property, office equipment, and computers normally belong in the five-year class. These assets normally are depreciated using the 200 percent declining balance method. This class fits most real estate capital assets, except improvements.

Most five-year property is depreciated under what is called the half-year convention. Unlike the midmonth convention, which applies to improvements, the half-year convention is relatively straightforward. It is assumed that all property placed into service at any time during the first year is subject to one-half of the allowable depreciation rate for that year.

The usual method for depreciating five-year property is the 200 percent declining balance method. This allows for twice the amount of depreciation that would be allowed under the more conservative straight-line method, and it switches to straight-line in the fourth year. Allowing for the half-year convention, the normal percentage claimed each year for depreciation under

---

[*]Assets placed into service prior to 1987 were usually depreciated under the original Accelerated Cost Recovery System (ACRS).

TABLE 4.3 Normal Percentages Claimed for Depreciation, Five-Year Recovery Period

YEAR	PERCENTAGE
1	20.00%
2	32.00
3	19.20
4	11.52
5	11.52
6	5.76

the five-year class is summarized in Table 4.3. Note that the 200 percent declining balance reverts to straight-line after the third year.[*]

Under GDS and alternative systems, a number of additional recovery periods can be used. However, most instances of capitalized assets for real estate fit into one of two recovery periods, the 27.5-year period for improvements and the five-year period.

Depreciation is summarized and reported on Form 4562. This is a two-page form, as shown in Figure 4.5. Part I of the form is for the expensing of assets. Assets are expensed by writing them off in the year they are placed into service. This provision can be used for up to $20,000 of assets. However, assets used for real estate investing are specifically excluded from the expensing election, so this section does not apply to that activity.

Part II of Form 4562 is used for reporting the majority of real estate–related depreciation. Lines 15b and 15h are the most common lines used. If you have more than a single property to report, it is a good idea to attach a supplementary exhibit. It should include your name and social security number, the tax year, and identification as an attachment to Form 4562. The columns should correspond to those columns shown in Part II, Section B (GBS). The total of depreciation claimed each year is summarized on line 21 and then carried over to Schedule E, where each property's deductions are listed in detail.

Most real estate investors use only one section on the second page of Form 4562: Part VI, Amortization. You are required to amortize certain legal fees and points that are spread out over the period of a loan. (Some financing arrangements include loan origination fees, but they are included in the loan proceeds; in that case, the points have to be amortized.)

---

[*]The 5-year recovery period extends over 6 years because only a partial deduction is allowed in the first year.

Form **4562**	**Depreciation and Amortization** (Including Information on Listed Property)	OMB No. 1545-0172
Department of the Treasury Internal Revenue Service (99)	See separate instructions. Attach this form to your return.	**2001** Attachment Sequence No. 67
Name(s) shown on return	Business or activity to which this form relates	Identifying number

Part I   Election To Expense Certain Tangible Property Under Section 179

Note: *If you have any "listed property," complete Part V before you complete Part I.*

1	Maximum dollar limitation. If an ente rprise zone business, see page 2 of the instructions	1	$24,000
2	Total cost of section 179 pr operty placed in se rvice (see page 2 of the instructions).	2	30,645
3	Threshold cost of section 179 pr operty before reduction in limitation	3	$200,000
4	Reduction in limitation. Subtract line 3 fr om line 2. If zero or less, enter -0-	4	- 0 -
5	Dollar limitation for tax ye ar. Subtract line 4 from line 1. If zero or less, enter -0-. If married filing separately, see page 2 of the instructions	5	24,000

(a) Description of property	(b) Cost (business use only)	(c) Elected cost
6		

7	Listed property. Enter amount from line 27.	7	24,000
8	Total elected cost of section 179 pr operty. Add amounts in column (c), lines 6 and 7	8	24,000
9	Tentative deduction. Ente r the smaller of line 5 or line 8	9	24,000
10	Carryover of disallowed deduction fr om 2000 (see page 3 of the instructions).	10	- 0 -
11	Business income limitation. Enter the smaller of business income (not less than zero) or line 5 (see instructions)	11	
12	Section 179 expense deduction. Add line s 9 and 10, but do not ente r more than line 11	12	24,000
13	Carryover of disallowed deduction to 2002. Add lines 9 and 10, less line 12	13	

Note: *Do not use Part II or Part III below for listed property (automobiles, certain other vehicles, cellular telephones, certain computers, or property used for entertainment, r ecreation, or amusement). Instead, use Part V for listed property.*

Part II   MACRS Depreciation for Assets Placed in Service Only During Your 2001 Tax Year (Do not include listed property.)

Section A—General Asset Account Election

14 If you are making the election under section 168(i)(4) to group any assets placed in se rvice during the tax ye ar into one or more general asset accounts, check this box. See page 3 of the instructions . . . . ☐

Section B—General Depreciation System (GDS) (See page 3 of the instructions.)

(a) Classification of property	(b) Month and year placed in service	(c) Basis for depreciation (business/investment use only—see instructions)	(d) Recovery period	(e) Convention	(f) Method	(g) Depreciation deduction
15a 3-year property						
b 5-year property		3,000	5 yrs.	MQ	200 DB	750
c 7-year property						
d 10-year property						
e 15-year property						
f 20-year property						
g 25-year property			25 yrs.		S/L	
h Residential rental property			27.5 yrs.	MM	S/L	
			27.5 yrs.	MM	S/L	
i Nonresidential real property			39 yrs.	MM	S/L	
				MM	S/L	

Section C—Alternative Depreciation System (ADS) (See page 5 of the instructions.)

16a Class life		2,345			S/L	43.80
b 12-year			12 yrs.		S/L	
c 40-year			40 yrs.	MM	S/L	

Part III   Other Depreciation (Do not include listed property.) (See page 5 of the instructions.)

17	GDS and ADS deductions for assets placed in se rvice in tax years beginning before 2001	17	4,511.73
18	Property subject to section 168(f)(1) election	18	
19	ACRS and other depreciation	19	

Part IV   Summary (See page 6 of the instructions.)

20	Listed property. Enter amount from line 26.	20	65
21	**Total.** Add deductions from line 12, lines 15 and 16 in column (g), and lines 17 through 20. Enter here and on the appropriate lines of your return. Partnerships and S corporations—see instructions	21	29,370.53
22	For assets shown above and placed in se rvice during the current year, enter the portion of the basis attributable to section 263A costs 22	- 0 -	

For Paperwork Reduction Act Notice, see page 9 of the instructions.   Cat. No. 12906N   Form **4562** (2001)

FIGURE 4.5   IRS Form 4562.

Form 4562 (2001)   Page **2**

Part V   **Listed Property** (Include automobiles, certain other vehicles, cellular telephones, certain computers, and property used for entertainment, recreation, or amusement.)

Note: *For any vehicle for which you are using the standard mileage rate or deducting lease expense, complete only 23a, 23b, columns (a) through (c) of Section A, all of Section B, and Section C if applicable.*

Section A—Depreciation and Other Information (Caution: *See page 7 of the instructions for limits for passenger automobiles.*)

23a Do you have evidence to support the business/investment use claimed? ☐ **Yes** ☐ **No**   **23b** If "Yes," is the evidence written? ☐ **Yes** ☐ **No**

(a) Type of property (list vehicles first)	(b) Date placed in service	(c) Business/ investment use percentage	(d) Cost or other basis	(e) Basis for depreciation (business/investment use only)	(f) Recovery period	(g) Method/ Convention	(h) Depreciation deduction	(i) Elected section 179 cost
24 Property used more than 50% in a qualified business use (see page 6 of the instructions):								
USA 280F Van	11-16-01	100%	25,300	1,300	5	200 DB/MQ	65	24,000
		%						
		%						
25 Property used 50% or less in a qualified business use (see page 6 of the instructions):								
		%				S/L –		
		%				S/L –		
		%				S/L –		

26 Add amounts in column (h). Enter the total here and on line 20, page 1 . . . . . .   **26**   **65**

27 Add amounts in column (i). Enter the total here and on line 7, page 1 . . . .   **27**   **24,000**

Section B—Information on Use of Vehicles

Complete this section for vehicles used by a sole proprietor, partner, or other "more than 5% owner," or related person.

If you provided vehicles to your employees, first answer the questions in Section C to see if you meet an exception to completing this section for those vehicles.

	(a) Vehicle 1	(b) Vehicle 2	(c) Vehicle 3	(d) Vehicle 4	(e) Vehicle 5	(f) Vehicle 6
28 Total business/investment miles driven during the year (**do not** include commuting miles— see page 1 of the instructions)						
29 Total commuting miles driven during the year						
30 Total other personal (noncommuting) miles driven						
31 Total miles driven during the year. Add lines 28 through 30						

	Yes	No	Yes	No	Yes	No	Yes	No	Yes	No	Yes	No
32 Was the vehicle available for personal use during off-duty hours?												
33 Was the vehicle used primarily by a more than 5% owner or related person?												
34 Is another vehicle available for personal use?												

Section C—Questions for Employers Who Provide Vehicles for Use by Their Employees

Answer these questions to determine if you meet an exception to completing Section B for vehicles used by employees who **are not** more than 5% owners or related persons (see page 8 of the instructions).

	Yes	No
35 Do you maintain a written policy statement that prohibits all personal use of vehicles, including commuting, by your employees?		
36 Do you maintain a written policy statement that prohibits personal use of vehicles, except commuting, by your employees? See page 8 of the instructions for vehicles used by corporate officers, directors, or 1% or more owners		
37 Do you treat all use of vehicles by employees as personal use?		
38 Do you provide more than five vehicles to your employees, obtain information from your employees about the use of the vehicles, and retain the information received?		
39 Do you meet the requirements concerning qualified automobile demonstration use? (See page 8 of the instructions.) . . **Note:** *If your answer to 35, 36, 37, 38, or 39 is "Yes," do not complete Section B for the covered vehicles.*		

Part VI   **Amortization**

(a) Description of costs	(b) Date amortization begins	(c) Amortizable amount	(d) Code section	(e) Amortization period or percentage	(f) Amortization for this year
40 Amortization of costs that begins during your 2001 tax year (see page 8 of the instructions):					
41 Amortization of costs that began before your 2001 tax year			**41**		
42 **Total.** Add amounts in column (f). See page 9 of the instructions for where to report . . .			**42**		

Form **4562** (2001)

FIGURE 4.5 *(Continued)*

In order to keep records for depreciation calculations, as well as filing of the information itself, a depreciation worksheet has to be maintained. The IRS recommends using a form such as the one shown in Figure 4.6 for this purpose.

When you are dealing with several properties, year-to-year calculations of depreciation can become complex. Thus, it makes sense to prepare worksheets in advance, calculating each year's depreciation allowance. This enables you to fill out a worksheet for each tax year without also having to recalculate the deduction. For example, a worksheet for real estate deductions might look like the one in Figure 4.7. This worksheet provides for calculation of up to 27 years' depreciation. Another alternative, practical for assets other than improvements, is to develop a calculation showing not only the annual depreciation but also the applicable annual percentage. This is practical when using the 200 percent declining balance method available for five-year property.

It is also useful to show depreciation claimed to date, since the IRS form asks for prior depreciation claimed. Thus, a five-year property valued at $6,000 and depreciated under the five-year declining balance method, could be reduced to a worksheet as

Worksheet—five-year property

Asset: Pick-up truck

Purchase date: 2002

Price: $6,000.00

Year	Percentage	This Year's Depreciation	Claimed to Date
1	20.00%	$1,200	$1,200
2	32.00	1,920	3,120
3	19.20	1,152	4,272
4	11.52	691	4,963
5	11.52	691	5,654
6	5.76	346	6,000

State regulations differ from the federal rules in many states; thus, adjustments to calculated depreciation allowances often are required. Because federal and state depreciation requirements may differ, it might be necessary to maintain two sets of depreciation records. This applies not only to the calculation of annual allowances but also to the reporting of capital gains on the sale of a real estate asset. Because the reported

Description of Property	Date Placed In Service	Cost or Other Basis	Business/ Investment Use %	Section 179 Deduction	Depreciation Prior Years	Basis for Depreciation	Method/ Convention	Recovery Period	Rate or Table %	Depreciation Deduction

FIGURE 4.6   Depreciation Worksheet.

Property_____

Total Purchase Price	$_____
Less: Land	$_____
Improvements	$_____

Date Acquired   _____

Year	Depreciation	Year	Depreciation	Year	Depreciation

FIGURE 4.7 Worksheet, Annual Depreciation.

gain includes an adjustment for depreciation, the gain will be different as calculated under federal and state rules.

Elections and Rules

The depreciation calculations described in this chapter are the *usual* methods of calculation. The MACRS-prescribed methods for recovery period and calculation define the maximum rate for depreciation available under the law. A number of elections can be made, however, to extend depreciation over a longer period of time.

Rather than depreciating property under the guidelines of the MACRS, you can use the Alternative Depreciation System (ADS), which uses the straight-line method only. Under ADS, longer depreciation periods apply. Once the election is made, it is irrevocable. For real estate, the election to use ADS is made for each property. The two recovery periods are 12 and 40 years. Thus, as a general rule, improvements are depreciated over a 40-year period, and all nonimprovement assets are claimed over 12 years.

An election to claim *less* depreciation than you are allowed can be made for a variety of reasons. For example, you might not have a very large tax liability from one year to another and would prefer to defer depreciation write-offs to later periods, where they might be more valuable. For real estate investors owning numerous properties, the election can also make sense under the rule limiting losses to no more than $25,000 per year. By reducing depreciation on a number of real estate properties each year, it is easier to fall under the $25,000 limit each year and avoid carrying over passive losses that might never be fully used under the more generous MACRS rules.

For example, if you own four or five rentals and your total depreciable real property is $400,000, you are entitled to $14,545 each year when it is depreciated over 27.5 years. That is reduced to only $10,000 per year under the ADS rules. Considering that you can deduct only $25,000 per year, no matter how many properties you own, the reduced depreciation allowed per year can be an advantage. When you can take more than $14,000 in depreciation in a single year, you probably exceed the $25,000 ceiling when adding mortgage interest alone; that means you get no tax benefit from property taxes, insurance, utilities, and other investment expenses.

It can also make sense to defer depreciation deductions with future capital gains taxes in mind. If you anticipate holding properties for only a few years, remember that any gains will be increased by the amount of depreciation that you claimed or that you could have claimed. That means that you might not realize the benefit of depreciation because you exceeded the $25,000 ceiling, yet you are required to recapture the full amount available. Anticipating the possibility that your deductions might place you above the deductible ceiling, the longer, 40-year recovery period could make a lot of sense, not only immediately but even more so in the long run.

While this chapter explored depreciation rules as well as tax reporting and calculations in the most general sense, the tax rules are complicated. Your state's rules might be vastly different from the federal rules, meaning that your records have to reflect two sets of calculations to comply in both cases. As is always the case when it comes to tax rules, you need to consult with a qualified tax professional to ensure that the methods you use to set up your books, keep records of transactions, and report income and expenses are in compliance with current requirements.

CHAPTER 5

Selling Rental Property

When you own investment property, you need to operate with a long-term plan. Just as owners of mutual funds need to have an exit strategy, real estate investors also need to work with established goals. When will you sell? What is the objective?

Some investors will sell when they are able to achieve a specific percentage of return; others want to enjoy tax benefits for a number of years or just accumulate equity toward retirement. Others give up on real estate after working for many years with tenants, because it is difficult to travel for an extended period of time. They find out that, with tenants, they have to be in town almost all of the time. This group concludes that owning rental property is appropriate in their 30s and 40s but that it becomes a burden after those decades.

Strategies for Selling Property

Given that everyone is different and operates from a different set of assumptions, you need to develop a strategy not only for acquiring real estate but also for when and why you will dispose of it. This involves setting specific goals identifying the timing for the sale of real estate, based on what you hope to achieve by owning it. Stockholders do this regularly as part of their well-managed portfolios. Sales take place to bail out of a losing situation, or when profit goals have been met. If the sector loses strength in the market, stockholders move their capital out of stocks previously thought to be promising and seek other companies for their investments—all with the purpose of maximizing the potential for gain while reducing exposure to market risk.

Real estate investors need to take the same approach. To say that real estate is *always* a viable investment would ignore the realities. The cyclical nature of real estate mandates that even a long-term hold is going to be subject to strong growth periods, stagnant times when prices are not moving, and possibly even periods when values are falling. This is not to say that you should speculate in real estate, moving in and out of positions with regularity. The cost of high-volume trading makes this impractical as an investment strategy in the real estate market. It does mean, however, that you need to watch the market and make judgments about whether to keep property based on your goals. For example, if you want to maintain a growth pattern of 10 percent per year, is it practical to hold real estate? This goal is not as difficult to reach as it might seem. It can consist of several features. Remember, yield can be based either on the total value of property or on the amount actually invested. Because the majority of real estate is financed, it is a highly leveraged investment, so the cost of interest has to be offset by rental income just to maintain a breakeven situation. Assuming that this is possible, how can you achieve a 10 percent return each year?

Part of that 10 percent return can consist of tax benefits. These are not difficult to compute. Look at last year's personal income tax return and divide the total tax liability by taxable income. For the year 2000, these values are found on the reverse side of IRS Form 1040, lines 57 (total tax) and 39 (taxable income). The result is your effective tax rate.

The net loss reported on real estate investments reduces your tax liability. Your effective tax should include both federal and state taxes. For example, your rate may be 27 percent. That means that you saved 27 percent of the net loss reported from real estate. If you had the maximum of $25,000 in real estate losses for the year (due to depreciation, interest, and other expenses), your tax savings was $6,750. This is important because yield on real estate investments should include the important tax benefits, one of the primary features of real estate investing. If you have $80,000 invested in down payment and improvement capital, the $6,750 in the example represents nearly 8.5 percent yield , on invested capital. If the total value of investment real estate you own is $250,000, then yield on market value was 2.7 percent for the year.

The tax benefits are a major part of yield whichever way you calculate it. If your goal is to reach or exceed 10 percent per year, you gain much of that benefit in tax reduction alone. By tracking the government's estimates of real estate values, you also get a fair approximation of increases in property values. However, it will be far more accurate to get this information from your local Multiple Listing Service (MLS), since it keeps track of *local* price trends, which are related directly to your investments.

As long as you are meeting or exceeding your goal of earning 10 percent per year, real estate investing continues to make sense. This does not necessarily mean that you need to sell your investment properties as soon as yields fall short of that goal, however. Remember, when you sell an investment, you need to do something with that capital. Chances are, if real estate does not yield 10 percent, you will have problems finding another place to put your money that will meet that goal—especially considering the major role that tax benefits play in real estate.

It is more likely that you can improve investment performance by exchanging a current investment property for another, perhaps one with better cash flow, more potential for growth in value, or both. Some properties are maximized as investments over a relatively short term, after which it makes sense to move your money to other properties. For example, if you follow the advice to buy the worst house on a good block, what happens after you make your cosmetic repairs? Within two or three years, that property might be at a par with other values in the area, and, if all property values have risen, it might be time to sell and move on. Perhaps you will be able to find another situation similar to the first one. Before doing so, however, you need to judge whether the current property has, indeed, maxed out in the sense of reaching its immediate potential—*and* that you can do better moving your investment capital elsewhere. You also need to be aware of the tax liability that will be involved in selling one rental property and replacing it with another. Later in this chapter, the like-kind exchange rules will be discussed, showing you how you can sell a rental and buy another with no current-year tax liabilities. (This is a federal tax provision; tax rules in your state will not always conform, so it is possible to defer a tax liability for federal income tax and remain liable for state taxes.)

Rules for Owner-Occupied Housing

As a homeowner, the federal tax rules are very favorable when you sell your home. A major change in the rules took place in 1997, allowing you to sell your home and pay no federal income taxes whatsoever—if you meet the qualifications.

Before 1997, homeowners were required to replace a sold home with another one of equal or greater value in order to avoid taxes. This meant that a family trying to move to a smaller house could not do so without a tax penalty, so trading down meant paying tax on part of the sale. The replacement home had to be bought within two years from the date of sale. When people were 55 or older, they could take advantage of a one-time exclusion up to $150,000 in profit on the sale of a primary residence. Thus, as a general rule, it was difficult for people to avoid taxes indefinitely when selling their homes.

Under provisions of the Taxpayer Relief Act of 1997, those rules were eliminated, and homeowners were provided a significant form of tax benefit when selling their homes. A family can now avoid *all* federal taxes on as much as $500,000 of profit on selling their homes (a single person is entitled to a $250,000 exclusion of profit). To qualify, they have to have lived in the home as a primary residence for at least two out of the past five years. It is no longer necessary to replace the sold house, and no age limitations or requirements apply. Furthermore, the exclusion can be used as many times as you like, as long as you meet the two-year rule every time. You cannot exclude profit on more than one primary residence within a two-year period.

Thus, you can buy and sell a home every two years, profit every time, and never be liable for federal income taxes. For primary residences, there is now an important tax advantage in the federal rules. For those whose homes would be sold at a profit above $500,000 ($250,000 for single people), the excess is taxed. This means that the more affluent homeowners will be taxed on large profits from very expensive homes, excluding only the maximum of $500,000 for a married couple and being taxed on any excess.

With these new rules in place, an interesting question arises for real estate investors. Can you convert an investment property to a primary residence, live in it for two years, and then sell without being liable for federal tax? The rules state that a primary residence has to meet the definition: You must have lived in the property for at least two of the past five years. Thus, in most instances where investment property is converted to a primary residence, the profit can be excluded up to the maximum, with an important exception: Any depreciation that was claimed while the property was used as an investment would be taxed at ordinary tax rates, under the recapture rule. If you are planning to convert investment property to a primary residence, you should first consult with a tax advisor to ensure not only that you know in advance how the decision affects your taxes but also so that you will be able to properly document the property's change in status.

Establishing a property as your primary residence is a relatively easy thing to do. First, you can have only one primary residence at a time. Second, the two years do not have to take place consecutively. For example, if you live in the property for the first six months of a four-year period, you have met the requirement. In cases in which you move in or out of a property, you need to be able to demonstrate that it did serve as your primary residence. One way to prove this is through payment of utility bills. As long as you were paying your own water, sewer, gas, electric, garbage disposal, telephone, and cable television bill for a property for a period of time, that establishes that you were using it as your primary residence.

Rental Property Conversions

To convert a rental property to a primary residence, you need to physically move to the home. This means that tenants are moved out and utilities transferred into your name and that you are able to establish the date that you began living in the property.

Another important step in documenting the change is the division on your tax return between itemized deductions and investment expenses. Personal deductions are claimed on Schedule A as itemized deductions, but rental expense deductions are placed on Schedule E. Thus, if you convert a rental to your primary residence during the year, you need to carefully split interest and property tax deductions between the two schedules. You also need to attach a worksheet to your tax return, breaking out the expense and showing how it was calculated. For example, assume that you used a property as a rental for the first four months of the year and then converted it to your primary residence for the remaining eight months. Your worksheet would have to break out the deductible interest and property tax expenses accordingly:

Description of Expense	Schedule A Itemized Deduction	Schedule E Investment Expense
Mortgage interest		
1/3		$3,000
2/3	$6,000	
Property taxes		
1/3		400
2/3	800	

In completing Schedule E, you also need to specifically exclude deductions for the eight months of primary residence use that are deductible only when the property is being used as an investment. For example, homeowners' insurance premiums are deductible as an investment expense on Schedule E, but the same premiums are not deductible for your primary residence. Thus, in the example, only one-third of the annual premium can be deducted. All other expenses, including depreciation, are deductible only as they apply to the rental period.

Conversion in the other direction requires a similar level of clear and complete documentation. When a primary residence is converted to investment use, you need to carefully divide deductible expenses between Schedule A (itemized deductions) and Schedule E (investment expenses). The need to establish the change-over date is just as critical in this case, since the conversion also sets the starting point for deductions as investment expenses, including not only interest and taxes but also insurance, depreciation, and other items that would be prorated. For example, utilities you pay as a landlord are deductible as investment expenses, but they are not deductible on your primary residence.

Conversion of property from rental to primary residence, or from primary residence to rental, occurs frequently. Careful documentation helps avoid questions later in the event of an audit or even an inquiry letter from the IRS. Conversion often presents a practical alternative to selling a property that no longer serves its original function. For example, you normally would sell a primary residence that is no longer suitable for your family; as an investor, you can convert it and rent it out. While this move can create positive cash flow, especially if you have a fixed-rate mortgage that has been in effect for many years, you also have to plan carefully. Because the sale of a primary residence is not taxed, conversion to rental use creates some tax limitations:

1. *You lose the tax-free advantage of selling your primary residence.* You can avoid all taxes as a married couple on up to $500,000 in profit ($250,000 for single people) as long as you have lived in your home for two of the past five years. When you convert to investment property rather than selling, that advantage no longer applies after expiration of the federal residency requirement.[*] For many families, the tax advantage associated with the sale of a primary residence is too valuable to give up, so some long-term tax planning is important before simply converting the property. Fortunately, under the rules, you still have three years to decide to sell the property. If you were to do so, you would be taxed only on depreciation recapture during the applicable period.

2. Depreciation might be considerably less on a long-held primary residence converted to investment use than it would be on a newly purchased property. Depreciation is always based on the purchase price, regardless of current market value, so converting your primary residence might involve a smaller tax benefit than you would like. For example, let's say that you bought your current home for $80,000 about 10 years ago, with about $50,000 for improvement value and $30,000 for land. The property is worth $150,000. Under the tax rules, you can claim depreciation of only

---

[*]The expiration would take place at the end of three years. At that time, you would have used the property for two of the past five years. After that, the exclusion of taxes would no longer apply.

$50,000, the original cost of improvements to the land. That's $1,818 per year. If you were to sell your primary residence and received $150,000, it would be tax-free; you could then turn that capital around and buy a newer rental property for $150,000. If the same improvement-to-total ratio applied, the improvement value would be $93,750. On that basis, you could claim annual depreciation of $3,409 (straight-line rate for 27.5 years).

Conversion is a complex matter with tax ramifications. You need to exercise careful tax planning whenever you are thinking about undergoing a conversion in either direction. Checking with a tax expert is an important part of the process, including a review of how the decision affects your state tax status as well as under federal rules.

Tax-Free Exchange Rules

Real estate investors are given special consideration under federal tax rules. They not only can deduct depreciation on their investments but also can write off up to $25,000 per year in passive losses. No other investors are allowed to use passive losses in this way. As a real estate investor, you also have a special benefit when you sell investment property. You can defer all of the tax if you replace sold property under the like-kind exchange rules.

The rules for deferral of gain on like-kind property are spelled out in Internal Revenue Code section 1031; thus, these transactions are referred to as 1031 exchanges. The provision does not allow you to escape tax, only to defer it. You can sell a property and replace it with another, and the taxes are paid later, when you sell the replacement property. In fact, the gain can be deferred indefinitely by replacing one property with another into the future.

A few limitations apply, however. First, the clock begins running as soon as the sale closes on a property. You have to identify a replacement property that is going to be purchased through a 1031 exchange within 45 days. The sale has to close within 180 days from the sale of the other property. Most important of all, the replacement property has to be purchased for a price at or above the sale price of the property being replaced. If you go through a 1031 exchange for a property costing less, the difference is taxed.

The 1031 exchange is available only for investment property. You cannot handle the sale of your primary residence through such a technique. In fact, under the revised tax rules, you cannot defer the gain on your primary residence under any circumstances. The exemption from tax of the first $500,000 in profit (for a married couple) is absolute. Under the 1031 exchange, you can defer the gain on investment property as long as it meets the definition of a like-kind exchange. Fortunately, that means the replacement of investment real estate with other investment real estate, so you can sell a single-family house and replace it with a commercial site; you can sell a duplex and replace it with raw land; or you can exchange a building lot with a condominium. Any of these are considered a like-kind exchange as long as they are used as investment real estate.

You cannot qualify for a 1031 exchange if either subject property is exchanged through a lease-option or similar arrangement. The sale has to be clean in the sense that title is exchanged within the 180-day period and the value is bumped to a higher level.

When the exchange takes place, profit is deferred and taxed at a later date. The basis of the new property is reduced to the extent of deferred gain. For example, assume the following facts about a series of property transactions: You bought an investment property six years ago for $80,000. The value of improvements is $60,000, and land is assigned a value of $20,000. Over the past six years, you have taken deductions for depreciation of $12,000. You recently sold this property for $142,000. Closing costs were $9,850. Your profit on this sale was

Sales price		$142,000
Less: closing costs		− 9,850
Adjusted sales price		$132,150
Purchase price	$80,000	
Less: depreciation	−12,000	
Adjusted purchase price		$ 68,000
Net profit		$ 64,150

If you replace this property through a 1031 exchange, you can defer the federal tax on the gain of $64,150 as long as you follow all of the rules. For example, since the property sold for $132,150 (adjusted for closing costs), you need to replace it with a property selling at that level or above to defer all of the gain. If you purchase a new property for $135,000, for example, the entire gain is deferred; however, the basis in the new property (for tax purposes) is reduced by the amount of the gain:

Purchase price of replacement property	$135,000
Less: deferred gain on 1031 exchange	− 64,150
Adjusted basis in the new property	$ 70,850

Since the basis in the new property is reduced by the deferred gain, there will be a much higher tax liability if and when that property is sold. Of course, it can also be replaced under a later 1031 exchange as well.

To illustrate how the deferred tax is later paid, assume that the replacement property is later sold for a profit of $50,000. The tax would be assessed on the $50,000 *plus* the deferred gain of $70,850. For example, if the depreciable portion of the replacement property were $100,000 and you held it for six years, you would have claimed about $20,000 in depreciation deductions, so the outcome might look like this:

Adjusted sales price		$207,000
Basis	$70,850	
Less: depreciation	20,000	
Adjusted basis		– 50,850
Taxable gain		$156,150

Of course, you could replace this property for another under a 1031 exchange and defer all federal taxes as long as the purchase price exceeded the $207,000 sales price. Or you could invest in a property costing less and be taxed on the difference.

The need to continually replace property to avoid taxation is a problem, of course, because every investment plan should include an exit strategy. At some point, it becomes desirable to sell and get out, even if that means paying taxes on the final profit. Given the significant tax consequences of having to pay taxes on a deferred gain, the 1031 exchange delays the liability but makes it worse later, so a long-term plan should include a realistic approach that recognizes the problem of future tax liability.

An interesting twist on this entire discussion arises when a real estate investor converts investment property to a primary residence. Given all of the facts in the previous example, what happens to the replacement property and its taxation if it is converted prior to sale and held for at least two years? Under the current tax rules, you are not taxed on the first $500,000 of gain on a primary residence in which you lived for at least two of the past five years. The exception, of course, is that depreciation claimed for rental use of the property is subject to recapture at ordinary rates, so no matter how else the gain is treated, you would be taxed on the depreciation on sale of a converted primary residence.

As to treatment of the remainder of the gain, the question becomes more complicated. On its surface, it appears that it would be possible to defer gain on investment property, and later convert that property to personal residence use, live in it for two years or more, and then sell without a tax consequence on the nonrecapture portion of the gain (up to the maximum allowed). However, the question is far more complex than this, and the assistance of a tax advisor is essential as part of your tax planning and reporting.

Long-Term Planning

The thorny questions relating to taxation of gain require considerable long-term planning. Not only are there a number of questions related to treatment under federal rules, but if you pay state income tax as well, the treatment of profits, depreciation, and reporting may be vastly different than under the IRS regulations. However, such planning is not limited to questions of taxes alone. You also need to plan well ahead for when and why you will sell your investment property.

Experienced stock market investors accept this premise in most cases. When they buy stock, they also know that they will sell at some point in the future: after a specified number of years, when a profit level is reached, or when a specified portion of value has been lost. Ironically, the same investors may enter the real estate market without defining the same basic ideas for exiting the investment. That is a mistake.

Real estate, like all other investments, should be purchased as part of a plan. You know how long you intend to hold the property, what you expect in terms of cash flow and tax benefits, and when you intend to sell. This assumes a pattern of growth in market value, an approach to equity accumulation combining market appreciation and repayment of a mortgage, and, of course, tax planning. You will decide at the time of sale how to defer taxes if appropriate, either through conversion or a 1031 exchange.

All of these matters require mapping out the investment, so that you have objectives. When those objectives are reached, you sell. If you are not ready to sell because of market conditions at the time, you have to make a decision: continue holding the property, sell and take less profit than you expected, or place the property under professional management, for example. The planning process is an essential part of the successful investment plan for any form of investing, because goal setting provides structure and certainty to the overall plan itself. Without a plan, you have no basis for arriving at a decision later on or for judging how well you are proceeding along the path. Some investors, accustomed to the ease of trading in and out of stock and mutual fund shares, find real estate more awkward; thus, they do not develop the exit strategy they need. Their attitude might be to take a wait-and-see approach.

The illiquidity of real estate—in other words, the difficulty and expense of selling—makes it more essential than ever to develop a comprehensive plan identifying the aspects of your investment and the reasons you will sell later, including the following:

1. *The holding period.* You need to arrive at a time period you allow for the property to season, expressed in terms of years you intend to hold

the property. This can be five years or more. In typical markets experiencing rising real estate prices, it takes several years for the investment to season for a variety of reasons. First, any improvements made to the property will not add value for two or more years; second, the relatively high cost of buying and selling offsets modest gains. It takes several years to season a typical property, unless an unexpected hot market takes place and prices run up dramatically.

2. *Net profit expectations.* Identify your expectations for a specified net profit, expressed on a per-year basis or overall (also define the basis for computation, either on amount invested or on the more traditional market value approach). Remember to include three important components: the reduction in taxes resulting from deductions of passive losses, on both federal and state taxes; the accumulation of equity through repayment of mortgage debt; and the growth in market value based on historical averages.

3. *Tax planning.* Develop your personal tax strategy, including estimating the value of passive loss deductions each year when used in conjunction with other income, and tax consequences of selling. Tax planning should include not only anticipating the current year tax advantages but also estimating future-year liabilities. A competent tax advisor is essential in helping you anticipate tax questions and plan for them now. The tax issue is such a significant part of the real estate investment equation that you need to devote considerable thought to it.

4. *Method of sale and related tax consequences or benefits.* You have available a variety of options, including an opportunity for 1031 exchange deferral or conversion of rental property to primary residence, if appropriate. However, these options are accompanied by a series of important questions: Is a particular option legal? What will the tax liability be under one option, compared with another? Which option best suits your personal financial plan?

5. *Personal goals.* Finally, how does the whole question of outcome fit within your personal plan? The lifestyle choices you make, and directions you select for accumulating your estate, should dictate your financial plan. One of the potential traps in real estate investing is that the tax restrictions end up dictating the plan. It should be the other way around. If selling real estate would mean the loss of tax benefits, or a one-time tax assessment, that has to be faced realistically. It is a mistake to stay in the market beyond the time your plan indicates, just to avoid tax consequences. In the ultimate analysis, quality of life is far more important than after-tax profit. Some investors make the mistake of allowing the tax aspects of real estate to trap them into situations they do not really want. You are wise to recognize this going in and to make a conscious decision to avoid that mistake.

Reviewing the Market

In considering the purchase of real estate, you might need to wait for the right market conditions; the same is true when you sell. The conditions can include the supply and demand not only for real estate but also for the tenant market and for financing. All three markets are cyclical, and each has its own characteristics.

Real Estate Market

The real estate market is subject to changes in supply and demand, which affects the pricing in each region. This market is strictly regional, so national statistics reveal only the averages. You need to study what is going on in your area. As a seller, remember that, as a general rule, prices tend to rise and fall together; thus, if you sell today and buy a replacement property, you will be buying and selling in the same market. In this regard, it does not really matter whether real estate prices are relatively high or low.

However, the pricing structure in your area could be quite different for newly constructed homes versus older stock. In some areas, a brisk market could exist in new homes and, at the same time, previously owned housing could be in a slump. Such conditions tend to be temporary, but if you plan to sell one type of property and invest the proceeds in another, it is worth remembering and studying in advance.

As a seller, you are at a disadvantage when the market is slow, because there are too few buyers looking at available property. Track the number of months' supply of single-family properties to judge the relative condition of the market. If there is only a three months' supply of homes for sale, that indicates a strong market; however, if there is a full year's supply for sale, then the market is very slow. If the market is very brisk, you are in a good situation as a seller. You will be able to offer your property in a limited-supply market, and buyers might vie for the chance to bid on your house. In the best of all markets, offers may even be received *above* your asked price.

As a buyer, you have the advantage when the market is slow. You can choose from a fairly large inventory and make offers below the asked price. In these conditions, you are likely to find a good bargain if you research and compare carefully. In a strong market, you need to compete with other buyers for a limited supply of housing.

No matter when you sell a property, you will have to consider the advantages and the problems you will face when acting as both buyer and seller. Depending on where your area is in the cycle for real estate, you are likely to need to compete with others in a market that is limited in some way, either for buyers or for sellers.

Tenant Market

An entirely separate market will be found for rental units in your area. It is separate because, no matter how brisk the market for real estate in general, the supply and demand for rental housing are driven by different factors. If there is an excess of rental units in your area, then you may have problems locating tenants. As a buyer of investment real estate, it might be necessary to wait until this situation changes. As a seller, the problems with higher than average vacancies might be primary in your decision to sell.

The market for rentals affects the pricing of investment property— specifically, multi-unit housing. This includes duplexes, triplexes, and higher-unit buildings as well. However, single-family housing can be sold either to another investor or as an owner-occupied property. As an investor, you also need to be aware that a different demographic of tenant will be interested in single-family housing than in apartment units. As a general rule, tenants looking for a house are willing and able to pay more rent per month than are those looking for apartments. Thus, when you judge the market for rentals, keep in mind the kinds of tenants that will be looking at your specific property. For example, you cannot judge the health of the demand for housing rentals by studying trends in apartment occupancy.

Financing Market

The third market is related to the supply of money. Lenders are actively looking for borrowers when the money supply is high, but the same lenders are not going to make borrowing easy when they do not have the money available to lend out. Like other markets, the money supply is cyclical. Interest rates are forced up or down by the relative degree of money available to lend, as well as the need to borrow money. Thus, as a seller, you need to consider what the current money supply means if you plan to turn around and borrow money again. If you have a loan on the property you already own, it is locked in according to the terms of your contract. However, if the market is far different today, you might have to pay higher interest, driving up your costs; it is even possible that you will not be able to qualify for financing if the market has changed drastically.

Before deciding to sell and replace property, it makes sense to find out the condition of the market. Talk to the loan officer at your bank. Ask about prequalifying and compare today's rates with the rate you are paying on the current property. Be aware that, if rates are higher, then you are going to be penalized by selling your property and replacing it. By the same argument, however, if rates are lower, then your costs will go down as well.

Preparing Property for Sale

Once you decide to sell your investment property, you need to prepare it for sale. When you sell your owner-occupied house, you probably are aware of all of the needed repairs and take care of them as part of your normal routine. However, as the owner of investment property, you do not live in the house and you probably are not as aware of all of the small but important maintenance problems that need to be fixed.

Preparing a property for sale requires a complete top-to-bottom inspection to ensure that all systems are in working order; a review of cosmetics, such as landscaping and painting; and an action plan to put the house into good enough shape to present to the market.

Typically, after a period in which tenants have occupied the property, you should expect to need some fixing-up expenses, probably including the following:

- Inside wall repairs and painting
- Carpet cleaning
- Complete cleaning of kitchen and bathrooms
- Possible outside painting
- Landscaping update and maintenance

This probably serves as a minimum for the kinds of repairs and maintenance required when the property goes on the market. You face a different set of decisions when you sell with tenants in the house. Can you expect cooperation in showing the property? Are the tenants keeping the house in good order, inside and out? And do properties show better when empty? All of these important questions have to be addressed. Furthermore, depending on market conditions at the time you are planning to list your property, how long would the property need to remain empty before you could reasonably expect an offer? Remember, the longer you leave the property vacant, the more income you lose from month to month.

The rental agreement is yet another consideration dictating when and how you sell. If you have an ongoing lease in effect, you need to disclose to potential buyers that the current tenants have to go with the property. This limits your market to other investors, because anyone looking for a house to move into will exclude your property if they will be required to honor your current lease. Another alternative is to try and break the lease. If you have other properties available, you could ask tenants if they would be willing to transfer their lease. If the alternative property is larger, better located, or more modern, a tenant might be willing to move if the rent is not increased, especially if you offer to pay their moving expenses as well.

That decision has to be based on how anxious you are to execute a sale before expiration of the lease. If you anticipate placing a property on the market within a year, limit lease terms to one year or less or rent on a month-to-month basis only. When tenants occupy your house within the terms of a lease, you cannot force them to move without cause just because you want to sell your property; you are committed to keeping your part of the bargain through to the end of the lease term. Thus, the question of *when* to sell probably has to be deferred if you have a lease, unless the tenant is willing to discuss an arrangement with you for moving out of the property early.

Even if you rent on a month-to-month basis, meaning you can give notice whenever you wish, the decision still remains whether to place the property on the market while it is occupied. You will need to depend on the cooperation of your tenant if real estate agents will be showing the property to prospective buyers, doing walk-through inspections for other agents, and perhaps even holding one or more open houses for the property. All of these actions are designed to market your property, but they also are disruptive to the tenant. You are going to expect your tenant to keep the property in good shape, perhaps more so than the ordinary care that tenants are required to exercise; thus, you place the tenant in the position of being asked to help you sell your property, in which event they will be given notice and required to move.

Aggravating the situation, some real estate agents will not be considerate of your tenant, trying to show the property without the required notice, not showing up for appointments, and expecting tenants to accommodate their needs in every respect. You need to research your state's tenants' rights laws and insist that all agents follow the right procedures. Laws usually dictate the required notice tenants have to be given, as well as other conditions.

SIDEBAR

To review landlord-tenant laws in your state, check the web site *http://rhol.org/rental/ltlaw.htm#us*—this site provides links to other applicable sites for the laws by state.

In choosing a real estate company through which to list your property, compare policies for showing the property. Does the agency have one person to coordinate appointments with agents and their clients? Will there be a lock box, or will the tenants allow the property to be shown only when they are at home? How much advance notice is required (it is usually at least 24 hours)?

Also, be sure that the agent you pick is completely professional and knows the provisions of the landlord-tenant laws in your state. For example, most states' provisions cannot be waived as a condition of renting to a tenant. If a property is on the market and a tenant leaves, a new tenant cannot be asked to waive a notice requirement as a condition of renting the property, for example. You can make arrangements with a current tenant informally, but those arrangements are not enforceable under most states' laws. For example, a landlord has a tenant and decides to sell the house. During the sales period, the landlord receives a notice that property taxes are being increased. He shows the notice to the tenant and says, "Normally, I would pass on this increase to you. However, if you will agree to allow me to show the house without the required notice, I will leave your rent at the same level." As long as a tenant agrees informally to such an arrangement, it may work well. However, the tenant continues to have the right to insist on proper notice, and the landlord has the right to pass on rental increases from time to time. Thus, there is a two-tier arrangement to keep in mind. The ruling tier is what the law requires, and the secondary tier is the arrangement that can be made between cooperative landlord and tenant, each recognizing the convenience and benefits of the other. The informal contract provides that the tenant waive the right to notice in exchange for lower rent, and the landlord cedes rental income in exchange for getting around the required notice. While the agreement is not enforceable under the prevailing law, both sides may agree to operate according to its terms.

Tenants and the Sale

A cooperative tenant facilitates the sale and makes your task easier. Such a tenant accepts the required notice and allows real estate agents to walk through the home, showing it to prospective buyers. The tenant keeps the property neat and clean inside and out, so that a good impression will be made.

Resentful or uncooperative tenants can have the opposite effect. Not only do they make it difficult to show the house, but they also create a negative impression. If the landscaping is out of control and the insides poorly maintained, a would-be buyer is going to have difficulty seeing around the mess. Rather than seeing the property's potential or permanent features, the would-be buyer is distracted by the obstructive tenant and his or her environment.

As long as your tenant works with you to help present your property in the best light, you will not have any problems presenting your house to the market. However, in extreme cases, it will be necessary to evict the tenant and show the property in vacant condition. That enables buyers to openly discuss the property with the agent. It is always easier when tenants (and owners) are not present, because the buyer can ask questions and even criticize attributes of the property; however, when tenants are there, it is more difficult, especially if the tenant is hostile and uncooperative.

The rules for ending the tenancy agreement vary by state. A lease, of course, remains in effect until it expires, unless the tenant willingly gives up that lease early. A month-to-month agreement can be terminated with the required notice, and selling the property is a valid reason for giving notice in all states. However, some states make it easier to end a tenancy than others, and in areas where tenants' rights groups are especially vocal and organized, it is more difficult for landlords to end even a month-to-month tenancy, even for good cause. Your relationship with your tenant should be cordial enough that it will not be necessary to resort to legal action, such as eviction; however, even the most fair-minded landlord eventually runs into the intractable tenant who will fight to the bitter end to prevent being made to leave the property.

The relationship between landlord and tenant is always characterized by some degree of tension. After all, the tenant occupies and has possession of the property, and the landlord owns it. By its nature, the relationship can lead to conflicts and to dissimilar motives and desires on the part of each individual. The landlord-tenant relationship is not a friend-to-friend one, or a parent-to-child one. It is a business arrangement and has to be treated as such. Even in the most formal business relationship, the two sides can get along well together and coexist on friendly terms. However, to be realistic, it is essential to recognize that landlords and tenants do not always share the same goals, and an adversarial approach is possible. This is never more true than when you tell the tenant that you are planning to sell the property.

If you do decide to give notice to the tenant in anticipation of a sale, you need to ensure that the notice is adequate and that, in the event of a fast sale, the new owner is advised that the tenant has possession through the notification period. This period varies by state and in the method it is calculated. For example, a 20-day notice does not necessarily mean 20 days from the period of notification. It can mean 20 days *or* the next rent due date, whichever is the longer period. For example, rent is due on the first of the month. A 20-day notice given between the first and tenth of the month is effective on the last day of the month. However, a 20-day notice given after the tenth (in a 30-day month) would be effective the *following* month-end.

Your goals in providing tenants with notice should be to accommodate their needs to locate a new rental property, to make the move as smooth as possible, and to make sure that your rights to market the property are respected. In addition to protecting tenants while a house is on the market, the law also provides that tenants cannot prevent the showing of the property, given adequate notice. Both sides need to cooperate and to respect the rights of the other. Thus, as long as you provide a tenant with the required notice, the tenant is required to allow real estate agents, the owner of the property, and prospective buyers to enter the premises and take a look. The remedy when a tenant is uncooperative usually involves terminating the rental agreement with notice; if that notice has been given already, you might simply have to wait out an unreasonable tenant and defer the effective marketing of your property until the tenant has left.

Your own experience as a landlord working with tenants while you sell your house, should be positive. Most people will respond well as long as they are informed about your intentions in advance and are provided the respect of being kept informed as the matter moves along. Thus, if your tenant finds out you are planning to sell by coming home one evening to discover a "for sale" sign on the front lawn, that is a bad start. Let the tenant know ahead of time that you are planning to sell. If you receive offers and the tenant seems serious, let the tenant know that, subject to eliminating contingencies, the property might sell. For example, if you will be expecting a 60-day escrow, tell the tenant what is going on and let him or her know that, if all goes according to plan, you will be giving notice at a specific time in that process.

Many of the problems that arise between landlord and tenant can be avoided simply by telling the tenant what is happening and when you expect a decision to be made. By showing respect to the tenant, you will be able to avoid the problems that often characterize sales with tenants in the property. As the owner, take the responsibility for making the transition as smooth as possible for everyone: seller, buyer, *and* tenant.

Managing Your Property

CHAPTER 6

Recordkeeping for Rental Property

C lear and concise records are essential for you as a real estate investor. Not only do you need to track expenses over many years, but you also need the records to prove that your tax returns are legitimate in the event of an audit. You probably need help from a tax professional to prepare income tax returns and plan ahead to minimize taxes; however, you should be able to keep records on your own most of the time, without requiring outside help.

The *purpose* for keeping records varies, depending on whose voice you listen to. An accountant can produce a list of requirements for record-keeping beyond tax compliance: analysis of expenses, trend watching, budgetary controls, and more. In a practical sense, however, real estate is not an investment like any other, so the common utility of a recordkeeping system does not apply in the same way. A stock market investor may track return on investment every day; the same exercise makes little sense in real estate.

The most noteworthy reason for you to keep records is for tax compliance, and that reason is enough by itself. However, other reasons occur as well:

- You need to keep your checking account in balance each month, requiring a careful record of checks written and deposits made.

- For multiple rental properties, you will want to track income to ensure that rents are paid on time.

- The books help you see whether tenants have paid rent on time or have been chronically late. This information is useful when tenants leave and new landlords call or write for references.

- If a vendor writes, stating that a bill is unpaid, you need good records to be able to prove that you did send out a check.

- You may consider undergoing an expensive renovation. Historical records for similar projects provide a good idea of what it will cost, including expenses you did not think about ahead of time.

Records You Need to Establish

The basic requirement for keeping your books and records is that you be able to *prove* that your claimed expenses are legitimate. This is more complex than it seems at first. For example, to prove that you are claiming the right amount of depreciation, you have to be able to show at least three separate facts:

- The date you purchased the property
- The breakdown between land and improvements
- Its use as a rental property

These facts require that you keep records for closing on the property, the assessment for property taxes, and dated rental agreements. Most people do not consider these kinds of records to be a part of the bookkeeping source documents but, in fact, they are. A source document is any document that establishes the basis for a claimed expense. The commonly known types of source documents are vouchers, invoices, and receipts. However, for noncash expenses, such as depreciation, you need a different type of source document.

A set of books not only consists of a listing of income and expenses divided into their proper categories; it also has to serve as a place for establishing how and when expenses came about, so the source documents have to exist, but equally important, they have to be retrievable with little trouble. You have to be able to put your hands on the right document when you need it.

Beyond the basic requirement that you be able to prove an expense, you also need to be able to keep your investment books and records separate from your personal records or the records of other business ventures. The easiest and most efficient way to meet this requirement is to set up a checking account specifically for real estate transactions. In this separate account, follow these rules:

1. Deposit *only* rent income or transfers from your personal account. If rents are not enough to cover payments, you may need to put ad-

ditional funds into the account periodically. This is preferable to paying investment expenses from another account.

2. Pay out only investment expenses from the account, no others. Do not mix payments between investment and personal expenses.

3. Pay out *all* investment expenses from the account.

4. Identify all payments as they are made.

5. Be sure you have a source document for each payment, in the form of an invoice or a receipt. If one is not available, write a brief note explaining the expense and place it in your files.

6. Deposit all rental income into the account and identify it by source (tenant and property), especially if you operate more than one rental. They have to be broken down at the end of the year on your tax return.

7. Keep all of your source documents in one place. Set up files for recurring expenses, such as utilities, insurance, and mortgage payments.

8. Also set up files for each property, and keep important paperwork in the files. This includes the closing statements from purchase, title insurance and report, mortgage paperwork, and any other documents given to you when escrow closed.

9. Keep files for rental paperwork on each property. This includes all rental applications (even from the ones to whom you did not rent) in the file as part of your permanent record for the property.

10. Maintain a file for bank records. Keep monthly bank statements, deposit receipts, canceled checks, and all other banking records in this file.

This collection of records should not overwhelm you. The only danger involving records arises if you do *not* keep your files well organized. Most of the recordkeeping you need to do involves setting up adequate files and placing the proper pieces of paper in each one.

Recurring income and expense records are relatively straightforward. It is somewhat more complex keeping records for renovations and other capital improvements. Such projects tend to be characterized by a large volume of invoices and receipts and the necessity for some degree of cash payments. The best way to deal with cash payments is discussed later in this chapter. Keeping records for capital improvements requires setting up separate files that (1) isolate all of the expenditures by type and date, requiring the filing of receipts, and (2) establish proper records for the purpose of depreciation and as part of the permanent records for the specific property.

Remember that each capital expenditure has to be capitalized (set up as an asset) and depreciated over 27.5 years, in most cases. If you are undergoing a capital project over several months, this requirement is complicated, because improvements are depreciated for the first year, using the midmonth convention. Thus, expenditures in each month are calculated during the first year using a separate factor. For example, you own a rental property and you have it rented out to a tenant. At the same time, you are performing capital improvements, which extend over four months, April through July. You spend the following amounts on improvements during this period:

April	$1,495
May	4,062
June	5,573
July	2,117

As described in Chapter 4, the applicable multiplier for each month's depreciation changes to reflect the timing of expenditures.[*] Applying those multipliers, the first-year depreciation for improvements would be broken down as

April	$1,495 ÷ 27.5	= $54
	$54 × 0.7083	= $38
May	$4,062 ÷ 27.5	= $148
	$148 × 0.6250	= $93
June	$5,573 ÷ 27.5	= $203
	$203 × 0.5417	= $110
July	$2,117 ÷ 27.5	= $77
	$77 × 0.4583	= $35

Using the midmonth convention, the first-year depreciation for this project would be

$$\$38 + \$93 + \$110 + \$35 = \$276$$

---

[*]Depreciation begins when an asset is "placed into service." Depending on the nature of improvements, it might be necessary to begin depreciation only on completion of the entire renovation. Some improvements can be placed into service as money is spent, whereas others are not treated that way until the end of the job.

To arrive at this relatively small amount, a lot of recordkeeping and calculating is involved. However, the records serve a purpose beyond the first-year depreciation calculation. They also prove that the money was spent and that you are entitled to claim depreciation; also, when you sell your property, the value of improvements is added to your basis and depreciation is recaptured and taxed. Thus, the records you set up for capital expenditures have importance over many years, and those files need to be well organized and maintained, not only now but for documentation of capital gains in the future, perhaps many years later.

Considering the small amount of first-year depreciation applying in the example, a simplified approach is to assume that the entire project was not subject to depreciation until it was completed. Thus, the total spent is considered to have been placed in service in July, and depreciation for the first year is

$$\$13,247 \div 27.5 = \$482$$
$$\$482 \times 0.4583 = \$221$$

The depreciation calculated under this method is only $55 lower than under the more detailed method. This is an example of how taking the easier course can save time and trouble for very little added expense.

Paperwork and Organization

The essence of a good bookkeeping system is organization. You do not require special skills or training to keep a simple, well-organized record of your investment transactions; however, you do need to set up records to document your transactions and create a system to keep the paperwork in order.

It seems that the process of buying and maintaining a rental property requires very little paperwork. It is often surprising, however, to experience the volume of documents that accumulates over only a few years. It begins with the closing documents and only grows from there. Included in these records are rental application forms and contracts, receipts for ongoing expenses, deposit slips, bank statements, and documents for any improvements you undertake on your rental properties.

The bookkeeping itself should be kept at a very simple level. Most of it can be executed in your checkbook and then summarized on a monthly page. For those with no formal bookkeeping or accounting training, the simplified record is based almost entirely on keeping the checkbook in a consistent, legible, and orderly manner. All deposits are identified and broken down so that you can easily identify the sources of all funds. All checks are written down, in the checkbook as the checks are issued and are identified by type of expenditure. The balance is kept and double-checked regularly, and the account is reconciled as soon as the bank statement arrives each month.

When transactions fall outside of the bank account, they are documented properly and kept in an orderly manner. For example, you might buy a few dollars' worth of hardware from time to time for work on a small improvement or as part of ongoing maintenance. Most people don't carry around their investment checkbooks, nor do they want to write a check for a small amount. However, those small amounts add up over time, especially when you work on a project for several weeks. Thus, it is important to save documents and get them into your system, but without making it so complicated that it takes up a lot of time and effort.

The following are some guidelines for handling cash expenses:

1. Save the receipts for everything and write a description on the receipt as soon as the purchase is complete. The description should include the type of expense and, if you own more than one rental property, a property identification.

2. Put receipts in an envelope, so that they can be summarized periodically.

3. Summarize the receipts and make an entry into your books, either by writing yourself a check or through a special entry on a monthly worksheet. (This worksheet is described more fully in the next section.)

When you write a check for cash expenses, the amount of the check should agree with the total of the receipts you accumulate, so the check is made payable to you, and the expenses are broken down in the checkbook by account type. This breakdown can include supplies, for example, identified by property; postage expenses; gas and oil for a truck used exclusively for investment property maintenance; and other small expenses. This method is simple, and it gets all expenses into the checkbook system. The consistency you achieve with this method is desirable, because any exceptions to the standard procedure should be avoided. It is the exceptions that cause trouble in a recordkeeping system.

The second method involves monthly summaries of noncheck expenses. The month's expenses are summarized, but they are entered onto a summary worksheet instead of being reimbursed. This method serves the same purpose and might end up being more practical because everyone's bookkeeping method and personal style is different; however, it is important to remember that, whichever method you choose, the thoroughness of documenting expenses is always the goal; if you can achieve that while keeping things simple, you have the best possible system.

The failure of a system arises from organizational problems. If the paperwork is just too complex and takes up too much time, it simply does not work. The purpose of keeping records is not to create a bureaucratic mess for yourself but to do just the opposite: to take charge of the papers and keep them in an orderly way, so that you do *not* have to deal with them more than once. The following are some guidelines to keep in mind concerning the organization of your system:

1. Setting up *more* files to solve paperwork problems does not make matters better; it only aggravates a poorly organized approach. You need to make the system work logically.

2. Consider writing out the titles of the files that you absolutely need and then setting up those files. Don't solve new problems or deal with exceptions by creating new files; instead, try to organize things so that you need to deal with as few steps as possible.

3. Remember that exceptions to your procedure are where trouble usually begins. Work to eliminate or reduce the occurrence of exceptions.

4. Keep up with the filing chore and record transactions as they occur, rather than waiting too long. Once things pile up, it is more difficult to regain control. However, maintaining a system as you go makes it all work more easily. Bookkeeping is like weeding: A well-organized and properly planned garden is easy to maintain if you work at it for a while every day, but if you let it go, the weeds take over and you will never recover control.

5. Keep in mind the purpose of keeping books—to document business transactions, so that you can completely document your tax return, keep track of expenditures, and keep your checkbook in balance. Beyond that, any requirements for your books should be as simple as possible.

It makes sense to start out by making a listing of files that you absolutely need. Include files for blank forms that you use, such as rental applications, rental contracts, and statements of condition. Following is a summary of the files you probably need to set up:

- *Blank Forms*

  Rental applications forms

  Rental agreement forms

  Statement of condition forms

- *Property-Specific Files (One for Each Property)*

  Rental file (contains applications and contracts plus tenant correspondence)

  Documents (closing papers, title insurance, deed, etc.)

  Appraisals

  Documents for capital expenditures and improvement projects

- *Bank Files*
  Monthly bank statement
  Deposit slips and canceled checks
  Bank reconciliation

- *Expense and Payment Files*
  Supplies
  Utilities
  Telephone
  Auto and truck expenses
  Advertising
  Office expenses
  Mortgage payments and records
  Credit card payments (for cards used exclusively for investment expenses)

- *Tax Files*
  Copies of personal tax returns
  Depreciation worksheets
  Documents supporting your tax calculations

In addition, your own circumstances may dictate other files that you need to set up. The preceding list is a starting point only, and you may discover that you need additional files. As a skeleton of your organizational system, this serves as the basic requirement for an effective and efficient system.

Documenting Expenses

In order to remain in control of your system, it's important that you work on it as part of a recurring routine. Don't let it get away from you. The majority of the recordkeeping chore can take place in the checkbook as you record deposits and write out checks. Make sure that all of the important information is written down and that it explains each transaction completely. For example, a description written briefly as "Supplies" doesn't tell you which property it related to or what specific supplies they were. It could be that supplies are part of a capital improvement that has to be capitalized or that the total transaction includes supplies for more than one property. The description has to be adequate for the tax reporting that you will need to do at the end of the year.

The transactions that take place outside of your checkbook should be kept to a minimum. They are unavoidable, but avoiding exceptions to your routine reduces the chances for error or that your books will become overly complicated. The following are four ideas that will help reduce the need for cash expenses:

1. *Open an account with your local supplier.* It makes your job easier if you can charge your purchases during the month, and then write a check for the entire balance on receiving a bill at the end of the month. If your local building supply store will allow you to do business on that basis, it can eliminate any need to buy with cash. Be sure that you identify every transaction, so that you can break down a monthly payment by property.

2. *Carry your investment checkbook with you.* Use the checkbook as much as possible and avoid using cash. Also be sure that you write down a complete description of the transaction, including the amount and type of expense.

3. *Use one credit card exclusively for investment expenses.* If you have several credit cards, dedicate one for investment expenses and for nothing else. This enables you to isolate expenses and makes the documentation easier. The monthly statement from the credit card company, plus your receipts, helps you keep a consistent record of expenses not paid through your checkbook. By using the credit card, you also avoid cash payments.

4. *Use a separate checking account for investment activity.* All deposits and checks relating to your real estate investments are thus isolated from your personal expenses. This makes it easier and more sensible to write yourself a check in reimbursement of investment-related cash expenses. The separate investment account makes sense even if you have only one property, as it can also be used for other investments as well; it becomes increasingly important to isolate and separate expenses and income as you expand to more than one rental property.

The monthly transactions, whether strictly from your checkbook or including cash expenses as well, should be summarized on a monthly worksheet. The example in Figure 6.1 is one way to organize this worksheet. This summary enables you to organize your checkbook expenses by type. It also provides a breakdown by property. As a means of double-checking math, make sure that the total of income agrees with the total of deposits for the month. Also make sure that the total of expenses agrees with the total of checks written (adjusted for nonexpense payments, such as principal on notes or expenditures for improvements). The investment activity worksheet summarizes only income and expenses. It excludes the following:

Investment Activity
Month_____

	Property: ____	Property: ____	Property: ____	Total
Income				
Advertising				
Auto and travel				
Cleaning and maintenance				
Insurance				
Legal and professional fees				
Management fees				
Mortgage interest				
Other interest				
Repairs				
Supplies				
Taxes				
Utilities				
Other: _____				
_____				
_____				
Total expenses				
Net (income less expenses)				

FIGURE 6.1 **Monthly Summary.**

- Deposits that are not rental income (for example, it might be necessary to deposit additional funds to cover the monthly expenses)
- Spending for nonexpense items; these include principal on mortgage notes and payments for improvements and other capital assets
- Payments to yourself, which are not deductible

Prepare an investment activity summary each month and periodically for the year-to-date of all investment activity. For example, a quarterly year-to-date summary would include the past three months (plus previous year-to-date totals). This worksheet helps you prepare for income tax reporting in several ways:

1. It enables you to judge the level of income or loss that will be reported. This is very important because tax-reported losses are limited to $25,000 per year for most investors; thus, if you track the year-to-date loss throughout the year, you will be able to judge whether or not your loss is likely to exceed that level.

2. The worksheet is useful for tax planning overall, so that investment activity can be coordinated with planning for tax purposes for all income, including wages, stock market profits and losses, and all other forms of income that is taxable.

3. It helps you summarize your records on an as-you-go basis, rather than waiting until the end of the year, when the task would be overwhelming. It always makes more sense to keep records throughout the year, rather than all at once, just before you prepare your tax return.

4. The worksheet provides a convenient summary, collecting *all* deductible expenses in one brief report. This includes cash expenses run through the books by way of reimbursement or added separately.

If you have cash expenses in addition to expenses paid through your checking account, they can be handled in one of two ways. First, you can write a check to yourself as reimbursement for cash paid out. This payment is broken down by category and documented with receipts kept in your expense files. Second, you can add cash expenses into the monthly summary by using a simple worksheet like the one shown in Figure 6.2. This format should be used when cash expenses are extensive. The total from the checkbook is entered and cash expenses added to it; then the adjusted total is used for the investment activity worksheet. While this step might seem rather formal, it shows the steps you went through to arrive at a monthly and year-to-date total in each expense category. At the end of the year, you will not recall steps like this unless they are properly documented, so the worksheet provides a valuable trail, which saves a lot of time and reconstruction later.

The simplified monthly worksheet and periodic year-to-date summary are really all you need to meet the legal requirements for recordkeeping. As long as you keep all of your receipts and can prove how and where you spent money on deductible investment expenses, you do not need to hire an accountant to keep track of where you spend your money. You probably need professional advice for annual tax preparation, but you can keep your own books without any specialized training.

Expense Worksheet
Month_____

	Checkbook	Cash	Total
Expense_____			
Property:_____			
Property:_____			
Property:_____			
Expense_____			
Property:_____			
Property:_____			
Property:_____			
Expense_____			
Property:_____			
Property:_____			
Property:_____			
Expense_____			
Property:_____			
Property:_____			
Property:_____			
Total expenses			

FIGURE 6.2 Expense Worksheet.

Balancing the Bank Account

Your investment bank account should have only a limited number of transactions, so balancing the account should not be complicated. The exception is during periods when you are undergoing extensive remodeling and other improvements. Then, the volume of activity will be far higher than average.

During the usual periods of activity, you should experience only the following payments:

- Mortgage payments (usually only one per property each month)
- Utilities
- Supplies
- Insurance
- Property taxes
- Repairs

Thus, in a typical month, you should have only six or seven payments each month. Even if you operate four properties, that is still fewer than 30 checks, in most situations.

Keep your investment checking account in balance by examining the bank statement every month and identifying the outstanding items. Remember, balancing your checking account is nothing more than identifying timing differences and correcting errors. Timing differences include deposits in transit (money you put in the bank that has not shown up on the current statement) and outstanding checks (checks written that have not cleared as of the bank's statement date). Beyond that, you need to account for math errors and to identify items recorded incorrectly in your accounts. The adjustments have to be made to both the bank side and your checkbook side, as follows:

- *Bank Adjustments*
  Ending balance
  Plus: deposits in transit
  Less: outstanding checks
  Plus or less: any bank errors

- *Checkbook Adjustments*
  Ending balance
  Plus or less: any math errors
  Less: bank charges

If you identify and make these corrections, you should find both sides in agreement. This assumes, of course, that you begin the month with a good balance, one that has been adjusted from prior months. It also assumes that you have entered all corrections needed to the checking account side—math errors, bank charges, and other problems have to be adjusted in order to create a good balance forward.

If you void a check in the current month, the amount of the check should be added back into the running balance. If the voided check was written in an earlier month, two steps are needed. First, add the check amount back to your running balance; second, remove the voided check from your list of outstanding checks.

As you begin each month's reconciliation, check off the items on the bank statement as you find them. Begin with timing differences from last month—outstanding checks and any deposits in transit. If checks remain outstanding, they need to be relisted on this month's outstanding list. Then check off each deposit and check on the bank statement against the items in your checkbook.

Next, list the current month's outstanding checks and deposits in transit. Then deduct any bank charges that appear on your statement. If your adjusted balance does not agree with the adjusted balance on the bank side, go through the month and double-check all of your math. If you discover errors, these have to be written into your checking account *and* listed as adjustments on the reconciliation.

Also be sure to double-check to ensure that the amount you wrote down for each deposit and check agrees with the amount reported by the bank. A transposition error, for example, will throw your account out of balance, and adjustment will be needed. This occurs, for example, when a check is written for $135 but you record it as $153. Your account will be off by $18, in that case.[*]

The Bank reconciliation worksheet shown in Figure 6.3 is a useful form to use. It enables you to identify corrections and timing differences as they adjust either the bank's side or the checkbook's side. When your reconciliation is complete, the adjusted balances should agree.

	Bank	Checkbook
Ending balance	_____	_____
Plus: deposits in transit	_____	
Less: outstanding checks	_____	
Plus or less: bank errors	_____	
Plus or less: math errors		_____
Less: bank charges		_____
Adjusted balance	_____	_____

FIGURE 6.3 Bank Reconciliation Worksheet.

---

[*]Transposition errors are fairly easy to find. The sum of a transposition error's digits always add up to 9; thus, if you are out of balance by $18 (1 + 8 = 9), $27 (2 + 7 = 9), or $36 (3 + 6 = 9), you probably have a transition error.

Items like deposits in transit (money put into the bank but not yet shown on the statement) and outstanding checks (checks you wrote that have not yet cleared your bank) are typical timing differences and should adjust the bank side. Bank charges, math errors, and excluded items are errors in the checkbook, and should be listed on the right side of the form.

Remember, too, that when you find an error, it is not enough to merely list it on the form. You also need to adjust your checkbook balance; otherwise, the error will be carried over to the following month.

Balancing your investment account is important not only because it establishes exactly how much money there is in your account but also because it provides a double-check on your bank and against the possibility of fraud from the outside. Check amounts can be altered, for example, and passed through to your account without the change being caught; thus, a stolen check can find its way through the system, resulting in money going out of your account in error. Such an incident should be reported to the bank and to the police at once; you also are entitled to reimbursement, since cashing an altered check is a bank error.

Banks do make mistakes, even with automated banking systems. Checks not belonging to you can be charged against your account or a deposit amount put in for less than the amount actually deposited. Reconciliation helps you make sure that such errors do not go undetected. It also helps you find the inevitable transposition and math errors you will make from time to time.

How Long to Keep Your Records

Keeping track of monthly expenses and double-checking your bank account balance are essential steps in any bookkeeping system. You also need to determine how long you have to keep records. For most situations, records that establish business transactions have to be kept at least three years from the due date of the tax return. For example, if your due date is April 15, you need to keep records until April 15 three years later. For example, for the tax year 2001, the return is due on April 15, 2002, so these records have to be kept until April 15, 2005 (three years from the due date). A word of caution is in order: If you file for an extension of time to send in your tax return, that extension also extends the three-year deadline. For example, if you do not have to file your tax return until August 15, you have to keep the applicable records until August 15 of the third year out.

Even with this minimal requirement of three years' retention, you probably need to keep some of your real estate records for longer than three years. The record of income and expenses reported each year meets the three-year rule for the most part. However, if you plan to defer the gain on property with a like-kind exchange, the records establishing your basis in the property (and its use as an investment) have to be kept at least three years following the sale of a replacement property. That can be many, many years into the future.

That means you need to keep closing statements from escrow from the beginning of your investment activity. Because the gain is deferred when you replace property, you need to be able to establish the adjusted basis for the replacement investment property. You also have to be able to prove that it was used as an investment for the entire period, meaning some records have to be kept showing rental income, utility records, or other ways to document the fact that you did not use investment property as your own residence.

The following are some guidelines for record retention when involved with investment property:

1. Keep *all* bookkeeping records for no less than three years from the due date of the income tax return, including extensions.

2. Keep all purchase and sale records of properties no less than three years following the due date for the year of property sale (if the property is not replaced).

3. If property is sold and replaced in a like-kind exchange, keep all purchase and sales records for original and replacement properties until the replacement property is sold, plus three years.

4. Organize storage so that files are easily retrievable. Mark boxes by year and type of record. Don't take up current file space with old records. Use sturdy file boxes and remove older files from your office space.

5. Avoid mixing records between years. This makes it easier to identify when specific records can be discarded. It also helps you avoid throwing away records in error that you need to keep.

6. Keep all correspondence related to bookkeeping and property purchase or sale under the same guidelines for transaction records.

7. Keep all rental agreements no less than three years after a tenant vacates the property, including rental application, lease or rental contract, and inventory of condition forms.

8. Keep applications from everyone, even those to whom you do not rent, for three years. An applicant might come back and apply again, and you may want to compare information, or questions might come up regarding your tenant selection—for example, you might be accused of discriminating, and the methods you use to pick tenants should come from information you gather on the application form.

9. Keep all of your correspondence with tenants or applicants for at least three years.

10. When in doubt, keep records longer than you need to, rather than throwing them away.

A bookkeeping system can be simple and easy. However, even though investment records can be simple from month to month, you will still accumulate a lot of records over the years. The essence of an efficient system comes down to how well it is organized. Keep only the current year's information within immediate reach and remove all other records to storage. Maintain files so that they are manageable. Bulky file material can be stored outside of the file, with only a note to yourself about where other material can be found. When you remove files from your filing cabinet, return them as soon as you are done working on them. Don't let files pile up all around the house, but invest a little time keeping a well-organized system. This small investment of time will pay off in increased efficiency.

Allocating Expenses between Properties

Whenever you own more than one investment property, it is necessary to allocate certain expenses. Some expenses can be specifically assigned by property; others cannot. For example, expenses such as interest, property taxes, utilities, and insurance can be identified by the subject property. In those instances, expenses should be assigned to the property without question. However, some other expenses present a problem because they cannot be identified as belonging to only one property. These have to be allocated on some reasonable basis. For example, if you own a lawnmower, which you use on several properties, it should be capitalized and depreciated. The annual depreciation has to be split among all of the properties. If you buy office supplies to keep records, there is no easy method for determining how much of the total expense relates to each property. The expense of consulting with an accountant or attorney usually does not refer to a single property, but is more general.

The preceding examples demonstrate that certain expenses cannot be easily assigned to properties without being arbitrary. Admittedly, just about any method you select for allocating expenses is going to be arbitrary. The best solution is to use one method consistently; that also enables you to justify the way that expenses are assigned.

One method is to simply divide expenses evenly among several properties—one-third to each of three or one-fourth to each of four, for example. However, an alternate method, allocation on the basis of gross rental income, bears a degree of logic. For example, you own four properties and need to allocate several expenses that do not apply to any one specifically. The year's gross rental income on the four properties was

Property	Income
1	$ 6,180
2	5,700
3	8,224
4	5,002
Total	$25,106

Rounding out the percentages, the applicable portion of the total is

Property 1 = 24%

Property 2 = 23%

Property 3 = 33%

Property 4 = 20%

The calculation involves dividing each dollar amount by the total. For example, property 4 realized $5,002 for the year:

$$\frac{\$5,002}{\$25,106} = 20\%$$

Expenses are then assigned to each property on the basis of the income breakdown. This method is reasonable in the sense that higher-income properties receive a higher share of the allocable expense. This does not always mean that the net profit or loss is also evenly distributed; however, a fair distribution is not the goal in allocation. The goal is to achieve a breakdown that makes sense, even when expenses are not specifically related to any one property.

If you have more than one property, but acquired one part-way through the year, the rent should be annualized, so that the breakdown remains consistent and reasonable. For example, using the same dollar amounts as in the previous example, what if property 4 were acquired at the beginning of the fourth month? That would mean that the total of $5,002 would represent only nine months of income, whereas the other three properties would represent a full year.

To annualize, divide the partial-year income by the number of months you owned the property and multiply the result by 12 to represent the annualized total. This produces a dollar value that would be the 12-month equivalent if that property had been owned and rented out for the full year. In the example, the $5,002 income represented only nine months' time.

The annualization in this case requires dividing $5,002 by 9, and multiplying the result by 12:

$$\frac{\$5,002}{9} \times 12 = \$6,669$$

The allocation formula then has to be revised:

Property	Income
1	$ 6,180
2	5,700
3	8,224
4	6,669
Total	$26,773

The allocation would then show the following:

Property 1 = 23%

Property 2 = 21%

Property 3 = 31%

Property 4 = 25%

You need to allocate because the federal tax reporting form requires that the details be shown for each property. This occurs to accommodate verification for specific expenses. For example, mortgage interest deductions claimed should agree with the dollar amount reported for each property by each lender, and depreciation for properties should agree with the depreciation reported on a separate schedule. The allocation of relatively minor expenses complicates the whole reporting system; it is one of the small but important details required of every real estate investor who owns more than one property.

Depreciation presents a special problem because some depreciable assets cannot be assigned to a single property. For example, depreciation on a pickup truck has to be allocated using a logical method, and the allocation should be consistent from one year to the next. Thus, the claimed total will be spread over many properties each year, even though there is no logical relationship between the depreciation and each property. The important thing, however, is that the "Total" column for reported depreciation agree with the total reported on the depreciation form that is attached to your tax return.

Apply consistent allocation methods for both federal and state tax returns, even when your state applies different deductibility standards and you have to make adjustments. The consistency of allocation makes it easier for you to trace back through your records and establish the logic of your thinking at the time.

Perform allocations on a worksheet and save the worksheet. Each year's allocation system will be needed the following year, when you will go through this step again. The worksheet should be kept with your other tax paperwork.

It can be said that recordkeeping is a necessary evil for the real estate investor. However, as long as you follow the steps outlined in this chapter, the bookkeeping and tax-reporting chores should not take up a lot of your time, and the major expense should be periodic consultation with your tax advisor. The books and records are far easier to maintain for real estate investing than for most other types of investing, particularly those with a higher level of trading volume, such as the stock market. Calculating net profits is easier for real estate investors than for mutual fund investors, for example. It is a matter of setting up the records efficiently, keeping the files orderly and current, and not letting the chore get away from you.

CHAPTER 7

Landlord and Tenant

At the core of all investments are the characteristics that distinguish them from one another. Stocks change in price rapidly and are traded with ease on the auction marketplace. Options and futures require specialized knowledge and a thorough understanding of unique market risk. And when you own rental properties, you have to develop a relationship with tenants.

Even if you hire a management company to deal with the landlord-tenant issues, you remain responsible for the success of your investment, and that depends on the careful selection of tenants who are suitable for the property, and vice versa. It requires careful screening to ensure that a tenant can afford the property and does not have a history of negative tenancy (evictions, for example). While you need to make sure you avoid renting to people who want to set up a drug operation or another illegal activity, you also have to be aware of groups protected under the law and make sure you do not violate the rules by discriminating. For example, it may be that your property is large enough only for one or two people. However, is it proper or legal for you to state in your ad that no children are allowed? Because your house has steep stairs, it might not be practical for elderly tenants, but can you forbid the elderly from applying? These questions are legal ones. You might have a completely valid reason for rejecting a tenant, but you have to make sure that your reasons comply with the law and, of equal importance, that you document your reasons to protect yourself.

It is reasonable to reject an applicant because family income is too low to afford the rent you require. However, you have to apply the same standard to *all* applicants. If a rejected applicant can make the case that you used income as an excuse to discriminate for other reasons, such as race, then you could end up with a legal fight on your hands. If you follow the law, you can avoid such problems. However, your paperwork also needs to be designed so that you can show that your tenant selection process is based on a reasonable and legal test.

Matching tenants to properties is a matter of checking references and background information, verifying information provided by applicants, and eliminating unqualified applicants or those whose references do not check out. If you accept an applicant with a history of trouble—whether with other landlords, with credit, or with the law—then you should expect to have similar problems as well. As long as you screen tenant applicants and check all references thoroughly, you should be able to avoid problems for the most part; at the very least, you can eliminate some tenants based on what they reveal in the application process. Others reveal enough in what they do not tell you. For example, if they do not provide you with a landlord reference, then you have no way to check on their history.

When problems do arise, taking immediate action to correct them is invariably better than ignoring them until small problems becomes large, expensive ones. Part of the maintenance of properties has to include the monitoring of your tenants, keeping an eye on the condition from a distance and making sure that no problems are evolving that would require your full attention later.

The Application Form

The application process is where it all begins. Insist on getting a written application from every prospective tenant. Those who do not want to fill out the form probably would not qualify based on recent history, so the form itself works as a screening device. You will give out many blank forms that will never be returned. The form should be thought of as a place for gathering basic information about applicants, and you should definitely check *all* references before agreeing to rent to anyone.

Figure 7.1 is a typical application form. It provides all of the information you need to check out an applicant's references and rental history. As a first rule, insist that every applicant fill out a form. If more than one adult will be applying as a cotenant, ask for an application from each person.

Remember, when applicants leave out information, that in itself can be very revealing. If it is only an oversight, it can be corrected. But applicants who don't remember their landlords' telephone numbers or addresses, or who will not provide their social security numbers or give you permission to obtain their credit reports, are letting you know that they do not want you to have the information for a reason. Often, the reason is that they know you won't want to rent to them if you discover their history.

Rental Application

Property address_____   City_____

Name_____   Social security number_____
Driver's license number_____
State_____   Telephone: Home_____
                            Work_____
                            Message_____

Name and branch of your bank_____
Your account number_____ Type Checking_____
Savings_____

Current home address_____
City_____
How long at this address?_____ Rent amount $_____ per month
Reason for moving_____
Landlord's name_____   Telephone_____

Previous home address_____
City_____
How long at this address?_____ Rent amount $_____ per month
Reason for moving_____
Landlord's name_____Telephone_____

Your nearest relative_____ Telephone_____
Person to contact in an emergency_____
Telephone_____

Have you ever been evicted? Yes_____ No_____

Names and relationships of all persons who will live in the
property with you:

_____   _____
_____   _____
_____   _____
_____   _____

Any pets? (Describe)_____
Do you own a waterbed? Yes_____   No_____

Occupation_____ Monthly income_____
Employer_____ Telephone_____
How long have you been with this employer? _____

Supervisor name_____
Do you grant permission to obtain a copy of your credit report?
Yes_____ No_____

Signature_____ Date _____

FIGURE 7.1 Rental Application.

The form begins with the property address and city. This information enables you to later identify the property an applicant had in mind when filing the application with you. File all rental applications in the applicable property file for later reference. Applicants are next asked to provide essential information about themselves: name, social security number, driver's license number and state, and telephone numbers. All of this information is essential in order to qualify a person as a prospective tenant. If the person does not complete these sections, ask for the additional information. The social security number is necessary for a credit check. The driver's license number enables you to check on past rental and criminal records, if you want to go to that extent in checking out an applicant. It is easy and costs nothing in most areas. A visit to the county courthouse is worthwhile. In most jurisdictions, the primary court system (most often called superior court) contains records for all people against whom any actions have been filed. This includes eviction notices and any criminal complaints. You can ask the superior court clerk to check on a name; you might need also to supply a driver's license number, or a search might be performed on that number itself. In most states, the information is available to the public and is free of charge. Finding out whether a person has a record of evictions certainly is important to you, and you probably will not want to rent to someone with a history of evictions. Similarly, knowing a person's criminal record is important, especially if the individual has convictions for drug offenses. Because the person will be in possession of your property, you will want to take steps to eliminate anyone who might use that property for manufacturing or selling drugs.

Asking for the name of the person's bank and the bank account number seems, at first, to be out of place on a rental application form. However, it is essential to discover whether a person even has a bank account. The lack of a bank account by itself does not make someone a poor prospect to occupy your property; however, in combination with other information, it can be revealing. First of all, it is unusual for a person to not have a bank account, so you might wonder about the reason. Some people have outstanding judgments against them, so they do not want to risk having their bank accounts seized. That information might come out in a check of civil and criminal records or an examination of a credit report. Even lacking these records, if a person does not list a bank, it can tell you a lot. It can be a sign that the individual has had problems with planning out a family budget for the month; this can also translate into chronic problems getting the rent to you in time.

Perhaps the most important information of all comes next, the listing of current and past home addresses. Included in these sections are the length of time the person lived at each address, the rent paid per month, the reason for moving, and the landlord's name and telephone number. These sections are essential and have to be filled out; you need to telephone the current *and* past landlords and speak with them.

Contact the current landlord to verify information and to find out what type of tenant the person was, whether rent was paid on time and whether any problems came up in the relationship. Remember, though, that a current landlord might withhold some negative information, perhaps fearing that, if the individual does not find a new place to live, he or she will not move. Thus, while the current landlord reference often reveals information that you need to know, you also have to get in touch with the previous landlord. Given that the applicant no longer resides in that person's property, you are more likely to get the full truth from that person.

What if the applicant does not supply you with enough information to get a reference, either positive or negative? For example, some people will claim that they lived with their parents, rented a room with a friend, or have lost their landlord's name and telephone number. Your position should be that, if you cannot check references, then you cannot rent to the person. Some people are smooth talkers with a lot of problems in their past, and they have mastered the art of appearing mature and responsible. Appearances aside, you still need to be able to check references, and the application is worthwhile only if it is filled in completely and if you follow through by tracking down all of the information.

Having the nearest relative's name as well as an emergency contact could become important information in the event that something were to happen to the tenant. An accident, for example, could lead police to your door to locate a relative to let him or her know what happened. Any criminal activity at your property could also necessitate having this information. Additionally, if an applicant is unable or unwilling to provide you with these names and telephone numbers, that alone should make you suspicious. One reason for asking these questions, like so much of the application form, is to see if applicants are willing to provide you enough personal information for you to find out about them.

One big advantage to using a form is that it makes it difficult for people to lie or leave out the truth. It is unlikely that a person would forget about being evicted, so asking whether or not someone has ever been evicted is an important question. It also is easy to check if the eviction occurred in the same state in which you live. Most states provide information free of charge on evictions filed in the court. An eviction is an extreme step for a landlord to take and usually happens only after all other solution attempts have been exhausted. From the landlord's point of view, a tenant who would have to be evicted probably is also a person whose troubles disqualify him or her as a likely tenant prospect.

Your rental agreement should list all of the people who will be living in the property, so this information should be asked for on the application. If your property is suitable for only a limited number of people, a particularly large group is inappropriate and should be eliminated just on that basis. Asking for this information also helps support your position later if an applicant pulls an often-used switch on you: One person makes the application and all of his or her references check out, but someone else ends up living in your property, and that person does not qualify. Another form of the switch occurs when one or two people apply for the tenancy, but it turns out that many more people end up residing in the property. These are serious problems for you as the landlord. Having a tenant who did not apply in the first place, you have no specific contract with the person in possession of your property. That situation has to be corrected immediately, even if that means giving the tenant notice and finding someone else. And when too many people live in a property not designed for those numbers, it invariably ends up badly for the owner/landlord. Finally, you need to ensure that you are dealing with individuals who have integrity and have not deceived you during the application process. Providing incomplete and misleading information on the application form should make you suspicious and often will be accompanied by the exact problems you were hoping to avoid in taking the application in the first place.

Asking for identification of pets is important, especially if you do not allow pets in your property. Some rentals are simply not appropriate for pets or for certain types of pets, such as large dogs. If your property is a single-family residence, the pet issue will come up many times. One reason that tenants want to rent a house is so that they can get a pet; thus, while a tenant might not have a pet when he or she applies, you might discover one later, so the rental agreement needs to be very specific about your pet policies. If you do allow pets, you may also want to require an additional security and cleaning deposit. Pets can damage a property easily and quickly, especially if you provide carpeting and property is furnished.

The question concerning waterbeds might seem dated. However, if your rental is off the ground floor, a waterbed is a potential hazard. When filled, these beds are quite heavy and can damage the structure itself. A waterbed leak can also cause severe damage to your property, even if it is a one-level apartment or house. Many landlords will not accept tenants with waterbeds, which also should be spelled out in your rental contract.

The questions about employment should also be filled in completely, and you should verify the information: whether the person has the job, monthly income, length of employment, and job title. Beyond this basic information, employers usually will not give out additional information.

From your point of view, it seems only logical that you would like to deal with tenants who are employed and whose employment information checks out.

The applicant should give you permission to request a credit report, even if you end up not asking for one. Some landlords require an application fee, which covers the cost of getting an automatic report. This is a problem for many tenants, who are being asked to pay money without any assurance that they are being considered seriously as tenants. While you might not want to actually get a credit report in every case, it is interesting to discover whether an applicant will give you permission. You might need a separate form to be completed in your state to get permission to get the actual credit report. One alternative is to ask the applicant to provide you with a credit report at his or her expense. However, if you check out all of the other information on the rental application, you probably do not need to also get the credit report.

Finally, the application form should be signed and dated. An applicant who does not sign the form might be reluctant because some information supplied to you is false.

Screening Tenants

How do you screen an applicant? Remembering that you cannot discriminate unfairly, you often have to decide from among several qualified tenant prospects, especially if demand is high for rentals in your city or town.

The attributes of a worthwhile tenant go beyond the obvious—employment, stability, and a clean record. In addition, every landlord desires a tenant who also has the following qualities:

1. *The tenant is a good match for the property.* The ideal situation is one in which the tenant seems to be a good match for the property. This is important because only when the tenant and property suit one another is the tenancy going to last. A specific house and neighborhood dictate the kind of people that work out. For example, some neighborhoods are characterized mostly by young, single people, such as in a college town. Others may be primarily young families, share rentals, or retired folks. While these demographic groups certainly can be mixed, it makes sense to try and match people based on the character of the neighborhood.

The appearance, size, and condition of the property also attract a particular type of tenant. Some people want an isolated property far from town, whereas others prefer being close to the downtown core and do not mind a lot of traffic and other noise. Certain types of tenants like large yards, are not bothered by the appearance of an older property, or require fencing and as much quiet as possible. While you cannot insist on interviewing only the "ideal" type of tenant, when you have a choice between two equally qualified applicants, the selection can be made on your hunch about which applicant suits the property in more ways.

2. *The individual has a history of staying in one place for longer than just a few months.* The tendency to move around a lot is characteristic of younger tenants, and more so of single than married ones. You certainly cannot reject an applicant solely on the frequency of movement from one rental to another; however, it is an encouraging sign when you see that the applicant remained in one rental for several years. This indicates that the person had a good relationship with the landlord and paid rent in a timely manner and that no problems arose on either side make frequent moves necessary.

When you speak to the past landlord of a long-term tenant, there is more of a tendency for a positive report. This is reflected in the long-term nature of the tenancy, of course. That in itself makes the point that the individual takes care of property and would make a worthwhile tenant. As a landlord, you look for long-term tenants. The less often you have to turn over a property, the lower your overall costs and the less exposure you have to vacancies.

3. *The applicant seems to be mature and understands the relationship between landlord and tenant.* You cannot devise a question on your application form to discover whether an applicant understands the relationship between tenant and landlord. The truth is, many tenants do not understand the landlord's point of view. They never think about the fact that you have to make a mortgage payment and depend on rent to do so; if they do understand that, they still are going to be unsympathetic to your risks and concerns. Some tenants view their relationship with a landlord in familial terms, and the landlord too often is seen in a parental role, rather than as one side of a business arrangement. This is why the rental agreement needs to be extremely specific and spell out all of the terms and conditions and why some tenants—particularly immature ones—often run into trouble with their landlords.

More grown-up tenants have experience behind them, so that they really do understand how the tenancy is mutually beneficial if both sides do their parts. Some tenants have had negative experiences with landlords, so their trust level is low. However, the relationship works best if both sides operate in good faith. If you are honest and fair with your tenant, you can usually expect the tenant to reciprocate.

To screen tenants in the quest for the ideal one, what can you do? How can you look beyond the application and, on a practical level, how much investigation is worthwhile? You can check and verify employment and income, any record of criminal activity or past evictions, and the all-important past landlord references. For the most part, these take care of the basic questions that should be on your mind in reviewing applications. Beyond that, though, how do you pick one tenant out of two or more entirely qualified people?

Your own instinct should play a part in the selection process. While the landlord-tenant relationship is not a friendship and shouldn't be one, you can still rely to a degree on your first impressions about people. Body language, eye contact, firmness of a handshake, the way that people express themselves—all of these add up to an overall impression. When people are being completely straightforward, it usually is apparent. This is reassuring, so an applicant who makes an overall good first impression is likely to operate as a good tenant as well.

However, some applicants have a very poor background but are expert at conning other people. They imitate the behavior of honest people with their body language and communication skills. This is why you always need to check references, and why you need to reject an applicant who cannot supply you with references to check. For example, one landlord met up with an applicant who could supply only one landlord reference. During the tour of the empty house, the applicant made a pointed comment that he and his wife could not move in on Sunday morning because they had to be at church. The landlord's hunch was that this comment was directed at him in order to make a particular impression but that it was not sincere. He ignored his hunch and called the only landlord reference given to him, which was very positive. However, it turned out that the so-called landlord was actually a friend of the applicant and not a landlord at all. The tenant lasted only three months and had to be evicted for non-payment of rent. It turned out the couple was also under investigation for welfare fraud and drug charges. This example is an extreme one, but it demonstrates how a smooth-talking con artist can disarm an unsuspecting landlord. That tenant's application contained adequate information for the landlord to discover past problems. A check for past criminal convictions and rental evictions would have saved the landlord the trouble and financial loss that came from renting to the applicant. If the landlord had listened to his own hunches, he would have been more careful and more thorough than usual; instead, he made the mistake of being too trusting.[*]

---

[*]This is an actual case history from the author's experience as a landlord.

Danger Signals

As you interview applicants, listen carefully to the statements they make. Beyond what is written on the application form, or what information is left off, an applicant often will say things that provide you with insights about the person. These insights also serve as danger signals to you. For example, some people think they need to sell the landlord on how much they like the house, as well as on their ambitious plans for gardening and decorating. Experience shows, though, that, the bigger the plans an applicant expresses, the less gets done. It is more likely that the applicant who expresses a desire to transform the garden will not even mow the lawn. The belief that the landlord has to be sold on the would-be tenant is a distraction. In fact, approaching the question as an investor, you seek someone who will pay the rent on time, take good care of your property, perform maintenance specified in the contract, and use the property only in legal ways. You want to avoid tenants who are late on the rent, abuse your property, do not perform maintenance, and use your property to manufacture or sell drugs. This distinction makes your selection process far easier, because it gets around the subtle details of whether a tenant has plans to work the garden.

Another danger signal is the applicant who wants to barter for part of the rent. For example, if the tenant offers to paint the house for reduced rent, you have a twofold problem. First, the tenant probably does not know how to paint professionally; most people think it's fairly easy to paint a house, but they do not do a good job, so there is no good reason to agree to let a tenant paint, inside or out.* Second, an individual who tries to barter to reduce rent is letting you know that he or she cannot afford the rent you are asking; thus, if you agree to rent to the person, you are going to have trouble getting your rent each month.

Another danger signal arises when tenants want to bring in other people to share the rent. For example, two or more friends want to apply together. Remember, people will not rent under those circumstances except in one situation: when none of the individuals can afford the rent alone. As soon as a disagreement arises, one of the tenants will move out, and, almost at once, you will find it increasingly difficult to get your rent. You may need

---

*Tenants offering to paint your property present you with a dilemma. As a general rule, you should never agree to let tenants perform such work. Landlords may agree to let a tenant paint a room and will even supply the materials if the tenant agrees to do the work. However, because it is usually a bigger job than the tenant thinks, it is not usually done correctly. Some tenants will even ask for compensation after the work has been done, which only leads to tension between you and your tenant. In other words, keep the relationship simple and clean. Don't agree to let tenants perform any extra work on your property.

to rent in share situations, especially if you deal with a lot of young singles, but you need to be prepared for frequent turnover when friends fight or the college semester ends, whichever comes first. Turnover among college-age tenants is very high. You may wish to avoid that market, if possible, in favor of families with children, for example; however, landlords do not always have the luxury of being able to select their demographic tenant base. If you need to deal with a variety of tenants in terms of age, marital status, and income, be prepared to deal with the characteristics and problems of each group.

The tenant faces the same dilemma as everyone else—wanting a nice place to live but needing to recognize financial limitations. As a landlord, you constantly need to balance your compassion against your better judgment. A tenant who cannot afford the rent that you need to charge may try to find ways to come to some type of bargain with you, such as trying to barter part of the rent for work. As a general rule, make a clear distinction between tenants and people you hire to maintain your property. The contractors, landscapers, and plumbers you hire expect to be paid by you, whereas you expect to be paid by your tenants. The tenant is not necessarily an expert in any of the areas you need to hire out, and experience shows that bartering agreements rarely work out. Chances are good that you will have trouble collecting rent *and* getting the work done.

Another problem with bartering is that the work the tenant wants to do is not usually recurring. Painting the house is not a monthly event, for example. One tenant offered to perform monthly landscaping in exchange for reduced rent. When the landlord pointed out that the tenant was obligated to maintain the lawn and grounds as part of the agreement, the tenant next asked for lower rent, anyway. Needless to say, this tenant was unable to afford the rent and had to seek a different house or apartment to rent.

When a tenant asks to pay the security deposit in installments, this is yet another troubling sign. If the tenant does not have the resources to come up with a security deposit and first month's rent, this means he or she cannot afford to move. From the simple point of view of basic budgeting, you need to wonder how this tenant will scrape together the monthly rent.

Also watch for signs on the application form. In addition to the lack of suitable references, avoid tenants who use parents as their sole reference, who are unemployed, or who claim to be self-employed with exceptionally high income but no verification. Providing a copy of their monthly bank statement would support the income claim, for example; however, self-employed tenants rarely offer any form of proof for such claims.

If tenants seem overly anxious to move in, that might be a sign they have been evicted from their current rentals or that another problem has not been disclosed. Some smooth-talking people realize that, if they pressure a landlord to allow them to move in before a scheduled availability date, this often means the landlord does not have time to check references. Don't give in to this pressure. For example, one tenant wanted to move in two weeks early, while the landlord was still painting and performing repairs. She offered to complete the work on her own. The landlord agreed. The work never was done, and the tenant would not allow the landlord access to the premises to complete the work. She changed the locks and stopped paying rent, making it necessary for the landlord to evict her. A check of the tenant's background would have shown past evictions, as well as numerous short-term rental arrangements, many ending badly.

Tenants who cannot afford to rent your property on their own are constantly seeking suitable share arrangements. However, as simple as it sounds, it is very difficult to find compatible people with whom to rent a house. Even good friends can end up getting on each other's nerves in such a situation, and if one person is late on the rent, it places pressure on the other. From the landlord's point of view, shared responsibility for rent is a troubling situation, which probably will last only two or three months before the whole deal falls apart. Then the task of giving notice, cleaning up, and finding new tenants is on you again. Another problem with share rentals is that disagreements arise as to who is supposed to clean the house, perform landscaping, and do other chores. As a consequence, you often end up inheriting a month or more of uncompleted work on the property. In summary, the share rental might seem like a practical idea, but it usually does not work out for anyone—not for any of the tenants and certainly not for the landlord.

Lease or Month-to-Month?

Once you recognize the telling signs for tenants who will not work out, you will be able to narrow the field. You still need to decide, though, whether to offer a lease for six months, a year, or more or to rent on a month-to-month basis.

A month-to-month rental agreement is a short-term one that is renewed automatically each month unless one side cancels it. Cancellation is achieved by way of notice. A month-to-month rental agreement has the primary advantage of being flexible. Tenants who are not certain about whether they want to commit to a one-year lease can simply give the required notice whenever they want and move on; in such an arrangement, their obligation never extends beyond the next due date of rent. From the landlord's point of view, it is easier to give notice to tenants if problems arise, such as nonpayment of rent. The landlord provides the required notice to the tenant and ends the agreement quickly.

The tenant's primary disadvantage in a month-to-month agreement is that rent can be raised at any time. A landlord could raise the rent, in theory, every month. However, a wise landlord would not raise rent for a responsible tenant, knowing that, once rent exceeds the market norm, the tenant will move on. From the landlord's point of view, month-to-month often also means greater turnover in tenants, even the good ones.

A lease locks in both sides in many respects. Rent is set for the term of the lease and cannot be raised except on renewal, in most cases. Some leases include a formula for rent increases at specified times, based on increases in the landlord's costs—most often, property taxes. Thus, if property taxes rise, the increase is passed on to the tenant in the form of higher monthly rent. The landlord is also locked in to the agreement in the sense that the tenant cannot be given notice except for cause, such as nonpayment of rent or destruction of the property, so a tenant with a lease can settle in for the lease term without having to worry about being given notice to move.

If the owner decides to sell a house in which a tenant has a lease, the lease cannot be broken without agreement on both sides, so the new owner has to honor the terms of the lease until its expiration. This makes it impractical to market houses as long as the lease is in effect, because it limits the market. Most buyers would want to occupy the property as soon as the sale were completed, so a lease complicates the deal.

The landlord may desire a lease because it requires tenants to remain in the property and continue paying rent for the whole term. This usually is a full year for houses in many areas. However, if your tenant turns out to be unpleasant to deal with, then the lease can become a liability. Perhaps the greatest advantage to the month-to-month agreement is the flexibility it provides to both sides. You can give notice at any time, just as the tenant can.

Some landlords use leases because they know that some tenants would want to stay only for the short term, so the lease weeds out the less stable tenants by its very nature. In other words, if a tenant plans to rent for only a few months, a one-year lease would eliminate that person, and he or she would not even apply for the rental. Another weeding out effect is achieved by the amount of initial deposit you require. Most month-to-month agreements ask for a security deposit and the first month's rent. While the longer-term lease often has the same terms, some require the deposit plus first *and* last months' rent. This gives the landlord a lot more protection. If a tenant is late on rent, the landlord already has the last month on deposit. This also eliminates many of the poorer applicants. For example, if rent is $500 per month and you ask for a $700 cleaning and security deposit, a tenant needs $1,700 just to get in the door. Weeding out disadvantaged tenants in this way is unfair in some respects. It provides degrees of safety to the landlord but eliminates a large segment of potential tenants. As a consequence, you probably end up with a higher vacancy rate because it takes longer to find suitable and qualified tenants. The protection you gain with higher deposit requirements and longer-term leases may be offset by the simple reality of lost rent.

The Deposit Receipt Form

You need to set policies regarding the amount of deposit you require for renting your property. The deposit should be adequate to cover any likely damage a tenant might do to the premises, which you would then want to charge against that deposit. If the deposit amount is not large enough to cover cleaning and damage, then you could lose money. If a tenant does not clean and does some damage, that is money out of your pocket if your deposit is inadequate to cover it.

For most single-family houses, you should require at least $500 in security and cleaning deposit (less for apartments or smaller multi-unit properties). As a general observation, the higher the monthly rent, the higher the deposit should be as well. Don't expect to convert security deposits to unpaid rent; if a tenant does not pay the last month and intends to just let you keep the deposit, then he or she has no incentive to clean the place. In such situations, you might need to take the tenant's left-over junk and garbage to the dump—not only taking the time to clean up after a messy tenant but also having to spend your own labor and then pay to get rid of used furniture, empty bottles, and abandoned appliances. If a tenant is planning to leave, require that he or she pay the rent through the end of the period.

You should expect a higher deposit if the tenant has pets. Many landlords have a firm "no pets" policy because animals can do a great deal of damage to your property in a short period of time. Tenants always describe their own pets as "small and well trained," even when it is not true. A pet deposit can be $300 or more, depending on the age and condition of the house, whether it has carpeting, and the type and size of the pet.

The deposit should be kept apart from other funds, preferably in a special savings account or money market account. This separation of security deposits is required by law in some states. Check requirements in your state by referring to landlord-tenant laws and look for the procedures regarding handling of deposits.

Deposit Receipt

Tenant name(s) _____

Property address_____

Date of occupancy _____ Date of inspection _____

A deposit in the amount of $ _____ was paid by the tenant on this date as a security and cleaning deposit on the above property. The tenant acknowledges that the attached statement of condition accurately reflects the condition of the property at the time that the inspection was performed and that I was present at that walk-through inspection. I/we understand that the property is to be delivered in the same condition upon termination of my tenancy, and that I will pay all costs incurred to restore the property to its present condition, with the exception of normal wear and tear.

Tenant_____ Date_____

_____ Date_____

To be completed at the time of vacancy: _____

Date the property was vacated_____

Cleaning and maintenance:

Description	Amount

Deposit made: $_____

Less: cleaning and maintenance required $_____

Less: deposit held for unpaid rent $_____

Less: unpaid utilities $_____

Other_____ $_____

Balance due (to be paid within _____ days) $_____

Forwarding address of tenant:

Name_____

Address_____

City, state, zip_____

Owner or manager signature_____

Date_____

Tenant_____

Date_____

FIGURE 7.2 Deposit Receipt.

A deposit receipt should be filled out, signed, and kept in your files, with a copy provided to the tenant as well. The deposit receipt often is part of a larger statement of condition, or it can be a separate form that makes reference to an attachment. A deposit receipt form is shown in Figure 7.2. The receipt form serves two purposes: (1) documenting the original receipt and the terms that go along with it and (2) returning the money to the tenant later when the tenancy is over. It begins with the details—tenant name, property address, date of occupancy, and date of inspection. The inspection should be done with you *and* the tenant together. In this way, any questions about the condition of the property can be answered as the inspection proceeds. The inspection and occupancy dates might be the same, or the inspection can take place within a few days before or after occupancy.

The deposit amount is written in next, at the front of the paragraph referring to the attached statement of condition; beneath this, the tenant should sign and date the form. The original should be kept in your files and a copy provided to the tenant.

The second part of the deposit receipt is completed when the tenant moves out of the unit. It documents the items that needed to be repaired, cleaned, or replaced. Normal wear and tear excepted, you probably will need to perform some work, such as carpet cleaning. If the tenant cleans the appliances and leaves everything in good shape, he or she should get back the majority of the deposit. This form provides space to spell out exactly how the balance is computed; it should be signed by you and the tenant. Note that the form asks for a forwarding address for the tenant. As a matter of practice, you should mail the return deposit to the tenant; this gives you time to make sure that all utilities have been paid up and that no undiscovered problems need to be paid for, due to the tenant. This also provides you with a record of the forwarding address. This is important in case mail arrives and needs to be forwarded.

The deposit has to be returned to your tenant within a reasonable period of time, dictated by state law. Check your state to determine how long this period is, checking the current law; also read the terms in that law relating to how you are expected to segregate the deposit and how security deposits can or cannot be converted to cover unpaid rent.

The Statement of Condition

The statement of condition is a very detailed listing of the condition of your property. It has to be filled out at the time you inspect the property. The inspection is most effective if you perform it with your tenant, so that any questions can be answered on the spot.

Statement of Condition

Property address_____ Date_____
Tenant name_____Phone_____

	Move-in Condition	Move-out Condition	Estimated Cost
Outside entry:			
Door/knob/lock			
Light fixtures			
Doorbell			
Inside entryway:			
Door/knob/lock			
Light fixtures			
Walls			
Ceiling			
Flooring			
Windows/screen			
Window coverings			
Closet			
Living room:			
Light fixtures			
Walls			
Ceiling			
Flooring			
Outlets/jacks/switches			
TV Cable			
Windows/screens			
Window coverings			
Heat/thermostat			
Fireplace/screen			
Closet			
Dining room:			
Light fixtures			
Walls			
Ceiling			
Flooring			
Outlets/jacks/switches			
Windows/screens			
Window coverings			
Closet			
Cabinets			

Condition codes, move-in: C = clean   D = dirty   N = not working   P = present
SC = scratched   ST = stained   M = missing
Condition codes, move-out: C = clean   CC = cleaning completed   SC = spot cleaned
RE = repaired   RP = replaced   NP = needs paint
T = torn   FP = needs full paint   NC = no charge to tenant

FIGURE 7.3 Statement of Condition.

	Move-in Condition	Move-out Condition	Estimated Cost
Statement of Condition Page 2 Property address_____Date_____			
Kitchen:			
Light fixtures			
Walls			
Ceiling			
Flooring			
Outlets/jacks/switches			
Windows/screen			
Window coverings			
Cabinets/hardware			
Sink and faucet			
Disposal/drain			
Dishwasher			
Range			
Hood/fan/light			
Refrigerator			
Microwave			
Hallway:			
Light fixtures			
Walls			
Ceiling			
Flooring			
Outlets/jacks/switches			
Window coverings			
Closet			
Master bathroom:			
Light fixtures			
Walls			
Ceiling			
Exhaust fan			
Door			
Flooring			
Outlets/jacks/switches			
Mirrors			
Counter			
Medicine cabinet			
Towel bar(s)			
Windows/screens			
Window coverings			
Sink/faucet			
Toilet			
Tub/shower			

FIGURE 7.3 *(Continued)*

Statement of Condition

Page 3

Property address_____Date_____

	Move-in Condition	Move-out Condition	Estimated Cost
Bedroom_____ :			
Light fixtures			
Walls			
Ceiling			
Flooring			
Outlets/jacks/switches			
Windows/screen			
Window coverings			
Closet			
Bedroom_____ :			
Light fixtures			
Walls			
Ceiling			
Flooring			
Outlets/jacks/switches			
Windows/screen			
Window coverings			
Closet			
Bedroom_____ :			
Light fixtures			
Walls			
Ceiling			
Flooring			
Outlets/jacks/switches			
Windows/screen			
Window coverings			
Closet			
Bathroom #2			
Light fixtures			
Walls			
Ceiling			
Exhaust fan			
Door			
Flooring			
Outlets/jacks/switches			
Mirrors/counters			
Medicine cabinet/ towel bars			
Windows/screens			
Window coverings			
Sink/faucet			
Toilet			
Tub/shower			

FIGURE 7.3 *(Continued)*

Statement of Condition   Page 4

Property address_____Date_____

	Move-in Condition	Move-out Condition	Estimated Cost
Utility room, garage, carport:			
Light fixtures			
Walls			
Ceiling			
Flooring			
Door			
Outlets/jacks/switches			
Windows/screen			
Window coverings			
Washer			
Dryer			
Overhead door			
Storage area			
Backyard/patio:			
Light fixtures			
Storage			
Barbecue			
Lawn area			
Planted area/garden			
Fencing/gate(s)			
Sprinkler/timer			
Keys:			
House/mail			
Laundry/pool/other			

Move-in	Move-out
I acknowledge that the condition is clean, undamaged, and in working order, except as noted above.	I agree that I am responsible for any differences in condition between move-in and move-out except ordinary wear and tear and that the cost to correct those conditions will be deducted from my security deposit.
_____	_____
Tenant	Tenant

FIGURE 7.3 *(Continued)*

This form can be merged with the deposit receipt; however, because it is highly detailed, it works better when separated. The most practical design for the form also details the property's condition at the time of initial inspection, the condition on final inspection, (move-out), and the cost to make repairs if needed.

One version of the statement of condition is shown in Figure 7.3 . This four-page form seems complicated at first glance; however, it covers a lot of information and is not difficult to fill out—especially for properties that are already familiar to you. Each room is listed in the typical house, perhaps in greater detail than would be required for many rental properties. Each room's condition is listed in considerable detail at the time of the move-in inspection (column 1) *and* at the move-out inspection (column 2). Any differences in condition are charged against the tenant's deposit, except normal wear and tear. Note that, at the bottom of page 1, a suggested series of codes is provided for you to fill in the form.

Examples of normal wear and tear include deterioration of a carpet's condition due to traffic, walls needing painting after several years' use, and an aging appliance working at less than peak efficiency. Items to be charged against the security deposit include dirty appliances and fixtures, unclean carpeting or floors, and any other matter that would be the tenant's responsibility to keep in good order, found at move-out to not be the case.

The fourth page has a section for tenant signature at both move-in and move-out inspections. This form is a part of the permanent record of how you receive and repay deposits, and it is essential that it be filled in as completely as possible. By filling it in at the beginning of your agreement with the tenant, you document all conditions and get the tenant's signature acknowledging that everything is accurate. If, at move-out, any conditions are not the same, you have proof that the tenant is responsible for the cost of repairs. The completed form also helps you fill in a new statement of condition when a new tenant arrives on the scene.

You may need the completed, signed form in the event a tenant disputes your version of condition for a rental property. If you are taken to court, the completed statement of condition is compelling evidence, especially if it is signed by the tenant. Most landlords do not go to the trouble to complete a detailed form, but you need to protect yourself by including move-in and move-out inspections as part of your routine.

What if the tenant refuses to sign at move-out? That occurs either because of a dispute as to actual condition or when the tenant disappears and is not present at the time of inspection. In the latter case, you will find many conditions needing work. Tenants who simply walk away from the property (and their deposit) never clean and often are aware that they have left the property in poor condition.

When the tenant will not sign or is not available, be sure to document all negative conditions with a completed form and photographic evidence. Still pictures of dirty appliances, floors, walls, and other items in which you will have to invest time and money to fix are good evidence in the event that a tenant later demands the return of a security deposit. In cases of especially bad condition, taking a video record is a smart move, especially if the damages are extensive enough so that you put in a claim with your insurance company.[*]

As a strict policy, you should promise to return the security deposit only after completion of the statement of condition. You cannot withhold the deposit just because a tenant is uncooperative; however, the laws of each state provide you with a period of time, usually 10 days, in which to refund these deposits. This gives you time to check thoroughly for damage and to ensure that no unpaid utilities bills need to be paid. By requiring the tenant to provide you with an address and promising to mail the refund, you also acquire a forwarding address. This becomes important if utilities have not been paid at the time the tenancy ends but bills are not mailed until later. At that point, the balance owed can be deducted from the deposit. If any damages exceeding the security deposit are found, or if your insurance agent asks for the address in an investigation of a damage claim.

In practice, some landlords rarely get a forwarding address for their tenants. Some undesirable tenants want to get their security deposit and move away without providing a forwarding address, often because collection agencies are a step behind and are looking for them, or because they know that damages exceed the amount of their security deposit.

In one case, a tenant did not notify the landlord when the heating system stopped working, unaware that a backed-up drainage system led to flooding of the space under the house, including heating ducts. By the time the tenant moved out three months later, all of the inside walls and ceilings were covered with mildew and all the floors were damaged. The repairs exceeded the security deposit by several hundred dollars. The tenant called the landlord a month after leaving the property to ask for the return of his security deposit. Needless to say, the landlord refused.[**]

While most tenants are reasonable and will care for a property well, the occasional negative experience makes the statement of condition necessary. To protect yourself from abuse on the part of tenants and to protect tenants by documenting conditions before and after their tenancy, the form serves a dual purpose.

---

[*]Many of the damages that can occur due to tenant neglect are not covered by an insurance policy. As a general rule, covered damages have to be "sudden and unexpected." If damage takes place over several months, the "sudden" requirement will not be met. An example of covered damage is vandalism done by a tenant at the point of abandoning your property.

[**]This is an actual case history from the author's experience as a landlord.

Basic Rules for the Agreement

The agreement you enter into with your tenant defines the terms of his or her occupancy of your property. When a tenant agrees to pay you to live in your property, the agreement allows the tenant to take possession of it. This possession includes several obligations and rights on both sides, so your rental agreement has to include all of the necessary definitions and conditions to define those rights and obligations; it has to be a legal and binding contract; and both sides have to sign and acknowledge it in order for it to go into effect. While a verbal contract is enforceable, it is invariably difficult to establish later the actual conditions of the contract without the document itself. In real estate matters, virtually all agreements should be in writing to protect both sides. There is an old expression "a verbal contract isn't worth the paper it's written on." That applies to your real estate agreement, too.

Every contract has to have specific features in order for it to be valid. These features have to be included in your real estate agreement, whether a formal lease or the less formal month-to-month rental. These features include the following:

1. *Both sides have to be able to enter a contract under the law.* If either side cannot enter a contract—due to age or citizenship, for example— then the terms of an agreement might not be enforceable. Since housing is a necessity, a minor can enter a rental agreement; however, many contracts entered into by minors are voidable, meaning that they can be voided if the minor decides to back out.

2. *There must be equal consideration.* A contract requires that each side give and receive something of equal value. In exchange for the payment of rent, a tenant is given possession of a rental house or unit. If the value on either side were unequal, then the contract would not be valid.

3. *Performance is required.* Before the contract is considered enforceable, each side has to perform. The payment of the first month's rent and a security deposit, required by the contract, has to take place before the tenant has a binding contract, and the landlord has to deliver possession of the property to the tenant.

4. *There must be a meeting of the minds.* One reason that a written contract is so important is that, in the event of a dispute, the document settles most matters. As long as all of the terms are listed in the contract, most disputes can be avoided or settled easily. By signing a contract, the general presumption is that an agreement was reached. If a property were available and an individual were to express an interest in renting it, that would not meet the test for a meeting of the minds; there would need to be a discussion and written agreement as to the specific terms of the contract.

5. *The contract has to be legal and enforceable.* Each of the terms in your rental agreement has to be within the law to be enforceable. For example, if your state requires 48 hours' notice for you to enter the property with a tenant's permission, you cannot waive that requirement in your contract. An informal agreement between landlord and tenant might work; but in case of an outright disagreement, the contract and the law will decide the outcome. All terms within the contract have to be legal in order to be enforceable; you cannot waive what the law requires, even when both you and the tenant sign an agreement to that effect. If a contract requires 48 hours' notice to enter the premises, you can ask the tenant to waive the requirement; and if he does, then there is not a problem. However, you cannot write the waiver into the agreement and then try to enforce it.

Your contract has to contain all of these attributes in order to be enforceable. In addition to the legal requirements that create a valid contract, you also need to include the specific terms and conditions that are needed for a rental agreement:

- Name of tenant and landlord
- Property address
- Statement spelling out the amount of security deposit and rent prepayments
- Monthly rental amount, rent mailing address, late fees
- Reference to attachments (statement of condition, security deposit receipt, etc.)
- Specific requirements (for landscaping care and general maintenance, for example)
- Policies regarding pets
- Term of the contract (month-to-month or lease)
- Notice and conditions under which termination can occur

The Rental Agreement

The actual agreement you enter into with your tenant can be a relatively simple form taking up as little as two pages. However, all of the required elements have to be included, to protect yourself as well as your tenant. Any form you use should also be reviewed by your attorney to ensure that it conforms to all of the laws in your state.

A sample rental agreement is shown in Figure 7.4. This agreement covers all of the basics, beginning with the date and names of the owner and resident. Following this are 15 paragraphs taking up two pages. The agreement must be signed by the landlord and tenant in order to constitute a valid contract.

Rental Agreement

This agreement is entered into on this _____ day of _____ , 20 _____ between _____ owner (landlord) and _____ resident (tenant). In consideration of their mutual agreement, owner and resident agree as follows:

1. **Address.** Owner rents to the resident, and resident rents from the owner for residential use only, the premises known as_____.

2. **Rent and fees.** Rent is due in advance on or before the first day of each month, at $ _____ per month, beginning on the _____ day of _____ , 20 _____ . If rent is paid after the 5th day of the month, a late charge will be assessed at the rate of $ _____ per day. If a resident's check is returned by the bank, the resident will be liable for a returned check charge of twenty-five dollars ($25.00) plus damages, computed as: _____ .

3. **Termination.** This agreement may be terminated by either party by delivering to the other a written notice of _____ days. Any holding over beyond the termination date shall result in the resident's being liable to the owner for damages at the fair market rental value of $ _____ per day.

4. **Occupants.** Premises shall be occupied only by the following persons:

_____	_____	_____	_____
Name	Birthdate	Name	Birthdate

_____	_____	_____	_____
Name	Birthdate	Name	Birthdate

5. **Restrictions.** Without owner's prior written permission, resident may not keep or allow any pets, waterbeds, other liquid-filled furniture, or recreational vehicles on the premises. Resident shall not keep more than three vehicles on the premises, and all must be currently registered and licensed. Resident shall not violate any criminal or civil laws, commit waste or nuisance, or molest or interfere with any other residents or neighbors. Any such action may result in the immediate termination of this agreement.

6. **Alterations.** No decorating, repairs, or alterations shall be done to the premises by resident without owner's prior written consent. Decorations include but are not limited to painting, wallpapering, hangings, or murals.

7. **Inspection.** Resident has inspected the premises, furnishings, and equipment and has found them to be satisfactory and has been given a copy of a statement of condition. All plumbing, heating, and electrical systems are operative and deemed satisfactory.

8. **Maintenance.** Resident agrees to keep the premises, furnishings and appliances, yard and landscaping, and fixtures in good order and condition. Resident shall pay owner the costs to repair, replace, or rebuild any portion of the premises damaged by resident or resident's guests. Resident's property is not insured by the owner. Resident is not a co-insured and is expressly excluded from any insurance policy held by owner.

FIGURE 7.4 Rental Agreement.

9. **Utilities.** Resident agrees to pay for all utilities, services, and charges, except: _____ . Resident will contact utility companies before occupancy and shall register billings in his/her name.

10. **Security deposit.** Resident shall deposit with owner as a security deposit the sum of $ _____ , payable upon entering this agreement. Security deposit shall not be used by resident to pay the last month's rent. Owner may withhold amounts from the security deposit as remedy for defaults by resident for the payment of rent; to repair damages to the premises caused by residents, except, ordinary wear and tear; or to clean premises, if necessary upon termination of tenancy. No later than _____ days after owner's regaining possession, owner shall return the remaining portion of the security deposit to resident to a forwarding address supplied by resident upon termination of this agreement. Resident may not sublet all or part of the premises.

11. **Access to premises.** Owner or his/her agents or employees may enter the premises (a) in case of emergency, (b) when the resident has abandoned or surrendered the premises, or (c) to make necessary and agreed repairs or to show the property to prospective purchasers or tenants, lenders, workmen, appraisers provided resident is given reasonable notice of owner's intent to enter. Notice of _____ hours is deemed to be reasonable. Resident will not change locks without owner's prior permission; in the event locks are changed, a duplicate key will be given to owner.

12. **Smoke detectors.** The property is equipped with functioning smoke detection devices. Resident acknowledges that the device(s) was/were tested and in working order and that their operation was fully explained by owner. Resident shall ensure that the device remains in working order. If battery-operated, resident agrees to keep a working battery in the device at all times.

13. **Attachments.** Resident acknowledges by initialing below receipt of the indicated attachments, which are hereby incorporated into and are a part of this agreement:

      Statement of condition_____   Security deposit receipt_____

      Pet agreement_____   Other_____

14. **Entire agreement.** This agreement, with attachments described in 13 above, constitutes the entire agreement between resident and owner and cannot be modified except by written addendum signed by both parties. No promises or representations have been made except as set forth in this agreement.

15. **Legal action and notice.** If any legal action or proceeding is brought by either party to enforce any part of this agreement, the prevailing party shall recover, in addition to other relief, reasonable attorneys' fees and costs. All notices upon owner may be served at _____ .

The undersigned resident has read and understood this agreement and has received a copy of the full agreement and all attachments.

| _____ | _____ |
| Owner | Date |

| _____ | _____ |
| Resident | Date |

| _____ | _____ |
| Resident | Date |

FIGURE 7.4 *(Continued)*

Paragraph 1 of the rental agreement states the property address. Paragraph 2 defines the amount of rent and its due date each month, and it specifies fees and how they are charged. State law may limit the fee you can charge, or it might specify the dollar amount of fees you are allowed to assess for late rent payment. Paragraph 3 discusses termination of the agreement. Each state provides a specific number of days' notice required. Read your state regulations carefully, so that you know what the number of days actually means. For example, a "20-day notice" can mean 20 days from the date that notice is given, or it can mean 20 days *or* the next end of the month. Thus, if a tenant gives notice between the first and the tenth of the month, the effective termination date means the first of the following month; however, if the notice is given after the tenth, it means the first of the following month, so you need to ensure that you and your tenant understand the rules when the number of days is specified.

Paragraph 4 lists the occupants and their birthdates, which tells you their ages as well. You need to specify to the tenants that they cannot simply invite people to share rent with them unless the contract is amended to add their names to the rental agreement. (Also see paragraph 10, concerning subleasing.) As landlord, you have the right to restrict the number of people living in the property, based on its size and living space.

Paragraph 5 lists a number of restrictions. Waterbeds and other liquid-filled furniture should be excluded if your homeowners' insurance policy also excludes damage caused by leakage from waterbeds. Recreational vehicles and an excessive number of cars on the premises create a nuisance for your neighbors. Other restrictions may be added to this paragraph based on zoning in the neighborhood, for example.

Paragraph 6 limits the kind of alterations your tenant can perform. You need to control the painting and wallpapering of a house, for example, because tenants' tastes might not be suitable for the house in general, and a paint job could limit your ability to rent to someone else. Tenants also might not do such jobs with the skill and care required to maintain property value. As a general rule, don't allow tenants to perform any work on the property.

Paragraph 7 relates to the attachment of a statement of condition. This paragraph is very important because it specifies that the resident has taken part in the inspection or, at the very least, has looked over the form and agrees with what it states.

Paragraph 8 requires the tenant to maintain the property. By signing, the tenant also agrees to pay for any damages. It also specifies that the resident's belongings are not insured by the owner. Tenants often fail to maintain the yard, for example; under this paragraph, that is a violation of the agreement. You have the right to terminate the contract or to modify it by raising the rent to cover the cost of hiring someone else to perform landscaping.

Paragraph 9, concerns utilities. You need to spell out which costs, if any, you will pay and which ones are the responsibility of the tenant.[*] Paragraph 10 lists the security deposit amount, which is also listed on the security deposit receipt. It also specifies what the deposit can be used for and that tenants are responsible for any damages, as well as the fact that the deposit will be returned by mail *after* the tenant has left. Paragraph 11 provides that you have the right to enter the premises to inspect and repair damages, but only with the proper notice. This requirement varies between states, so make sure that the number of hours' notice conforms with your state's laws. Most states specify either 24 or 48 hours. Also in this paragraph is the provision that residents cannot change locks without the owner's prior permission.

Paragraph 12 discusses smoke detectors and the tenants' responsibility for ensuring that they are kept in working order. The exact wording in this paragraph might have to be changed based on your state's requirements. This paragraph is also necessary for insurance purposes; in the event of a fire, you need to ensure that you did all you could to provide working smoke detectors. Some tenants remove the batteries when the alarm goes off while they are cooking, for example, and never replace them; others fail to replace batteries that have gone dead.

Paragraph 13 lists any attachments that are part of the contract, including the statement of condition and security deposit receipt. If tenants have pets, you also need to attach a separate form spelling out the tenants' responsibilities and extra deposit requirements. Paragraphs 14 and 15 deal with legal issues related to the contract, specifically limiting the contract to what is written on the forms and providing tenants with an address for service in the event of legal action.

You and the tenant must sign and date the rental agreement in order for it to be a valid contract. Keep your contracts in a file dedicated to the specific property. The contracts should be kept indefinitely, even after the tenancy has ended, in case questions or claims arise later.

---

[*]Some utility companies offer landlords the service of having utility billings revert to their names automatically when tenants leave. While this seems like a convenience, it can work against you. That system makes it too easy for tenants to not make contact with the utility company, meaning you end up paying their gas or electric bill. It is much wiser to have utilities go out of your name the day your tenants take over. That gives your tenants incentive to have their utility billings set up.

Solving Typical Problems

Many problems can arise in the relationship between landlord and tenant. You can never anticipate all of the potential questions or disputes in the contract; you can only revise and update the form as new problems arise.

Most of the problems can be solved, as long as both sides act in good faith. An honest dispute can be handled informally, and having to resort to the police or the courts is an extreme step. In one instance, a tenant was ready to move out and the landlord performed a walk-through inspection. He then made the mistake of returning the security deposit, even though the tenant did not give him all of her sets of keys. Later that day, the landlord was in the empty house, cleaning it, when the tenant showed up. She refused to leave on the premise that the house was rented through the end of that day, and she claimed that the landlord had no right to be there. The landlord's position was that the security deposit had been returned and both had agreed that the tenancy had ended. The tenant called the police, who arrived and heard both sides. However, the tenant then decided to turn over the key and not press the matter.*

As a landlord, you need to recognize that tenants see the house as theirs as long as they are paying rent. At the same time, you are making the mortgage payment, as well as paying property taxes and insurance and repairing defects in systems. Thus, both sides have a point of view concerning a property, and these points of view can lead to disagreements. Some tenants are very easy to get along with and will allow the landlord access to the property, especially if something is in need of repair. Others are very unhappy about having the landlord in their house and will not grant permission without resistance. Even though the contract defines how these matters are to be resolved, tenants and landlords may still find this matter to be a source of ongoing conflict.

One tenant became unhappy when the landlord had to hire a specialist to replace a liner in a venting system for a gas heater. The contractor inspected it and showed the landlord that it was plugged and presented an immediate carbon monoxide poisoning danger. The landlord authorized the replacement immediately and asked the contractor to begin work that day. The tenant objected because there had been no advance notice, nor was he asked permission for the contractor to be on the premises that day.

---

*This is an actual case history. It led to instituting a policy that no deposit will be returned until the keys are in hand and the statement of condition was signed.

The landlord explained that it was an emergency and the work had to be completed right away. The work proceeded, but it led to tension between landlord and tenant.[*]

Conflict situations cannot be avoided. They are going to arise even when both landlord and tenant are fair-minded and reasonable people. Problems can be reduced if you make an extra effort to include the tenant in your plans, especially when those plans involve you or a contractor being on the premises and performing work. When possible, work around the tenant's schedule and be considerate of his or her desire for privacy and control over the property.

Many problems can arise early on in the landlord-tenant relationship. There seems to be a period of adjustment in which the tenant makes a lot of contact with the landlord, asking for small repairs or concessions. This period of time often ends without confrontation, or it might be necessary to write the tenant a letter, suggesting that the tenancy is not working out. In one case, the tenant moved into an older house on a full acre. He first complained that the house was run-down and needed painting. Next he said he couldn't mow the yard because he didn't own a lawn mower. Then, during a cold spell, he said the house was difficult to heat. The landlord wrote him a letter, which said in part:

> These conditions were known to you when you rented the house. The age and condition of the property are also reflected in the relatively low monthly rent. At the same time, I don't want an unhappy tenant. Based on these complaints, it occurs to me that you might need to look for a more modern rental and be willing to pay more rent as well. If you agree, I will be happy to waive the notice requirement and will agree with you to end the tenancy as of the end of this month. If you want to look for another place, please let me know and I will be happy to accommodate you.[**]

The tenant responded to this letter by saying he was very happy and did not want to move. He bought a lawn mower and attacked the yard with gusto. He remained in the property for more than three years and was an excellent tenant.

The initial period of adjustment recurs, not with every tenant but with many. You can recognize it and get through it with patience and understanding. And, of course, some tenants go through remorse and want to move out after only a month or two.

Some tenants have a period of adjustment related to payment of rent. Your contract specifies that rent is due on the first, and you should enforce

---

[*]This is an actual case history. From the authors landlording experience.
[**]Author's letter to tenant.

that rigorously. Otherwise, some tenants will let it slip further and further until they are too far behind to get caught up. Also enforce the penalty for late rent by adding late fees as specified in your contract.

The law provides that, when rent is late, you have the right to serve notice on your tenant. The precise timing and wording of this notice vary; many states provide for three days' notice. The one-page notice warns tenants that they have that period of time to remedy the problem, or they will have to leave. It is the last step before eviction, assuming that tenants do not respond. Most people do respond, however. This notice to pay rent or quit comes in many forms. A typical one is shown in Figure 7.5. Because the rules concerning this notice—its wording, title, and manner of serving it on your tenant—vary from state to state, a legal review is suggested before you actually use the form. You might have to pay someone to serve the notice on your tenant in accordance with local court rules, or you might be able to simply deliver it in person or tape it to the tenant's door.[*] The purpose of the notification is not to intimidate the tenants but to remind them that you mean business. The contract has to be enforced, or you will end up with chronically tardy rent problems. You need to make your mortgage payment on time, and that means collecting rents on time as well.[**]

Even when you find yourself in conflict with a tenant, dealing with the problems as soon as they arise is the wisest choice. Don't let problems go for any longer than necessary; if a tenant wants to test the limits to see whether or not a contract is really going to be enforced, respond according to the agreement. Don't be afraid to serve a three-day notice, and adamantly insist on getting your rent on time each month. With all of the benefits to investing in real estate, the relationship with your tenant may be the most difficult aspect. If you deal with young or immature tenants, which often is the case in cities with large college populations, for example, you may find yourself forced into a substitute parental role, whether you want it or not.

When tenants challenge you each month in one way or another, you need to question whether it is worth keeping them as tenants or replacing them. Chances are, in a healthy rental demand situation, you will be able

---

[*]The author used pleading paper to serve this form on past-due tenants. This is the paper used for legal pleadings, which has a series of numbers vertically on the sides of the paper. This seemed to have the desired impact, and merely serving the three-day notice solved the tardy rent problem in every instance.

[**]As a landlord, you will discover that tenants are not sympathetic to the argument that you have a mortgage payment to make and therefore rents have to be paid on time. Tenants either do not believe that you have a mortgage payment, or they simply do not respond to that argument. The unfortunate truth is that, as part of the natural adversarial nature of the landlord-tenant relationship, tenants do not understand the landlord's financial problems, nor do they want to, for the most part.

Notice to Pay Rent or Quit

Regarding the property at _____
(address) and under the terms of our agreement:

Notice from _____ (landlord) is hereby given to
_____ (tenant) that the rent is now
past due in the amount of $_____ plus $_____
in late fees through _____ (date).

　You are hereby given three days to pay past-due rent. If rent is not
paid within three days, you are given notice to quit possession of
these premises as defined under our contract.

_____　　　　　_____

(Signed)　　　　　　　　　　　　　　　　　(Date)

FIGURE 7.5　Notice to Pay Rent or Quit.

to find suitable tenants. Many landlords have found long-term tenants who pay the rent on time, take good care of the property, and respect the landlord and his or her concerns. At the same time, you might also have to occasionally bear down on tenants and remind them that you have a contract. The monthly challenge can come in the form of paying rent late, failing to maintain the yard, having unauthorized pets, disturbing the neighbors with late-night partying, making repeated requests for repairs, and causing any number of other problems. The wise landlord recognizes this as part of the overall attributes of owning rental real estate. Most first-time investors buy single-family houses because that is what they can afford; this is fortunate, because it also preselects a tenant base that often is easier to work with than the tenant base for apartment units. That means that the tenants are likely to be more mature, to have higher incomes than apartment-dwelling tenants, and to understand the higher level of maintenance required when living in a house. When several college-age tenants want to share a house, these observations do not necessarily apply; in fact, having several co-tenants might also only increase the problems with which you will deal each month.

　Some landlords have concluded that accepting younger, less mature tenants whose incomes also tend to be lower than average leads to too many problems. The solution is to work with more established tenants who have full-time jobs, care about their credit rating, and understand that the landlord has financial concerns. Working with this demographic group does not ensure that you will have fewer demands from your tenants, but it does increase your chances for avoiding some of the problems that usually are associated with the less mature tenant market.

The majority of people, including younger tenants, will be responsible and reasonable in their relationship with you. It takes only a few unpleasant experiences to create suspicion, but you need to realize that most tenants simply want housing that they can afford, that is comfortable, and that is managed by a landlord whom they can trust and work with. The most successful landlord-tenant relationships are based on mutual trust and responsibility.

CHAPTER 8

Rental Property Solutions

Once you enter into a rental agreement with a tenant, the process begins of managing the property. This is a balancing act between respecting the tenant's rights to privacy and exercising your right to monitor the condition of the land and improvements. For example, if you see that the yard is in disrepair, then you need to contact the tenant and remind the person that he or she is obligated to keep the yard in shape. Just by driving by the property, you can gain a general sense of how well it is being cared for. You do not want to see trash and used appliances littered around the yard, broken-down vehicles, broken windows, and high traffic levels. The new tenant is responsible for staying within the contract.

While you cannot demand entry once per week to check smoke detector batteries and perform a general inspection, you can tell a lot just from outward appearances. In most areas, for example, refuse collection takes place weekly, and people put out a large garbage can. Drive by the property on collection day and make sure your tenant is putting out the can. If there is no can, call the refuge collection company and inquire about the status of the account. If the tenant has not paid the bill and service has been stopped, you should be concerned. The family trash probably is being saved up in the garage or left in the backyard in these circumstances, and the longer you let it go, the more *you* will have to dispose of later. When a tenant cannot keep a utility account open, that is a sign of trouble.

Just by observing your property, you can generally tell whether your tenant is taking care of the inside, without having to see it for yourself. It is rare that people will let the outside appearance go bad, while keeping the inside of the house in good shape. As a general rule, if a tenant is going to let the property go into disrepair, it will take place throughout.

Using an Outside Management Company

One of the most common reasons that investors stay away from directly owned real estate is the range of issues involving tenant relations. It is true that the one-to-one relationship between landlord and tenant can be a problem and that the very nature of this relationship is adversarial. However, there are ways to avoid the problems that some people have experienced in working with confrontational tenants.

It makes sense for many real estate investors to work with a professional real estate management company. This is especially true in three conditions:

1. *Your own time commitments make it practical.* If you invest in real estate and hold down a full-time job, have a family, and want time to pursue other interests, tenant matters can serve as a disruption and inconvenience. Asking a management company to handle the problems or questions that come up not only protects your time and privacy; it also provides you with the peace of mind to know that someone is watching your property and protecting your interests.

2. *The service is affordable, given your cash flow situation.* Management fees usually run around 10 percent of rents collected. If your cash flow is very close, then management fees will be an out-of-pocket expense. While such fees are deductible on your tax return, you still have to come up with more money to pay expenses than you generate from rents. However, if rental demand in your area is high, you might cover all of your cash flow requirements by increasing rents. If, for example, your rental house has been going for $600 per month, a typical management fee can be covered by raising that rent to $670.

3. *You want a buffer between yourself and your tenants.* For some investors, having a buffer between themselves and tenants is worth 10 percent, even when tenants are relatively easy to work with—because the investor wants privacy and does not want to work directly with tenants. The management company usually handles everything, including payment of bills, hiring and supervision of repair persons, and, of course, any complaints from tenants. They advertise available rentals, screen tenants, and collect rents. Most companies also provide you with a monthly report summarizing all activity on your rental property.

One potential problem with using a management company concerns the federal tax rules allowing deduction of real estate losses. You can deduct up to $25,000 in losses per year under the sole exception restricting such deductions. However, the rules state that, in order to claim a deduction, you must spend at least 500 hours per year on your real estate investments. If you hire a property management company to handle everything for you, then it will be difficult to meet this rule. Even if you do accumulate 500 hours working on fixer-upper properties, viewing property for sale, and studying the market, you will still need to be able to document the time you spend in order to protect your ability to claim the deduction. Before hiring a property management company, you should consult with your tax expert to ensure that you will continue to meet the test that allows you to claim the loss deductions for your investments.

In selecting an adequate property management company, the factors to consider should include cost, reputation, staffing, and proximity to your investment properties. Cost may vary to a degree among firms; however, it is not always wise to select the least expensive service if that also means that some services are not included. For example, if a relatively small firm charges less but does not screen tenants for you, the service might not be a good bargain at all.

The reputation of the management firm can be checked by asking other landlords. In some communities, landlord associations meet monthly to discuss tenant issues, share information, and offer support to one another; this is an excellent source of referrals to property managers. Also check with the local banks and savings and loan associations that lend money on real estate and that know the market. You can also check with real estate brokerage firms; however, many of these offer management services of their own and will not be as objective as a firm that does not offer the service.

Is it a good idea to hire a real estate brokerage management company? That depends. Some companies manage properties because they also have a listing, so tenants are placed in the properties only while they are on the market. As with nonreal estate–operated firms, the level of service varies; since the real estate brokerage firm is in the primary business of selling real estate, property management often is treated as a secondary line of business. Some landlords have favored using firms that dedicate their staff effort to the singular task of managing properties for landlords or for real estate firms representing owners.

Staffing should be another consideration. Some property managers handle dozens of houses and apartments and have several people on staff. They also have relationships with specialists in various home maintenance needs—plumbers, electricians, landscapers, roofers, pest control services, and more—and they are fully up-to-date on landlord-tenant laws. Other property managers are operated out of the individuals' homes and there is no staff. Considering that fees probably are not much different between these two extremes, you probably receive more comprehensive services by working through the staffed-up firm rather than the smaller, less formal one.

The proximity of the property manager to your property is of equal importance. If you live in an area that is spread out over many miles, you should be concerned with the distance between the manager's office and the property. As an investor, you will quickly discover that, when you manage properties yourself, the task is far easier when you live close to your investment properties; it is far more difficult when they are farther away. A commute of a half hour or more to keep an eye on your properties, collect rent, or make small repairs is a hardship, compared with a distance of only two or three blocks. The same factors affect property managers; the greater the distance to a rental property, the less effectively they will be able to manage it for you.

A final consideration in picking a management firm is how diligently it performs the work. You need a management firm that carefully screens potential tenants. This should include checking all references, including investigating past evictions, criminal convictions, and credit history. A firm that does not perform these basic services is not worth hiring. In addition, you need a firm that will diligently market your vacant property. As a matter of practice, you should manage your own properties at least for a few months, so that you get a sense of what kinds of problems come up, what kinds of tenants you attract, and the condition and status of the rental market in general. By going through this, you will be in the position to know what *should* take place. For example, if you know that houses remain vacant for a month or less, that should also be the case with properties under management.

The truth, however, is that no one, not even a professional management company, is going to market your property as aggressively as you. When your property is vacant, you place ads in the newspapers, return phone calls, make appointments, and show the property as quickly as possible. When a tenant appears promising, you check references immediately, knowing that, if you wait, the prospective tenant will find something else. However, a management company might not take the same steps or work on the same schedule. Some companies just place a "for rent" sign on the lawn of a vacant house and wait for telephone calls, check references over several days, and then get back in touch with applicants. The problem, of course, is that people usually are looking for a rental fairly quickly, so the longer they are made to wait the greater the chances that they will not be looking by the time the rental agency gets around to them. Just as good deals in rentals are rented out quickly, good tenants also are picked up quickly by landlords. To compete in the rental market, you need to act quickly when you find a good tenant candidate; you also want to ensure that your management company works as quickly as possible to keep your property rented out at all times.

Managing Property on Your Own

Remember, you need to be able to establish that you spend at least 500 hours per year—about 10 hours per week—involved in management of your real estate holdings. This includes not only working directly on the property but also researching, viewing houses for sale, pricing materials, and interviewing tenants. By directly managing your property, you almost certainly meet the legal requirement; when you work with a property manager, it is more difficult. Thus, in addition to acquiring the experience you need to be an informed real estate investor, you also need to fulfill the tax and legal requirements of participation in managing your property.[*]

Perhaps the two areas where most landlords need to spend the most concentrated effort are in screening tenant candidates and in advertising properties on the market. Tenant screening is difficult because, when your property is vacant, you naturally want to find someone as quickly as possible. Anyone looking for housing is likely to be operating under pressure, so you need to exercise concern and to recognize that, if someone needs to find a place within the very near future, the person might not represent him- or herself as honestly as if that pressure were not a factor. You need to review applicants objectively and make a decision based on references, financial ability, and suitability for the property. For example, if your house is very small, it is not suitable for an exceptionally large family. In all of these decisions, you need to be aware of the federal and state antidiscrimination laws.

In reviewing tenant applicants, unfortunately it is all too easy to discriminate and break the law without any ill intentions. For example, you cannot discriminate against applicants just because they have children. At the same time, it is not suitable for a family with five children to live in a one-bedroom house, so the selection process has to be made not on the basis that there is no room for children but, rather, on the question of suitability. A young couple with a small child can rent a one-bedroom house and be quite comfortable; to exclude such an applicant just because they have a child places you in legal jeopardy.

With this in mind, it is important that you are able to document your reasons for selecting a specific tenant and, even more to the point, why another tenant was not selected. You are allowed to reject tenants because their income is not high enough to afford rent and because you are unable to verify income, check references, or perform other reasonable duties that take place during the application process. You need to keep notes

---

[*]There is no prescribed record keeping requirement for establishing time spent managing property. Your other records—receipts, invoices, bank transactions—form the basis for establishing how much time you spend.

when verifying income and references. If you reject an applicant because of negative information or statements made by a past landlord, for example, it is important to keep that person's name and phone number *and* to write down what the person said. Keep your notes as part of your rental file, in case you need them later.

One of the advantages of hiring a property management firm is that you do not have to worry about how applicant questions are asked or how references are checked. As long as the property remains rented and is well cared for and rents are paid on time, you can invest in real estate without the concern and risk that direct management involves. However, spending some time working directly with tenants is a worthwhile experience for every real estate investor.

The second area where new landlords need to put in extra effort is in advertising. It makes sense to place a "for rent" sign on the front lawn of your house. However, if you have tenants in the property, you should include the wording, "do not disturb tenants." Display your telephone number, so that prospective tenants will speak with you directly.

The "for rent" sign is not enough. You also need to advertise in the appropriate local newspapers. If you want to target a particular market, choose your newspaper accordingly. For example, if you have had poor experiences with college student tenants, don't place an ad in the student paper or a notice on the student center bulletin board.

A local daily paper is the best place to advertise. Begin your ad on Sunday (if there is a Sunday paper) and run it for at least a week. Don't skip any days; remember that advertising works only when it saturates the market for a period of time. In a market where rentals are in high demand, you may receive up to 100 calls during the week in response to a well-written ad for a well-priced rental property. You may want to leave a recorded message giving out the property address and asking people to drive by and look at the property; if they are still interested, they should then call back and leave their contact number. In this way, you get around having to speak to everyone who telephones, knowing that many will not want to rent in the area where the property is located. Don't bother advertising on radio or in other nonnewspaper media. It is a waste of money.

Local rent locator services may call you, and these can be a good source of applicants. These companies sell lists of local houses and apartments for rent, and the people who buy the lists then make calls to landlords. You can place an ad in the paper and the rent locator will call you; if you have had good experience with the company in the past, you can also call the company and give out the specifics—monthly rent, size of the house, and your telephone number, for example.

Even if you use a rent locator, you still need to advertise in the newspaper. Your ad should include essential information: rent, size of the house or unit, whether a washer and dryer are on the premises, and pet policies. These are the questions that come up most often. An ad should start out with monthly rent, since this is where most people begin looking, and most classified ad sections are arranged in order of rent. The following is an example of a well-written ad:

$650—house, central location, 1,500 sq. ft.
3 bdrm. 2 bath w/d no pets. 555-1221.

This ad provides a lot of information in only two lines. The same information, when arranged poorly, is not as likely to attract many responses. For example:

Big house 3 bdrms. 2 baths. $650 month.
W/d included, no pets allowed. 555-1221.

In the second ad, rent is not listed first, so the ad probably will appear at the end of the other rental listings each day. And because it leaves out the reference to location, either many people will not call or all will have the same question—where is the house? Remember, location is important in every rental ad, especially for people who have to commute to work or school. Those who do not own a car will also want to know how close the property is to transportation lines.

To gain skill at writing short, effective ads, study the ads in your local paper. See which ones attract your attention and which ones do not sound interesting. Seeing what other people write is the best way to figure out what to say, or what not to say. For example, leaving off the rent amount will limit the phone calls you get and does nothing to screen the calls you do receive. Forgetting to put in your telephone numbers (a common mistake) gets you no calls at all, of course. Include all of the necessary elements in your ad, and you are likely to receive many interested calls.

Needing to Watch the Property

The distance factor can never be ignored when you invest in rental property. Being far away from the property may be the most overlooked problem of being a real estate investor.

Every small business owner discovers the problem of operating remote locations. A store in which the owner watches over merchandise, employees, and traffic every day can be highly profitable; however, when a second store is opened in another city, it is not likely to run as smoothly. Less profit and more problems with merchandise and employees have to be expected, because the owner cannot be there to watch things every day.

The same problems are found in real estate investing. It might seem that placing a reliable tenant in a house in a different city should not be a big problem. However, you need to expect to have more problems with remote properties than with those close by. Even going to the property to fix a minor problem will involve time and travel. A 30-minute trip represents a 1-hour round trip just to go to the property, so even a routine drive-by to see that the yard is being cared for is out of the way for you.

The following are some points to keep in mind about the location of property:

1. The farther away the property, the more problems you will have managing tenants.

2. It is easier to fill vacancies closer to home.

3. Distant properties are likely candidates for placing under management, assuming you can find a trustworthy property manager.

4. You need to be aware of real estate economics in more than one location when you invest in remote properties.

First-time real estate investors often underestimate the need to be aware of the economy in remote areas. Even within one small county, the economy of two different areas can be quite different. Remember, real estate cycles are extremely localized; national statistics are only averages and cannot be applied to your region or city. By the same argument, the economy within one area of your county can be vastly different from that of another area. For example, one county has a population of 120,000. Half of those people live in the largest city of the county, and the remainder live in the more rural outlying areas. A small town far removed from the city has an agricultural economy. This includes many dairy farms and berry-growing operations. A third area of the county is dominated by a large industrial employer. In this case, three distinct economic groups co-exist within a single county. It is likely that workers in the city, agricultural families, and industrial employees have vastly different economic factors at work. The consequence is that a positive change in one area might have little to do with the other two; however, a negative change can adversely affect all three economic groups. For example, what would happen if the industrial facility were to close down? It is likely that the other two groups would suffer. However, if an employer relocates in the city and creates new jobs, that is not as likely to have a direct, positive impact on the agricultural and industrial sectors.

The preceding example is typical of the economy in many areas. The point here is that, in order to invest in real estate in such a county, you need to be aware of the differences in the economy among the demographic and economic regions. Thus, if you have bought two or three rental properties in the city, you know about rental demand factors, the age groups in the tenant base, the market value of rentals, and the other realities of rental housing in the city. This does not mean that you should expect the same factors to be in play in the agricultural community or within the industrial base. All of the factors affecting your city-based market, for rentals as well as in real estate valuation, are likely to be far different in the other areas. The example concerns the economic differences within a single county. Imagine how much more complex the comparisons are likely to be when you invest in property outside of your own county. You would need to become familiar with all of the factors likely to influence real estate values and tenant demand levels. These include three primary elements:

1. *Tenant base.* Is rental demand driven by a large college-age population, working families, or the retirement market? In areas where a lot of new employment is occurring, companies import executive and management people, and higher-level rentals are in demand. In towns with large student populations, demand for share rentals or apartments can be high, but demand for single-family housing can be remarkably low at the same time. It is also important to remember that rental demand cycles are different for single-family housing than for multi-unit properties. The single-family tenant usually belongs to a far different demographic group.

2. *Political mood in the area.* Is the current government of a city or county progrowth or antigrowth, for example? If the current government is progrowth, a lot of construction may be underway, both residential and commercial. The real estate economy is probably in better health than the average because of the political factor. If the current government is antigrowth, that probably means that a limited supply of rental housing is relatively expensive, because demand tends to increase over time, regardless of the political mood. Antigrowth sentiment does not prevent growth; it tends to make growth occur in a more expensive manner. From the investment point of view, antigrowth political sentiment is good for investment value, even though it has a severe negative impact on the local citizens.

3. *Building trends.* How many new housing units were constructed last year? How long did they remain on the market? In a robust economy, housing is grabbed up as quickly as units are completed. This is the upswing timing in the real estate cycle. In an economy that is slowing down, housing tends to take longer to sell, and completed units may

have to be reduced in price. This is not a good time to get into a new area; the economic slow-down tends to affect real estate market values as well as rental demand.

Given these three primary factors affecting the economy of an area, it is obvious that investing in remote real estate is more complex than investing at home. You know these factors locally because you are there. You read the papers. You speak to other people where you live. The knowledge you have about real estate has been accumulated over time. It is far more difficult to gain the same level of expertise about another area. And when you consider how subtle changes in economic factors within one county can create completely different markets, you can appreciate how complex it is to gain an understanding of local markets for rental property.

Just as investors in the stock market need to study the fundamentals of a company before they invest, real estate investors need to study the fundamentals of property by area. A stock investor reads financial reports, looks at earnings and dividend histories, and judges the volatility of a stocks. This individual also considers sector strength, the company's position relative to its competition, and many other financial factors. Real estate investors have to do the same type of research, but they are not handed an audited financial statement about the economic and demographic forces at play in an area.

Considering how difficult it is to gain insights into property values and all of the factors influencing supply and demand, the idea of buying property outside of your immediate area is troubling. That does not mean that remote investments are poor ideas or that you won't make a profit buying property in another town. It does mean that the level of research will be more complex, and managing the property will be more difficult. As an absentee landlord, you will need to exercise perhaps a higher level of diligence with tenants than you do with the tenants a few blocks away, if only because of the distance factor.

Catching Problems Early

You might define a landlord as the person who needs to recognize small problems and to solve them before they become large problems. The typical stockholder in a publicly listed company has nothing to say concerning management of the company; control applies insofar as one has the ability to buy or sell shares, based on information and changes in market price. A landlord, in comparison, *is* the company. The decisions you make affect the investment value of your property.

Looking for small problems and solving them early has to take place in at least two areas: the condition of the property and the status of the tenant. The condition of the property includes the maintenance requirements associated with all houses: the need to keep plumbing and electrical systems in working order, to repair leaking roofs, and to do away with hazards, for example. Preventive maintenance involves taking out a tree that is threatening to fall on the house, cutting dry brush away from outside walls, and putting in proper drainage during the dry months to prevent flooding later.

The status of the tenant requires a different sort of policing on your part. You need to keep an eye out for telltale signs of emerging problems. These may occur early on, even during the application process. An applicant who does not have a bank account, one who wants to barter part of the rent, or one who cannot come up with the required deposit, for example, is an indication of more trouble coming your way later. Any applicant with these attributes, not to mention one who lacks suitable references or elicits negative reports from references, should be used as the basis for disqualification. Only by making that decision early on can you select suitable applicants and avoid the kinds of problems every landlord dreads.

Once your tenant is in the property, the most likely early warning sign is late payment of rent or partial payment with a promise to deliver the rest later. A tenant who cannot plan ahead so that all of the rent money is available on the first of the month probably cannot afford your rent level or cannot manage his or her money well. In either case, you need to correct the problem swiftly and permanently. Most tenants, on realizing that you insist on prompt payment of rent every month, will find a way to plan for that and will make payments on time. The majority of tenants will prove to be faithful in their rental payments, even if they are consistently late by a day or two. The few whom you need to chase after each month are likely to present you with other problems as well.

Some examples of early signs of trouble, such as household garbage being piled up in the yard or garage, have been mentioned previously. Also look for signs that the yard is not being maintained according to your agreement with the tenant. If you let this condition go, it will be difficult, if not impossible, to correct it later. You need to contact the tenants at the first sign of maintenance problems and insist that they take steps to keep their end of the contract. A tenant may have an excuse such as, "I don't own a lawn mower." However, you have a contract with the tenant; he or she needs to find a cheap, used lawn mower or to hire someone else to do the yard work. Some landlords lend used mowers to tenants, so that excuse is taken away. It is true that tenants often do not think about buying yard maintenance equipment; however, if they want to rent a house instead of an apartment, they also need to spend money to buy the equipment they need or to hire someone else.

Also look for signs that the tenant is not keeping the property neat. Trash in the yard should be considered an alarming sign. Not only is it disturbing to your neighbors and unsightly on the outside, but you can be assured that the inside of the property will be far worse when you can see litter on the outside.

Another sign of trouble is the acquisition of a pet, when the contract specifies (and the tenant agreed) that no pets were allowed in the house. Some tenants think that when they get a house, they also need a cat or a dog. The correct procedure, of course, is to talk to the landlord first and pay any additional deposits if required. However, some people overlook this step and just go out and buy a pet. It is an extreme sign of danger when the tenant gets more than one pet.

One tenant was given notice when the landlord discovered that she had six cats. When told that the cats had to go, she refused, so the landlord gave notice. When she left, she was behind in the rent, and the inside of the house was full of junk, requiring at least three truckloads of discarded belongings be taken to the dump. The clean-up took more than a day and cost the landlord money. The combination of lost rent and cleaning exceeded the deposit, not to mention the landlord's time.[*] In this case, the tenant's act of getting numerous pets told the landlord that there was trouble brewing, a belief that was reinforced when the tenant left a big mess behind. There should be little doubt that, given time, this situation would have become far worse. When tenants begin moving away from the observation of their contract, it invariably deteriorates, so any sign whatsoever of emerging problems should be taken as a sign of worse things to come. You will be better off with a period of lost rent due to vacancy than you will in putting off solving the problem.

Some landlords make an arrangement with the local utility company that any past-due billings are to be sent to the tenant *and* a copy sent to the landlord. This service is valuable and many local utilities offer it, recognizing that it is more likely that they will collect past-due accounts with the landlord's help. From your point of view, when tenants are 30 days or more past due on their water and sewer, electricity, gas, cable, or telephone bills, rent may be next on the list. By ensuring that past-due utility bills are paid, you can prevent losing rent in the near future. If the tenants are unwilling or unable to pay their past-due bills, they should be given

---

[*]This is an actual case history from the author's experience as a landlord. When told she would have to move if the cats were not given away, her response was, "My aunt died." The attempt to get sympathy and a delay in termination of the rent did not work.

notice. This is especially good advice for utilities whose unpaid balances go with the property. In other words, if tenants leave without paying their bills, you end up being responsible. This is usually true for garbage pick-up, water and sewer, and other municipal utilities. Your policy should be to telephone a tenant as soon as you receive a past-due notice and advise the tenant that the bill has to be paid within one week or you will terminate the rental agreement.*

Planning Maintenance

Tenant status requires that you watch your property continuously. The outward appearance of the house reveals a lot about what is going on inside. You cannot violate your tenant's right to privacy with constant demands to enter the premises, but you can see what you need to see just by driving by. A different level of planning is required for the more predictable maintenance functions.

If you live in an area with especially cold winters, you will need to plan for winterizing the rental property. Don't expect your tenants to winterize. Even when you build the requirement into your agreement, tenants will not necessarily take the basic steps needed to protect your property. The usual steps include adding temporary insulation, such as wrapping pipes beneath the house or placing protective devices over outside faucets. You should plan a prewinter inspection of your rental property, even when winterizing is the tenant's responsibility. A brief visit to the property is preferable to an emergency call to the plumber due to burst water pipes.

Also plan for periodic maintenance of the systems. Your heating system should be checked every year and the filter removed and cleaned or replaced. This is required more frequently if you live in a warmer climate and have air conditioning as well as heat. While your tenant should be responsible for keeping gutters clear, you should check periodically to ensure that this is being done. You may end up having to do some maintenance on your own, especially if an otherwise excellent tenant simply does not want to get up on a ladder and remove leaves and debris from the gutters.

If you live in warmer climates, you should also do an annual inspection for signs of termites and other pests. If you do not know what to look for in your region, it is worth hiring a pest control specialist to perform an

---

*This is a practical idea in a month-to-month rental situation. If you have a longer-term lease with your tenant, build a provision into the lease specifying that any unpaid utility bills are a violation of the agreement and are grounds for giving notice. However, before adding such a clause to the lease, check with your attorney to ensure that it is enforceable; if not, require a larger deposit to protect yourself against the cost of having to pay a tenant's utility bills.

inspection periodically. Depending on the area and the likelihood of infestation, an inspection and necessary spraying might be needed as frequently as once per year. Typically, an inspection costs about $50, money well spent to prevent severe damage. Such damages are not covered under most homeowners' insurance policies, so investing money to have an inspection is a wise form of preventive maintenance.

Some preventive steps are required if a house has special problems. If, for example, your house is in a heavily wooded area, you need to clean out gutters more frequently than once per year, and you need to treat roofs to prevent moss from taking hold, either by installing a zinc strip or spreading a special powder on the roof.

In warmer climates, houses exposed to the full sun need outside painting more frequently than the typical five- to eight-year cycle that most houses experience. The same house might also require a higher level and cost for yard maintenance, including watering, lawn mowing, and measures to prevent losing plants to dry, warm weather.

Each house has its own maintenance requirements, and you need to be aware of and schedule preventive maintenance steps. Older houses require more frequent maintenance and probably cost more than newer-built housing. Many landlords end up with older property, because the pricing, condition, and terms make these houses more practical and suitable as rental property, especially when you start out investing in real estate. Thus, the maintenance schedule you develop should be tailored to the house—its age, condition, and special circumstances or problems.

Under your contract with a tenant, you have the right of access to your property for maintenance. You need to give your tenant the required advance notification—in most states, 24 or 48 hours—in an emergency, the advance notice requirement is waived. What can you do, though, if your tenant does not cooperate? Because your rental agreement should spell out your rights as well as the tenants', you can always refer to the document in a discussion with the tenant. Also point out that the law supports the clause providing you with access to perform maintenance. It is helpful if you can supply your tenant with a summary of your state's landlord-tenant law in such circumstances, and many states publish brochures or booklets summarizing the provisions affecting tenants and defining their rights. Ultimately, a reasonable tenant will acknowledge your right to access as well as the need for maintenance; these steps make the home safer and more secure, as well as protecting your investment. By the same argument, an unreasonable tenant might take the position that he or she does not want the landlord to enter the premises; if that persists, you may need to give notice.

The extreme case occurs when tenants change the locks without permission from their landlords and without supplying the landlords with a duplicate key. This is a violation of your contract and is specifically disallowed. Thus, if a tenant does change the locks, you need to take immediate action to get a key or end the rental agreement. The right to access is an absolute requirement for you as a landlord; it is not only your right but also your responsibility to be able to get into the property when necessary. In an emergency, for example, fire or police personnel will expect the landlord to have a key.

Most landlords are able to develop a good working relationship with their tenants, even if it comes down to an uneasy truce. As long as you operate within the terms of your contract, respecting your tenants' privacy and contacting them only when necessary, most people will be reasonable in their role as tenants. The less frequent case of confrontation and expense is the experience you will remember, of course, but it is an exception, and that is important to remember.

The combined need to monitor property condition and tenant status are intrinsic aspects of being a real estate investor. It is rare that a property or tenant will require no maintenance or monitoring on your part. If you are fortunate enough to find a property and a tenant that takes little of your time, then don't disturb that situation. However, even in the best of situations, continue to keep on eye on your property from afar. It is better to ensure that nothing has changed by driving by the property from time to time than to discover a problem after it is too late.

CHAPTER 9

Managing the Investment Aspects of Real Estate

The investment aspects of real estate include everything except tenants and related matters. When dealing with tenants, you face several risks: extended occupancy in a soft rental demand market, a litigious and unreasonable tenant making endless demands and withholding rent, and an inability to attract the tenants that you believe are a good match for your property. For assuming those risks, you are entitled to receive rent, which is intended to cover your mortgage payments and other costs.

The balance between risk and opportunity has to be weighed in every investment before you decide whether it is right for you. Some people do not want to deal with the tenancy side of the equation, even while recognizing the significant investment opportunities of real estate. Others are willing to accept the risk and inconvenience of working with a range of tenants, in exchange for the cash flow, tax benefits, and long-term appreciation that real estate can bring, often to a far greater extent than those of other forms of investment.

Weighing risk and opportunity should include a study of not only the relationship between landlord and tenant but also the other side of the matter: the investment side.

Using Professional Help

When you buy and hold shares of stock, your contact with outside help usually is quite limited. You might invest on the advice of a stockbroker or financial planner, for example. In growing numbers, stock investors are using Internet-based discount brokerage services, meaning that no direct professional advice is used at all. Such investors may also perform their own research, using free online services, such as those providing annual reports and financial statements of publicly listed companies.

For stockholders, there is often no contact with professionals. For real estate investors, professional help is not only more frequent, but it often is an unavoidable aspect of being a real estate investor. In order to succeed, you need to develop a network of professional contacts of varying specialization. You need to work with people and firms that you know and trust, and you cannot afford to pick a name out of the telephone book. Professionals you are likely to need include the following:

1. *Accountant.* Because you have the right to deduct expenses, depreciate capital assets, and defer gain on property, real estate is unique among investments. It is the sole legitimate remaining tax shelter, the only one allowing you to deduct passive losses. However, the taxation and reporting of real estate transactions are complex matters, and you should consult with a professional accountant at the very beginning of your experience as a real estate investor. First, you should be sure that you understand how a particular transaction will affect your deductions and tax status. For example, if you own many properties, the sum of net losses could exceed your annual ceiling for deductions, or, if your adjusted gross income is higher than $100,000 per year, the benefits are phased out.

An accountant should be familiar with real estate taxation on both federal and state levels and should be willing to work with you in a program of year-round tax planning. For example, a decision you make today can be beneficial (or have negative consequences) in terms of what you owe in income taxes, so you need to consult regularly with a tax expert before proceeding. A periodic appointment for planning purposes should be adequate, so that your professional fees are not excessive. However, a competent accountant can help educate you about how to plan ahead, set up your books, document transactions, and make elections available to you under the tax laws. When you decide to sell an investment property, the accountant can also help you set up the proper methods to defer gains through a tax-free exchange.

2. *Attorney.* You need to consult with a real estate attorney from time to time. You may need advice concerning the specific landlord-tenant laws in your state, or you might need help if you need to evict a tenant. An attorney who understands real estate can help you in a variety of situations that can arise when you invest in rental property.

3. *Escrow agent or attorney.* Whenever you buy or sell property, you need to go through a series of steps: making a title search; getting title insurance; legally transferring title through the preparation of deeds, promissory notes, and other documents; recording documents; arrang-

ing needed inspections and payments for the cost of inspections; and more. This involves not only going through a series of steps and preparation of paperwork but also handling funds from buyer, seller, and lender.

In some states, the closing process is managed by licensed escrow agents working through an escrow agency, which often also includes affiliation with a title insurance company. The licensed escrow agent works for both sides and ensures that all money is transferred according to the contract and that all required documents are properly prepared, signed, notarized, and recorded. In other states, the same process is managed by an attorney who provides the same services but is not referred to as an escrow agent. To some, it might seem that any escrow company or attorney can do the job. However, if you transact a large volume of real estate business over time, it is always a good idea to develop a relationship with a firm in your area and to use that firm for all of your business, when possible.

4. *Insurance agent.* You need to insure all of your real estate, whether used as your home or as rental property. Some investors (and homeowners) make the mistake of failing to shop around and not recognizing the importance of service. If you place all of your emphasis on cost, you may find the lowest-priced insurance, but there may come a day when you need claims service as well; in that case, a professional and capable agent will be a valuable ally. You need to find an agent who provides excellent service as well as competitive prices and work with that agent for your insurance needs.

You also need to consider whether you need insurance beyond homeowners' coverage. Some companies market so-called mortgage insurance, which is nothing more than life insurance whose coverage is tied to the balance of your mortgage debt. Compare prices if you need to insure your life to pay off the mortgage in the event of your death. You may discover that you can get cheaper premiums buying a regular decreasing term policy, without working through an insurance company trying to sell mortgage insurance.

Another form of insurance you might be required to carry is called hazard insurance. Some lenders call it mortgage insurance, so you need to understand the distinction between this product and life insurance. Hazard insurance may be required by a lender if your mortgage debt is more than 20 percent of the purchase price of the property. This insurance protects the lender against default and is very expensive, adding to your total monthly payment. If you pay down a loan to the point that your equity exceeds 20 percent of the original price, you need to supply the lender with an appraisal. However, you might need to insist repeatedly on having the mortgage insurance canceled, even though you meet the requirement. Some lenders are hesitant to cancel the insurance, because it protects them. If you can negotiate a loan without hazard insurance, it can save you thousands of dollars. In some cases, it is worthwhile to put a higher down payment on the property or to borrow part of a down payment through a second mortgage to avoid having to pay hazard insurance.

5. *Loan specialist.* So much of the cost of property is actually interest that most investors should spend more time shopping for the best possible mortgage deal. Most people focus on looking for a bargain price of property and concentrate on squeezing a thousand dollars or so out of the price. Ironically, the same investor may fail to shop around for the best deal. In some cases, you are better off paying a higher sales price but getting a better financing package. Over the long term, the real cost of housing is found in the amount of interest you pay. In comparison, the difference of $1,000 to $2,000 in the sales price is insignificant. For example, a loan of 8 percent on $100,000 will cost you $264,000 over a 30-year term. You would save over $12,000 by negotiating that rate down to 7 1/2 percent.

With these facts in mind, it makes sense to work with a lender or mortgage broker who can find you the best possible deal. In the past, investors borrowed from their local banks or savings and loan associations; today, however, it is increasingly popular to use mortgage brokers representing lenders all over the country or even to find a lender online.

SIDEBAR

An online search of *mortgage lender* will result in locating many sources for competitive loans online. Four typical web sites that provide this service are
http://www.getsmart.com/
http://www.analysishomeloan.com/
http://www.thenetbusiness.com/
http://www.planetloan.com/

The days of personal banking may be gone. When it comes to finding the best mortgage for your investment property, it makes sense to find the best deal by searching on your own or by locating a mortgage broker who is willing to look for a good deal for you. In either case, you will end up working with one primary source, either in person or over the Internet. Your confidence in that person's integrity is critical, because finding the best mortgage loan will translate into a savings—or a cost—of many thousands of dollars over the coming years.

6. *Appraiser.* When you buy a property, the lender requires an appraisal in virtually every case. Some banks use their own appraisers, and

others hire local firms to do the job for them. Remember, an appraisal is an estimate of value, and appraisers have a lot of leeway in the conclusions that they draw. A lot depends on who hires them to do the appraisal and for what purpose. For example, a lender might tell an appraiser that the borrower's credit is good; the property should appraise well, assuming that its value is within a reasonable range. At the other extreme, an individual going through a divorce might hire an appraiser and would want as low a value as possible assigned to the property. This means that a spouse keeping the property will have less of a settlement with the departing spouse. Thus, while appraisers have to make their best estimates in setting values, they are influenced by the underlying purpose of the appraisal and by the individual who pays for the service. The appraiser finds comparable properties and adjusts values up or down, depending on a number of factors and variables; thus, a skilled appraiser is motivated not only to set values fairly but also to perform as well as possible for the company or person who will pay the bill.

7. *Home inspector.* A qualified home inspector is essential for you, both as a buyer and as a seller. On either side of the transaction, you may be required to have a third party inspect the property, looking for any defects, especially those invisible to the casual observer. If you find a professional inspector to evaluate properties you are buying or selling, that can be a valuable relationship. An objective inspection should be done by someone who is experienced and licensed by the American Society of Home Inspectors (ASHI), who cannot also offer to perform needed repair work, who will not even refer you to someone to do repairs for you, and who provides you with a written report explaining the findings during the inspection. These qualifiers ensure that the appraiser is objective.

8. *Contractors.* You need to work with a variety of contractors while you own investment real estate. Even if you do not specialize in the fixer-upper market, the time will come when you need to hire a pest control specialist, a plumber, an electrician, a roofer, a carpenter, a landscaper, or another contractor. Be sure that the person you hire is currently licensed and in good standing, is bonded, and has local referrals. Check those referrals and check with your local Chamber of Commerce and Better Business Bureau. Search on the Internet to see whether your state's licensing board publishes any information about contractors in your area. Also be sure that you contact the contractor, not the other way around. Legitimate contractors do not go door-to-door, telling you work is needed on your house, they don't make special discount offers in exchange for showing your house as a model, and they do not solicit work over the telephone. If you are able to find licensed, qualified people to work for you, then you will know the work will be of high quality and dependable.

9. *Real estate agent.* Finally, you will work with at least one real estate agent. It makes sense to use the same person whenever you want to sell property, as long as he or she has worked well for you in the past. Many investors find agents when they begin looking for property by going to open houses or by walking into real estate offices. This method is hit-or-miss at best; you are better off asking for referrals and locating an experienced agent who specializes in investment property. Most agents do *not* specialize in that way, so you need to qualify agents carefully.

Finding a qualified agent is more difficult than it might seem at first, because you cannot know whether someone can help you until you go through a buy or sell transaction. However, you can tell if someone has a professional attitude by how smoothly a transaction goes. You might also conclude that it makes sense to work with different agents when you are in the role of buyer or seller. Some agents specialize in getting a lot of listings, whereas others work more closely with buyers and take them to properties listed on Multiple Listing Services. An agent who has a lot of his or her own listings is motivated to show you only those properties, because if you buy one, it doubles the commission. The commission usually is split between the listing agent and broker on one side and the selling agent and broker on the other; thus, when a listing agent also sells the property, the compensation is doubled. The agent gets both sides.

Remember that agents always work for the seller. While they are legally obligated to protect a buyer's interests, too, their commissions come from the seller's proceeds. As a matter of common sense, when you are in the role of buyer, be sure you protect your own interests. Remember that anything promised to you verbally also has to go into the contract; if it is not in writing, it is not part of the deal.

Finding and Screening Professionals

The best way to find qualified professional help is to ask for referrals from other investors or professionals and see which names come up. Retain professionals who give you a sense of confidence. Follow these general guidelines when looking for professional help:

1. *Ask for referrals.* It makes no sense to retain someone based only on a meeting. Considering the expensive nature of professional help, you need to contact more than one person, compare prices or fees, and check them out. Rather than depending on luck, ask your banker, realtor, or accountant to refer you to competent sources for assistance. That invariably works out better than other methods.

2. *Check licensing and experience.* Don't take someone's word for it that he or she holds a current license or required designation. Check it out. Contacting industry groups is easy with access to the Internet; even without a computer, the telephone still serves as a useful research tool. For example, you may feel confident because a contractor has a state license number on his or her business card, but how do you know it is current or even valid? Investing a little bit of time may save you a lot of grief; make sure all licenses and designations are solid; if you discover that any are not, don't retain the person.

3. *Make changes if things do not go well.* Smart investors cut their losses. If you end up hiring someone who does not work out, fire the person without any remorse and find someone else. Typical problems include doing unacceptable work, overbilling, not returning telephone calls, and not finishing a job. These problems are not acceptable, and when you think about the financial size of your investment, you should insist on using only top professional help.

4. *Pay attention to your hunches.* Never ignore your instincts. If you have a negative sense of a person, find someone else. Most people know that their first impressions usually are correct; if they ignore those impressions, they often regret it later.

Problems with Co-investors

An aspect of investing that is not often discussed is the problems of buying rental property with someone else. This usually is a spouse, but good friends, people living together, and business associates also can buy property held in joint tenancy, sharing ownership.

If you invest with a business partner, you probably will want to visit an attorney and draw up a contract that covers all of the bases that you can anticipate. However, when investing with a friend or a spouse, you might ignore this step. That could be a mistake.

Imagine the following situation. A husband and wife invest in rental property, buying four rental houses over a two-year period. They agree that, after five years, they should sell the property and invest the money elsewhere. They know that owning rental property means working with tenants, meeting ongoing maintenance demands, and putting occasional strains on the family budget; with so much invested in real estate, they agree at the beginning of the venture that it will be short-term.

After five years, the husband begins bringing up the subject of selling. He has gone through the cycle and has enjoyed the tax benefits of owning real estate, but now it is time to move on. However, the wife does not want to sell and refuses to agree to the idea, even to selling one or two of the properties. What now?

If the agreed-upon plan is entirely verbal, then the spouse who does *not* want to sell has all of the power. This places a strain not only on the couple's financial and investing situation but also on their entire relationship. If there had been a binding contract, the husband could, at the very least, insist on following the agreement and staying with the original deadline. There is no reason that a married couple cannot enter a legal contract as business associates; in fact, it can be the only safe way to invest in a long-term situation such as owning rental property.

The fact is, real estate investing can take up a lot of time, and you might get discouraged at times with unreasonable tenants, higher than expected occupancy rates, or problems with the house itself. An accumulation of problems eventually wears you down, so that the advantages—tax benefits, cash flow, and so forth—begin to pale in value. When you invest in real estate, as with any other choice, you need not only to understand the risks involved, but also an exit strategy. When will you sell? Will the decision be based on a specific date, appreciation in market value, or another event?

If you are going to invest in real estate with anyone else, even a spouse, follow these important guidelines:

1. *Decide at the beginning of the venture which person has veto power over the other.* It is not always a welcome idea, but the truth is that one person has to have the final word. Even in a business partnership that is owned on a 50-50 basis, each partner is deadlocked unless one is recognized as having the final say. Within a marriage, both partners have to agree to the same terms. One of the two has to have the right to make a decision that breaks a tie, and the other one needs to agree to this arrangement.

If this arrangement is not included in the contract and agreed on by both sides, there may be trouble later on. At some point, you will disagree with your investment partner. If neither has the express veto power, then both sides will want it; this only leads to a disintegration in the relationship. No matter what happens, someone is going to be unhappy. This can be avoided by agreeing in advance which side has the final word. This is the only practical way to co-invest.

2. *Draw up a written contract that specifies how or when you will sell property.* A sensible contract needs to be finite. It needs to spell out the terms under which property will be sold. This may be written into the contract on the basis of the time you agree to invest, a specific market value or percentage increase in value, or other event (such as a child graduating from high school and going to college). The written contract protects both

sides, and even within a marriage, enforcing the terms of the contract might be the only way to settle a disagreement about how to proceed.

3. *Keep to the contract unless both agree to modify it.* On a practical level, it is always easier on any relationship to negotiate your way through a disagreement. This is true for a business or investing venture, which still applies even when the partners happen to be married. The contract should provide the means for settling a disagreement. Thus, in that respect, it can help settle a dispute that otherwise could not be settled without one person's being unhappy with the outcome.

It is necessary to separate the investment relationship from the personal—advice more easily given than followed but essential if you plan to co-invest. Both sides need to protect their positions and to proceed with certainty. One side knows that the contract protects him or her in terms of having an exit strategy; the other side is required to accept that deadline, whether he or she is happy with it or not. The point is, without the definition about how or when the investment plan will end, the very idea of buying property together has been defined poorly and is likely to cause problems later on.

4. *Approach real estate investing in a practical manner.* When you buy stocks or shares of a mutual fund, you usually have an idea about when you will sell. For example, some investors are wise to take the step of defining exactly what will trigger a sell order. For example, you might buy stock with the idea that, if your market value doubles, you will take profits or, if you lose 25 percent, you will bail out. This defines how you plan to sell and is a practical exit strategy. Other investors plan to hold their stock market investments until a child graduates from high school, until they retire, or until they accumulate a specific amount to start a small business. In other words, they structure their investment strategies around specific investing goals; they then use the goals to structure the entire investment.

5. *Don't invest together if you cannot trust your partner.* Whenever you enter into a co-investing situation (or any other contract), that venture should be based on trust. You probably have various personal and professional relationships and degrees of trust with the people you know. Some people are good for their word, but others are not. Even within a marriage, some people know that their spouses cannot be trusted to keep a promise. This knowledge often is unspoken, but the fact is out there. Given such knowledge, is it wise to enter into a contract for real estate investing, or anything else?

It makes no sense to proceed under those conditions. In any contract, the good faith of both parties is the essential starting point. Even a contract that spells out all of the terms is only good for so much, because if the parties cannot trust one another, the whole venture is a mistake from its beginning. Before co-investing in real estate, be sure that your partner is trustworthy and that your ability to maintain a practical working relationship will not be jeopardized because someone changes his or her mind down the road.

Stocks can be bought or sold under most arrangements by a telephone call. Remember, though, with real estate the transaction is more complex, is more expensive, and—most important of all—usually requires the signatures of both people. Thus, when spouses or other co-investors own property together, they both have to agree to sell property as long as both are listed as owners, so the one who does not want to sell has the real veto power in this situation. Draw up a contract and have it reviewed by your attorney *before* buying real estate in co-ownership with anyone else. It is less expensive to see the attorney at the beginning of this process than it is to hire legal help later when a disagreement arises.

Even owning a personal residence with someone else can complicate matters. In a marital situation, divorce often means a forced sale, even when one side would rather keep the property. If you purchase a residence with a co-owner to whom you are *not* married, ending the relationship can be especially complicated. For example, if you move out of a house you co-own with someone else (not a husband or wife) and you want to dissolve the ownership of the property, it is easy if (1) the other person will buy out your interest at an agreed-upon amount, (2) the property is sold and the proceeds are split, or (3) the co-owner agrees to let you buy out his or her share. However, what can you do if your co-owner will not buy you out or allow you to take over the property? In this situation, you are still liable for mortgage and property tax payments and for keeping the property insured. However, you do not live there, and you have no way to force the other person to liquidate the property. You need to hire an attorney and go to court, and if your equity is not substantial, it might not be practical to go through the cost of litigating the matter.

Whether you buy rental property or a residence with someone else, be sure you have already defined how or when the investment will be sold. Put it down on paper. Check with your attorney beforehand, and if potential problems arise in which your equity would be jeopardized, avoid putting yourself in harm's way.

Real Estate Partnerships

As an alternative to buying real estate on your own, you can enter into a partnership with other individuals, or "entities" (meaning partnerships or corporations). There are various kinds of partnership arrangements that can be structured to operate an investment portfolio, and one might work for you as another way to buy rental property.

The relatively simple two-person partnership requires a determination as to who has the right to break a deadlock. It makes no sense to structure a 50-50 partnership, because inevitably a disagreement is going to arise. With that in mind, a three-person partnership is more practical, because there can be no deadlock as long as all three people vote. However, the more people involved in a partnership, the greater the risk that something will go wrong. For example, if you and two other friends decide to go into real estate investing together, what happens if one of the three wants out? That would require selling property or raising capital adequate to pay off that person's partnership share. Problems arise when property values have not risen enough to make it easy to buy out a departing member of the venture. You may need to give the third partner a promissory note, meaning greater strain on cash flow for the remaining two partners.

Income tax reporting is complicated for partnerships. You need to file an information return for federal taxes, called a Form 1065. This return asks for much more information than does the relatively simple Schedule E used for reporting individually owned real estate.

The partnership return is filed, and each partner is given a Schedule K-1, which summarizes his or her share of partnership ordinary income or loss, capital gains, and other items that have to be reported on their individual tax returns.

In addition to the more complicated tax reporting, there is also a question about the deductibility of passive losses. It might not be possible to deduct partnership losses the way that individuals can; consultation with a tax expert is essential before deciding to structure a real estate partnership. You could lose valuable deductions and tax benefits by forming a partnership.

The partnership formed between two or more individuals and operated by them—meaning that each partner contributes to the management of properties—is called a general partnership. Another way to invest is through a limited partnership. In this arrangement, two classes of partners are involved. General partners operate and manage properties, and limited partners contribute capital but have no direct say in how the partnership is operated.

If you invest in a limited partnership or a similar real estate management company, you probably will not be able to deduct passive losses for tax purposes. By definition, partnerships usually do not meet the rules allowing you to claim passive losses. Limited partners are not allowed to participate in managing properties, so their losses have to be carried forward and offset against passive gains in future years.

Yet another way to invest in real estate is through a conduit investment. The best-known examples are mortgage pools and real estate investment trusts (REITs). A mortgage pool operates as a mutual fund; however, instead of investing in stocks or bonds, the mortgage pool puts together packages of mortgages and sells shares to individual investors. You earn interest income in a mortgage pool, which is taxable, and you have no direct voice in the management of the mortgage pool, and certainly not over the structure of the mortgages themselves. The mortgage pool is not taxed, and all taxable income is passed through to investors (thus the descriptive name "conduit"). Most national mortgage pools are operated and marketed by what is broadly called the secondary market (see Chapter 1). Organizations such as the Federal National Mortgage Association (FNMA), also called "Fannie Mae," and the Government National Mortgage Association (GNMA), also called "Ginnie Mae," are the largest mortgage pool organizations. Mortgages written by commercial lenders are sold on the secondary market and formed into pools; then shares are sold to the public.

REITs are also like mutual funds in the sense that they are formed with investment capital from many people. REIT shares are traded publicly over stock exchanges, so they are more liquid than other forms of real estate ownership. REITs can also be subdivided into equity, mortgage, construction, and hybrid classifications. An equity REIT has equity positions in real estate, often large projects such as shopping centers or industrial parks. Mortgage REITs lend money secured by real estate. Construction REITs are generally the highest risk and are formed to finance the development and construction of real estate projects, usually commercial or industrial ones. A hybrid REIT combines features of the other classifications, usually involving equity and mortgage features.

While there are many ways to own real estate other than direct ownership, none supply the direct control and tax benefits that you enjoy when you own and manage your own properties. Considering the risks of working with tenants, not to mention the market risks found in all forms of investing, each person has to determine whether direct ownership of real estate makes sense. For many, the answer is that it does make sense, but not indefinitely. There comes a point when even the most ambitious real estate investor wants to sell and replace rental property with something else.

Solutions for Long-Term Management

What guidelines should you follow to effectively manage your real estate holdings? While everyone can identify his or her risk profile in terms of the types of investments that are appropriate, real estate investors, because they often need to stay involved for the long term, might find that their goals evolve over time.

All investment goals are dynamic. People change, as do their economic and personal situations, so it is also reasonable to expect that what works for you today might not be as attractive in the future. Typically, direct ownership of real estate makes sense for people who have an adequate income to gain approval for financing, the personal energy to manage and maintain properties, and the willingness to put up with tenants for the foreseeable future. As years go by and investors grow, they may discover that their personal time is taking a greater priority, and the desire to build equity is less of a priority. This can be expected to happen in the normal course of events, especially if you accumulate equity over many years— from real estate, savings, retirement funds, and other investments.

The following are 10 suggested guidelines for managing long-term real estate holdings:

1. *Review your goals periodically.* Remember that your goals should change over time. This occurs as your economic and personal status changes and as you gain experience as an investor. Review your goals regularly to ensure that you are still happy with the investment decisions you have made. Change your investments when you no longer have the goals you had when you made your original decision to invest.

2. *Trade undesirable properties for desirable ones.* Some dissatisfaction in a real estate portfolio comes from a problem with a particular property. Rather than getting out completely, you might consider trading that property for another. By selling one property through a 1031 tax-free exchange, you have no tax consequences. Your problems might be associated with the age, condition, or other features of the property, and trading it for another might solve the problem.

3. *Trade up when practical.* Build equity over many years by trading modestly priced properties for higher-priced ones, as long as the new property continues to work as a rental. Very high-priced single-family residences often do not work as rentals simply because the rent you would need to receive to pay your costs would be too high. However, you can trade single-family residences for duplexes, triplexes, and even apartment complexes. Cash flow improves when you trade for higher-unit properties, so think of trading up in terms of multi-unit investments.

4. *Diversify your overall portfolio.* Never place all of your available capital in real estate, or any other single investment. Diversify in terms of type of product among stocks, real estate, savings, mutual funds, and other products. Real estate, like other markets, is cyclical, so you might need to last through very slow periods; at the same time, the stock

market might be performing quite well, so it makes sense to have portions of your capital invested in various markets.

5. *Emphasize the best returns and remain flexible.* In deciding where to invest the larger segments of your capital, look for the best-performing markets. Remember to compare risks, so that a decision is based on the whole picture—risk/opportunity *and* potential return based on cyclical performance. Be willing to change your emphasis quickly as markets change, while also recognizing that, in general, real estate is a long-term investment, and you might need several years for the market to season.

6. *Remember that tax ceilings limit the scope of your plan.* An often overlooked aspect of real estate limits your passive loss deductions to $25,000 per year. Were it not for this limit, it would make sense to own dozens of properties. For many reasons, however, this is rarely practical. It makes more sense to own between one and four properties, which is a manageable level and normally will stay within the $25,000 loss level. When losses exceed $25,000, they have to be carried over to future years, and if you are experiencing negative cash flow, the loss of tax benefits makes the cash problem less tolerable.

7. *Consider transfers between personal residence and investments.* While you should keep your family's personal residence separate from your investments as a general rule, some situations make it practical to switch. For example, if you want to trade up and buy a larger, more expensive home, it might make sense to finance your new home as your personal residence and make your current home a rental property. In this way, you may qualify for more favorable interest terms and a lower down payment, and you avoid the cost of selling your home. In another situation, you might also reclassify a rental property as your primary residence. In consultation with a tax advisor, this might make sense if you plan to sell the property in two years or more, because any gain is tax-free, in most situations. (The exception, of course, is that depreciation is recaptured and taxed as ordinary income.)

8. *Remember that financing costs are more significant than sales prices.* If you lose out on an investment property because you and the seller are haggling over a few thousand dollars in the price, that is unfortunate. However, if you win the negotiation and save a few thousand dollars but end up with expensive financing, that ultimately will cost you far more. A 1/2 percent interest rate cut on a $100,000 loan will run about $12,000 over 30 years, so it makes sense to put your time and effort into finding attractive financing and paying a little more for the property.

9. *Never allow investment features to overrule personal priorities.* Direct management of investment properties often means sacrificing personal time

to work on fixer-upper houses, to deal with tenant problems, and to perform chores. This is fine, as long as you want to spend your time nurturing your investment, especially if you and your spouse work on properties together. As long as a husband and wife are sharing goals, they strengthen one another and can get considerable personal enjoyment working together on their investments. However, as personal goals change, those goals should take priority over financial considerations. Otherwise, it is not worth the trouble. What value is there in having equity building in your real estate portfolio if it places your personal relationships at risk? Your personal priorities should always come first.

10. *Consider mixing equity and debt positions in real estate.* Some real estate investors get out of direct ownership by becoming lenders. If you have built up considerable equity in a property, perhaps even paid off your loan in full, and you want to sell, you have two choices. First, you can sell the property and take the cash—a desirable option but one that presents a couple of new problems: you have to decide where to invest the funds, and cashing out usually means you also have to pay taxes on the gain plus recaptured depreciation. Your second choice is to sell the property on the installment method, spreading profits out over several years. (Check with your tax advisor to ensure that you qualify before deciding to pursue this course.) When you sell your property on the installment method, you also take back a note. When you do that, you become the lender. As with all types of investing, taking a debt position requires that you have the required risk tolerance level. You may have to chase down monthly payments, and, in extreme cases, you might even need to foreclose on a defaulted loan. However, if you own a property free and clear when you sell, consider the significant income you receive in interest payments by carrying the note yourself. It could equal or exceed rental income. You sacrifice the tax benefits when you transfer to a lender, of course; however, for many, that is an acceptable way out of ownership of real estate.

Anyone who goes into real estate investing needs to recognize that, over the years, his or her attitude toward the property is going to change. This occurs in many ways and for a variety of reasons. Positive changes in attitude result from an appreciated real estate market, good experiences with tenants, and positive cash flow. By the same argument, negative changes in attitude can be expected when the real estate market is flat or falling, when bad experiences with tenants change your outlook, and when a weak market results in negative cash flow. Your overall attitude toward directly managed real estate is going to change from one year to the next, based on the mix of your experiences, your profit and tax benefits, and the degree to which you enjoy the experience of owning rental property and dealing with tenants.

As an investor, you participate in the economy far differently than most consumers do. You provide affordable housing to those who are not yet ready to buy, you support your local economy through the taxes you pay, and you promote the health of the real estate cycle by owning property. In return for that, you are provided attractive tax benefits, an income stream, and a valuable asset, which is insured and which you manage directly. While the time might come when you will want to move on to other methods of investing your money, it is unlikely that you will ever find an investment that combines all of the advantages of owning rental property. As long as you enjoy the experience, it is worthwhile; as long as you are willing to hold on to your investments, you will continue to experience the benefits, both financial and personal.

CHAPTER 10

Real Estate in the Larger Portfolio

All investing plans have to consist of selection—not only of which types of investments to make but also of how much risk to assume. This should include the best-known market risk (the risk that value will fall), as well as other forms of risk found more prominently in some investments and less in others. For example, real estate should be thought of in most forms as a long-term investment. Capital is tied up for many years— the condition known as illiquidity. Stocks, in comparison, can be bought or sold with ease and a fast turnaround, at little cost, and in a ready and efficient market. Thus, the features of real estate define risk, and every investor has to search for a suitable investment, given the degree and type of risk that the individual is willing to take.

If you find real estate to be a good match for you—meaning it is a suitable investment and your financial situation supports the idea—then you next need to decide how to devise your long-term plan so that you will be in control of your program. It is not responsible just to begin buying up properties and see what happens, on the assumption that property values will always rise. This, unfortunately, is the way many first-time investors get into the market. It is seen all of the time in the stock market, but it also occurs in real estate. As values rise, more and more inexperienced investors want to get in on the fast money; however, all things being cyclical, it is most likely that, at the top of the market, the frenzy of new investors will also be at record high levels. Whereas some make a good profit in the short term, most will end up losing.

It is far more sensible to study the market, recognize cycles, identify risks, and proceed in a way that you can afford. Buy one property and manage it for a few months and then evaluate your situation again. If you think it wise to buy more properties later, then do so; however, when you start out, go slowly until you have had the hands-on experience to understand better what it's like to be in the real estate market.

Financial Planning for the Long Term

Real estate investors need to think in terms of several years. A speculator, of course, gets into an investment with the idea of making a lot of money and then getting out in a very short period of time. However, there probably is no real estate equivalent of day trading. When you buy an investment property, it is expensive and time-consuming. The process of closing may take four to six weeks, with that time needed to complete financing and inspections. You cannot close out most deals in only a few days.

For those accustomed to the fast pace of the stock market, real estate can seem relatively uninteresting. But you need to ask yourself whether you want to invest for long-term profits or for the excitement of the game. Those who want to play the game should recognize that they are more interested in speculation; those who want to develop equity over many years and build a financial base should consider real estate as *part* of their overall portfolios.

Responsible financial planning begins with a series of questions. Why are you investing? What are your long-term goals? How much risk is appropriate? You are going to need to answer these questions for yourself and, in the process, fine-tune the characteristics of your portfolio. This includes considering the following important aspects:

1. *Liquidity.* Real estate is illiquid because your capital is tied up in the property. You can get equity out only by refinancing or selling. When you refinance, you are replacing debt, so it should be done only when you can replace a current interest rate with a lower one. If, in the process, you are able to take out cash, then it might be sensible. However, liquidity is a constant problem when you own real estate. With that in mind, you need to ensure that you keep a portion of your investments out of real estate, so that you have some cash available.

2. *Diversification.* The old advice to not put all of your eggs in one basket usually is good, to an extent. However, diversifying too much can be a problem as well. If your overall return is low because you are too diversified, then you have not achieved the advantage that every investor seeks: beating the double effect of inflation and taxes. Real estate is an effective investment in beating inflation over time, and the yearly tax benefits only increase your returns. However, it is also important to keep a portion of your portfolio in other investments—typically, in the stock market.

Also called asset allocation, diversification should be a highly individual decision. No one can tell you what percentage of your portfolio should be in one place or another; it depends on your personal profile: income, risk tolerance, and goals.

3. *Product selection.* The all-important decisions you make about what kinds of investments to buy ultimately determine how much profit you make from your investments. The selection is not limited to a pick between real estate or stocks; it also has to involve the specifics. Which rental property or stock you pick, when you buy, how long you hold, and how you time the sale all enter into the picture. If you do your research of the fundamentals (whether in stocks or in real estate), you will be in the position to make an informed decision. However, if you invest based on rumors or the opinions of others, then you are likely to make mistakes. Never invest based on what you hear from a friend, stockbroker, real estate agent, or stranger in an Internet investment chat room. Do your own research, get to know where the values are found, and invest your money where you have a better than average chance of profiting from the decision.

4. *Financial situation.* Your current and future financial position will play a central role in determining what investment decisions you make. Your annual income, of course, has to be considered if you plan to invest in property that might be vacant for a month or two. You need to be able to afford to pay the mortgage while you advertise for a new tenant. You also need to have enough capital for the down payment. Besides income and available capital, many of the events that occur in people's lives affect their decisions and change their goals. Marriage, birth of a child, divorce, death, loss of a job, and changes in occupation or health—these are the major events that, planned or not, significantly affect your financial position and affect how you use your capital.

5. *Change.* More than anything else, change characterizes everyone's life. No matter how sure you are about today's priorities or tomorrow's goals, they are likely to change. Within 5 to 10 years, you probably will have an entirely different outlook on many things, and your financial situation and your portfolio will be different as well. It makes no sense to set goals today and expect them to remain unchanged; you can only proceed based on what you know today and modify your goals as your financial situation evolves.

The process of setting goals is crucial for everyone's personal financial plan. The plan really is nothing more than a road map for how you *think* you are going to achieve well-defined goals, so it has to begin with the setting of goals. This includes defining risk, which in turn limits the kinds of investments you will consider acceptable in your portfolio. Some people do not want to risk their money in the stock market because they fear that sudden and drastic losses will wipe out a large share of their estate. Other people see the same volatility and recognize that, by the same argument, stocks can rise in value and double a capital base in a very short period of time. The same distinctions are made by would-be real estate investors attracted to historical price increases, substantial annual tax benefits, cash flow from rentals, and insurance over their investments. All of these features, the combination of which is unique to real estate, attract investors to the landlord market. However, others will see the illiquidity of real estate, plus the requirement that they deal with tenants, the possibility that the real estate market will flatten out in their area, and the more immediate danger of low rental demand if an excess of rental units go onto the market. These risks have to be considered by everyone, and real estate is suitable only if you weigh the benefits and risks and then proceed, fully aware of both.

The Liquidity Problem of Real Estate

There are three aspects of liquidity that concern every real estate investor: long-term commitment of capital, marketability of real estate, and cash flow. All of these problems, while distinctly different from one another, are defined as liquidity characteristics of investments.

Long-Term Commitment of Capital

Most landlords have to finance the larger portion of their investments, so the down payment is committed for the long term. At the minimum, it is safe to say that you will need to hold onto properties for five years, just to allow for the accumulation of equity, even in a healthy market. To produce a profit and cover the cost of buying and selling, a five-year term is normal.

During that time, capital remains tied up in the investment. It cannot be retrieved except by selling or refinancing. Considering the costs involved, it is unlikely that you will break even before a five-term period had passed. At the same time, a long-term financing arrangement produces almost no equity during the first few years. Consider the balance remaining in a 30-year loan at the end of each year. Table 10.1 summarizes this in percentage form for several interest rates.

Not only is your capital tied up for the first few years, but equity builds very slowly during the same period. At the end of the fifth year, only 5 percent of the loan is paid off (at 8 percent interest). And the same loan is only one-half paid off at the beginning of the twenty-third year. Thus, given the slow pace of equity accumulation in long-term financing arrangements, equity is going to accumulate from market value growth more than from repayment of borrowed money.

TABLE 10.1 Remaining Balance Tables: 30-Year Loans

AGE OF LOAN (YEARS)	% BALANCE REMAINING				
	6.0%	7.0%	8.0%	9.0%	10.00%
1	98.77	98.98	99.16	99.32	99.44
2	97.47	97.89	98.26	98.57	98.83
3	96.08	96.73	97.28	97.75	98.15
4	94.61	95.47	96.22	96.86	97.40
5	93.05	94.13	95.07	95.88	96.57
6	91.40	92.69	93.83	94.81	95.66
7	89.64	91.15	92.48	93.64	94.65
8	87.77	89.49	91.02	92.36	93.53
9	85.79	87.72	89.44	90.96	92.30
10	83.69	85.81	87.72	89.43	90.94
11	81.45	83.77	85.87	87.75	89.43
12	79.08	81.58	83.86	85.92	87.77
13	76.56	79.23	81.69	83.92	85.93
14	73.89	76.72	79.33	81.73	83.91
15	71.05	74.02	76.78	79.33	81.66
16	68.04	71.12	74.02	76.71	79.19
17	64.84	68.02	71.03	73.84	76.45
18	61.44	64.69	67.79	70.70	73.43
19	57.83	61.13	64.28	67.27	70.09
20	54.00	57.30	60.48	63.52	66.41
21	49.94	53.20	56.36	59.41	62.33
22	45.62	48.80	51.91	54.92	57.83
23	41.04	44.08	47.08	50.01	52.86
24	36.18	39.02	41.85	44.64	47.37
25	31.01	33.60	36.19	38.76	41.30
26	25.53	27.78	30.06	32.33	34.60
27	19.71	21.55	23.42	25.30	27.20
28	13.53	14.86	16.22	17.61	19.02
29	6.97	7.69	8.44	9.20	9.98
30	0	0	0	0	0

Marketability of Real Estate

Another liquidity problem arises when you consider how real estate is bought and sold, especially in comparison with stocks and mutual funds. It takes time and costs a lot of money to sell real estate. You have to pay a real estate commission and other costs when you sell. Typically, expenses for a seller are going to range between 8 and 10 percent of the sales price with the combination of commissions and other fees. In comparison, stocks and mutual funds are highly liquid.

Marketability also refers to whether you can find a buyer for your property. Every seller has a price that must be reached to justify a sale. For some, it represents a modest gain; for others, it is the breakeven point after costs. In extremely slow markets, sellers have to take a loss just to sell their property, because prices are depressed and there is a high inventory of properties for sale. When buyers will agree only to bargains, sellers have to come down in their price.

In a very poor market, when it is impossible to sell and get all of your capital back out of the deal, the marketability of real estate is very poor. Stocks and mutual funds are efficient because the exchanges ensure that every seller will find a buyer. The price of stocks adjusts to reflect the numbers of buyers actually there, and specialists will buy stock for sale even when no buyers are available, so stockholders enjoy the efficiency of the auction marketplace. However, real estate investors do not trade at auction but, rather, in the supply and demand market. It might not be possible or practical to sell a property at the time you would like. It might be necessary to wait out the market and the real estate cycle. Today's high inventory of properties for sale and excess of sellers will eventually be replaced with a very low inventory and an excess of buyers. From the seller's point of view, that is the logical time to sell property.

Cash Flow

The third version of the liquidity question in real estate is the constant concern about cash flow. If you own a property without a mortgage and it requires little or no maintenance, then cash comes in from rents and very little goes out. However, if you have a very high mortgage payment that is not covered by rent, and your property taxes, insurance, and recurring maintenance bills are never-ending, then your cash flow is very unhealthy. This form of liquidity is the one of greatest concern to most investors.

Even in a strong market for real estate, the tenant market can be slow or poor. This is characterized by high occupancy rates. By the same argument, real estate prices can be very flat for a period of time while demand for rental units is very high. Occupancy is measured by percentage. Thus, if the market is described as having less than 5 percent occupancy rate, that means it is easy to keep rental properties rented. However, if the occupancy rate is 20 or 30 percent or higher, then the market for rentals is very unhealthy. Most real estate investors are in debt for their properties, so they depend on keeping rentals occupied most of the time, just to make cash flow. A large number of properties produce market rents adequate to pay mortgages, but with little or nothing above that. Landlords have to finance property taxes and homeowners' insurance out of pocket, which is offset to a degree by tax benefits.

In this situation, you face the risk of negative cash flow, especially if an occupancy occurs or an unexpected repair comes up. If a tenant leaves your property in poor condition, the security deposit might not be enough to cover the cost of repairs. In other words, there are many situations that can have a negative impact on your cash flow. Creating a situation where you have a positive cash flow from some properties to offset a negative cash flow in another is a form of protection; however, even a positive cash flow property can turn negative with unexpected expenses or an extended occupancy.

You create a positive cash flow in most cases by putting a higher down payment on a property. The more money you put down, the lower your monthly mortgage payment. At the same time, you can rent out a property at market rates. You also are likely to have more positive cash flow from duplex units than from a single-family house. It is not uncommon that a house rents for $700 or $800, whereas a duplex costing the same has each unit going for $500 or $600. Thus, for the same investment, it is possible to generate far better cash flow with a duplex.

Most landlords, especially first-time investors, need to accept the risk, at least in their first few years in the investment. Of course, they also need to be able to cover negative situations from savings or monthly income. Within a few years, though, the first-time investor needs to seek ways to improve cash flow, so that the exposure to this serious risk can be minimized and eventually eliminated.

The Goal-Setting Problem of Investing

Real estate owners, like all investors, have a better chance of success if they first define the scope of their investment plan. Goals need to be set, including an exit strategy for the real estate investment, and that strategy has to be followed. Otherwise, you only invite problems later.

Stock market investors face the same issue, more often for the short term. For example, an investor buys shares of stock and waits for the price to go up. If the price falls, the attitude might be "I have to keep this stock until I get back to where I started," so the investor is holding stock worth less than the purchase price. This individual did not decide in advance on a bail-out point, the price at which the stock should be sold to reduce further losses.

In a second possible scenario, the stock remains at or about the same price level. Now the investor might reason that "I have to wait out the market." However, capital is tied up in the stock, and if the dividend yield is relatively low, then there is no return being generated. Given the passage of time, this investor needs to define *when* the stock would be sold and replaced with other stock.

In the third possible outcome, the stock's price rises. Now the same investor might argue, "Now that the stock is rising in value, I don't want to sell and miss out on future profits." In this outcome, the stock cannot be sold and profits taken. The investor has not set goals for selling and taking profits.

In all of the outcomes, there is no logical way for the investor to sell. The all too common trap has been to set up the whole thing so that a sale cannot happen, either to take profits or reduce losses. And even when the stock rises, each price level becomes the new starting point to support arguments in the future against selling.

This brief description of stock market thinking also applies in real estate. When property values are stagnant, the investor argues, "I cannot sell now. The property needs to season." When prices actually fall, the argument is "I have to get back to my starting point." And when prices are on the rise, the argument is "Now that prices are going up, it would be foolish to get out of the market."

The solution, of course, is to set specific goals. With goals, you have rules to follow. They relate to return on investment within time frames and to the limiting of losses. Thus, you can sell an investment if it does not produce a return within a specific number of months or years; you can also sell if a predetermined percentage of capital is lost. Finally, you can sell on reaching a specific profit level. The goal gives definition and order to your investment plan. Without that, you have no way of knowing what you are trying to achieve, what kinds of time-related deadlines to impose on yourself, or when to leave the market. Remember, the exit strategy is just as important as the entrance strategy.

Investors who do not operate from the goal-related mentality are making a big mistake, because they have no way to know how to react to changes in the market. Because they have to make up their strategy as they proceed, they really have no strategy at all. In the stock market, it can be said that the bulls and bears take a back seat to the other market animals, the pigs and chickens. This is true because most investment decisions are based on greed and fear, rather than on logic and analysis. These arguments apply equally well in real estate, even though price changes and market demand tend to move more slowly.

Coordinating Real Estate with Other Investments

When you have a goal, you have developed guidelines for future action. Goals can also be thought of as policies within a larger context, the entire portfolio. You need to develop a plan for managing your investment capital over many years, including contingencies that you cannot know of today. Thus, part of your capital should be kept in relatively liquid investments, such as savings accounts, money market funds, or the stock market. If you need to access that cash, it is fairly easy to do. Another portion of your capital should be working in the stock market, either through direct ownership of shares or through mutual funds. The long-term portion of your investment can be placed in real estate or other markets with less liquidity.

The selection of investments and the division of cash have to depend on your personal wealth, income, tax status, and many other personal considerations. For example, if you enjoy your privacy and recreation time, you might not want to consider becoming a landlord. If you are married but having problems and you believe you might be heading for a divorce, it also makes little sense to encumber yourself with a long-term investment, which might have to be liquidated in the near future.

However, if you have capital available to invest and the resources to provide a cushion for any emergencies or, in the case of real estate, vacancies in your property, then real estate makes more sense. If you are paying a lot in taxes each year, the tax-sheltering aspects of real estate investing are especially attractive.

Thus, depending on your income and personal situation, real estate could work or it could be a mistake, not only in timing but also in the selection of property itself. No investment is worth its inherent risks if those risks are a poor match for the investor. With real estate, you have a poor selection if you don't enjoy working with tenants, cannot afford vacancies, or do not enjoy the experience. More to the point, if you are uncomfortable with the risks for any reason, then you should not have money in the investment. The comfort level for you as an individual should be a ruling factor in deciding whether to get into real estate. And once you have made the decision to proceed, your comfort level should determine whether or not to stay or to get out.

Coordinating real estate with the rest of your portfolio involves more than the relatively mechanical division of capital. Diversification means allocating some capital into each of several dissimilar investments. The idea is that, when one market falls, another is not vulnerable to the same forces and might even offset losses. In other words, the stock market might fall but real estate might rise at the same time. Experienced investors understand that diversification is far more complex, of course. Diversification does not just mean owning shares of several different stocks, spreading risk by buying through mutual funds, or even splitting capital between major markets, such as stocks, bonds, and real estate. A healthy economy tends to have a similar positive effect on investments in general, whereas a poor economy tends to bring down many different investments. To truly diversify, you need to manage your portfolio with a view to what is going to be likely to happen to your capital over the long term.

For many people, this means managing risk rather than just allocating dollars into various types of investments. One problem with scientifically engineered diversification is that overall return tends to be very low because a portion of your portfolio's value is always on the decline. Management of risk makes more sense than diversifying dollars. For example, if you own shares of two or three mutual funds, if you have equity building in a retirement program, and if you are buying your own home, then you already have a typical form of diversification *and* risk management. Under that scenario, you are not placing large amounts of capital at risk, nor are you putting too much capital into a single market, which could fall suddenly.

Moving beyond the typical portfolio, you might first consider building an emergency cash reserve, then beginning to buy certain stocks directly. From there, you can build toward investing in real estate for the long-term growth potential, current cash flow, and annual tax benefits. However, the decision should be made as part of your overall financial plan. The decision to buy real estate should be based on not only the desirability of tax advantages, for example, but also on considerations such as family plans and priorities, cash flow, available capital, and the rest of your portfolio. How much is invested in liquid areas, such as stocks and savings accounts? How much negative cash flow can you afford in the event of vacancy? How much time are you willing to spend working to repair investment property or working with tenants? These are the important questions everyone should ask before buying rental property.

Investments versus Your Own Home

As part of the big picture approach to investing in general, you need to consider all of your assets—stocks and mutual funds, retirement accounts, insurance policies, cash on hand, and your own home. Your home probably is the biggest investment you will ever make in terms of total value. It is both an investment and a basic necessity, so how does it fit into your financial plan?

There are many intriguing possibilities concerning the use of your own home *and* real estate investments:

1. *Converting your home to investment property.* If you are ready to move to a larger property, the first thought usually is to sell your home and replace it with another. However, an alternative is to use the property as an investment and purchase a new home as your primary residence. The major advantage in doing this is that you can qualify for financing for owner-occupied housing, which usually requires a lower down payment and offers low interest rates. If you have built up a lot of equity in your current home, you probably will be able to rent it out for positive cash flow.

The downside is that you lose the tax advantage of selling your primary residence. If you have lived in your home for at least two of the past five years, you are not subject to federal taxes when you sell. This applies up to $500,000 of profit, and you can take advantage of this provision as often as you like, except that you cannot sell a primary residence tax-free more frequently than once every two years. Another disadvantage is that depreciation is based on the original purchase price, not on current market value. If you have owned your home for many years, this can keep tax advantages at a minimum. You might be better off taking the tax-free sale and replacing your current home with a new rental property of similar current market value.

For many people, converting a primary residence is the easiest way to begin investing in real estate. It provides you with financing advantages because your newly acquired home will be your primary residence. It also lets you start out with a rental property you know well. You have been maintaining the property for many years, so you know its condition.

2. *Converting investing property to your primary residence.* The opposite strategy is to convert a rental property to your primary residence. You might do this in anticipation of selling a property in two years and taking advantage of current federal tax laws. In other words, even a house that has appreciated in value can be sheltered from taxation by converting it to your primary residence and living there for two years before you sell. Under those conditions, you escape federal tax on up to $500,000 in profit. However, you are still taxed on depreciation recapture for the years the property was used as a rental.

The advantage of converting investment property to residential is primarily in the tax advantages. You can also spend the two years fixing up a run-down property and preparing it for sale in order to maximize profit when it goes on the market. It is far easier to work on property while you are living there.

The disadvantage is that you and your family might not want to live in a particular house for two years. Landlords often recognize the value of a property as a rental, even though it does not fit with their own style, so moving into an investment property means you have to inconvenience yourself and your family for two years, just to avoid being taxed on profit at sale. If you do not mind moving, this plan works; however, for many families, the disruption of moving twice in two years, not to mention the change of neighborhood, schools, lifestyle, and friends, is too much disruption to justify the savings.

3. *Using home equity to buy rental property.* A final way that you can use your home is by borrowing its equity for use as investment capital. You can apply for a home equity line of credit, for example, and access a significant amount of money, which then can be used as a down payment money for rental property.

The advantage in this plan is that getting the equity is relatively inexpensive, particularly if you go through the equity line of credit rather than a full-blown refinance. You pay interest only on the money you actually draw out, so you can have a $100,000 line of credit but not pay any interest until you write a check and take a draw. The convenience of this plan is its primary benefit. That convenience is also its primary disadvantage. You need to decide whether it makes sense to borrow home equity in order to invest. Study the cash flow to ensure that you will be able to afford the payments on the equity line in addition to your existing first mortgage. On top of this, you face the risk of vacancies and cash flow drain in your rental property. Borrowing money to invest invariably involves far higher risks; even though this approach characterizes real estate investing in general, the problem is augmented when you borrow equity from your home. It means you have a second mortgage on your home plus a mortgage on the rental property, so this places more strain on your family's cash flow.

While using your own home in one of several ways provides flexibility, it also involves some potential problems. You can switch primary residences to maximize tax benefits and create the best financing rates; however, what does it do to your family to move frequently? For the small financial advantages you get, it might not be worth the strain and inconvenience it places on your family relationships.

The question of whether it makes sense to mix investment and personal assets has to be answered by each person. Some families are more flexible than others. A young couple with no children certainly is more flexible than one with several children in various local schools, for example. Uprooting children and changing schools—moving away from friends and social activities—can be devastating to a child. A top-performing student may drop several grade points because of a move, and a happy, well-adjusted child can become withdrawn and depressed. Each family has to ask whether big changes are worth the investment value.

The same questions have to be asked between husband and wife. As long as both are happy with the plan to move around between properties as often as necessary to maximize tax and financing advantages, that is all well and good. However, if one becomes unhappy, it can make the investment plan impractical, not to mention the strain it places on the relationship. When couples find themselves in conflict over financial decisions, it has far-reaching consequences. The marriage itself can be threatened because one spouse insists on remaining fully invested while moving from one property to another, when the other spouse becomes increasingly unhappy with the plan.

Any investment strategy demands balance. Not only is balance important in terms of asset allocation, risk management, and cash flow, but it is also important in terms of personal and family goals. The security and well-being of you and your family should be the primary consideration; after all, the reason to invest and develop a long-term financial plan is supposed to be for security and future financial freedom. What good is that if you, your spouse, or your children are not also happy? It is a mistake to lose sight of what is really important, no matter how tempting the potential profit and tax benefits are in any investment.

Real estate certainly presents a package of advantages that can benefit many people. The long-term equity growth, direct management, tax benefits, and cash flow add up to a package that collectively appeals to a broad cross section of people. If you are in that group, there are many ways you and your family can benefit from getting into real estate. However, as with all investments, you need to define strategies for managing and eventually exiting from your investments. You need to understand how to balance personal priorities with investment opportunities. And you always need to keep an eye on what you are trying to achieve by investing your money in real estate, or elsewhere.

For the investor who has gone through the steps to define goals and identify an exit strategy, real estate can provide many benefits to a personal financial plan. If you go into the market with a clear idea of what is involved, how much capital you want to place at risk, and when you plan to sell in the future, then you are already well equipped to begin. By defining the desired end result, you have already avoided the most troubling risk of all, that of investing without a specific plan. Successful investing requires defining your long-term goals and creating a clear path.

Index